Management Culture in India

Management Culture in India

An Ethnographic Study

M. Romesh Singh

RAWAT PUBLICATIONS

Jaipur • New Delhi • Bangalore • Guwahati • Kolkata

ISBN 978-81-316-0820-3

Published by
Prem Rawat for **Rawat Publications**
Satyam Apts, Sector 3, Jawahar Nagar, Jaipur 302 004 (India)
Phone: 0141 265 1748 / 7006 Fax: 0141 265 1748
E-mail: info@rawatbooks.com
Website: www.rawatbooks.com

New Delhi Office
4858/24, Ansari Road, Daryaganj, New Delhi 110 002
Phone: 011 2326 3290

Also at *Bangalore, Guwahati* and *Kolkata*

Printed and bound in India

Contents

Foreword

This work by M. Romesh Singh adds to a long history of ethnographic studies in corporate organizations. The first ethnographic techniques, and the methods anthropologists use in studying human behaviour, were forged in the early days of anthropological research. They were the answer to how to study human behaviour in societies where the anthropologist did not know the language or the rules of how to behave. Today anthropologists continue to strengthen and add to this body of techniques to understand all human behaviour even in familiar settings.

Anthropologists in the United States began studying business organizations in the 1930s with a study of Western Electric's Hawthorne Works, a manufacturing plant in Chicago. Early research there led to the identification of the *Hawthorne Effect*: when scientists are measuring or recording the behaviour of human subjects, subjects may change their behaviour because they know they are being studied. These researchers were conducting the first ethnographic study of informal social organization in the work setting. The Hawthorne studies and Lloyd Warner's anthropological contribution to them were seminal to the realization by organization scientists that understanding human relations was crucial to understanding organizations and worker productivity. This realization led to the creation of *human relations* as a field of study. The use of ethnographic techniques in studying organizations was born.

Another milestone in the work of anthropologists using ethnographic techniques to study corporate organizations came in the 1950s with the work of Edward T. Hall who served as director of the US State Department's "Point Four" training programme. This was a training programme designed to teach technicians who would be working outside

North America about cross-cultural communication. He built a career in the field and eventually wrote several seminal works well known in business, in anthropology, in communication, and in many other fields (Baba 1995).

In the 1980s there was a surge of interest in ethnographic techniques and anthropological inquiry by business organizations and organization studies researchers. In 1987, the Institute for Research on Learning (IRL), funded from a variety of sources, including the Xerox Foundation, was founded. While the work at IRL was purposefully interdisciplinary and drew from fields such as economics, statistics, psychology, and computer science, it was heavily influenced by anthropology's ethnographic techniques from the beginning.

In the 1990s, anthropologists moved into the field of design. The anthropologists at Xerox were influential in the adoption of ethnographic techniques in this field. Doblin Group, E-Lab, Sapient, and other design firms employed anthropologists. In the Netherlands, Hans Tennekes, Koot, and others were establishing the field of business anthropology in organization studies while in the United Kingdom Paul Bates was defining the difference between the anthropological perspective on organizations and that of other organization specialists, and in France, Jean Francois Chanlet was publishing on the multiple layers of culture in organizations (van Marrewijk 2010).

Since 2000, the fields in business anthropology and the use of ethnographic techniques in business have further crystallized and grown. In 2005 anthropologist Eric Arnould and Craig Thompson published a seminal article in the *Journal of Consumer Research* in which they reviewed 20 years of consumer research, identified a research tradition that they called consumer culture theory (CCT), and explained how this research studied the cultural dimensions of the consumption cycle (Arnould and Thompson 2005). In design anthropology, the annual Ethnographic Praxis in Industry Conference (EPIC) began in 2005. This conference was again started by a group of anthropologists, including Ken Anderson at Intel, Tracey Lovejoy at Microsoft, Jeanette Blomberg at IBM, and Christina Wasson at University of North Texas. Goals for EPIC include the following: 'to promote public recognition of practicing ethnography as a profession and to support the continuing professionalization of the field' (http://epiconference.com extracted 2/7/12).

In Europe the increased interest in the field is demonstrated by added training programmes, and the European Association of Applied Anthropologists' Applied Anthropology Network annually organizes the event called 'Why the World Needs Anthropologists,' which is spearheaded by business anthropologist Podjed (Podjed, Gorup and Mlakar 2016).

The growth of business anthropology and the use of ethnographic techniques in Asia over the past 15 years is significant for the field. The International Union of Anthropological and Ethnological Sciences now includes the Commission on Enterprise Anthropology begun by Tomoko Hamada Connolly and Zhang Jijiao. Business anthropology conferences are being held across Asia. For example, the first International Forum on Business Anthropology was held at the Museum of Ethnology, Osaka, 2010, and the International Union of Anthropological and Ethnological Sciences has held several conferences, for example, in China in 2009 and 2011. In addition, Robert Tian has organized numerous conferences in China beginning with the First International Conference of Business Anthropology held at Sun Yat-sen University in Guangdong in 2012 (Chen and Zhou 2013) and has promoted the teaching of business anthropology across universities there . In India anthropologists are pushing to increase the training in business anthropology in departments across the country. As one of the world's largest consumer bases, India attracts multinational corporations and global businesses. Business anthropologists can be helpful in manoeuvring in this environment (Singh n.d.).

A further sign of the importance of the field and of its international nature is the birth of two journals of Business Anthropology. The *International Journal of Business Anthropology* sponsored by the University of Sun Yat-sen, China, and VU University, Amsterdam, is the result of the hard work of Robert Tian and its initial issue was published in 2010. The *Journal of Business Anthropology*, an open access journal hosted by the Copenhagen Business School, published its first issue in 2011 and is the result of the efforts of Brian Moeran and Christina Garsten.

Romesh Singh's book adds to this growing body of international literature and uses ethnographic techniques to understand business organizations. His ethnographic case studies of four organizations (Scientific Organization, Seacom Pvt. Ltd, HEC, and Telcom) highlight the importance of organizational culture and discuss management issues of concern in India. This book also attempted to trace the historical trends of management in India and importance and techniques of doing ethnography in business organizations. I am pleased to see this further development of business anthropology and the use of ethnographic techniques in India. Singh's work is a welcome addition to the knowledge base in business anthropology.

Ann T. Jordan
Department of Anthropology
University of North Texas, USA

References

Arnould, Eric J. and Craig J. Thompson. 2005. Consumer Culture Theory (CCT): Twenty Years of Research. *Journal of Consumer Research*, 31(4), 868–82.

Baba, Marietta L. 1995. A Biography of Edward T. Hall. *Journal of Applied Behavioral Science*, 31(2), 117–18.

Chen, Gang and Daming Zhou. 2013. Editorial Commentary: The Rise of Business Anthropology in China. *International Journal of Business Anthropology*, 4(1), 11.

Consumer Culture Theory Website. 2011. *About CCT*. Retrieved from www.consumerculturetheory.org

EPIC. 2011. *The Ethnographic Praxis in Industry Conference*. Retrieved from http//www.epiconference.com/

Podjed, Dan, Meta Gorup and Alenka Bezjak Mlakar. 2016. Applied Anthropology in Europe: Historical Obstacles, Current Situation, Future Challenges. *Anthropology in Action*, 23(2), 53–63.

Singh, M. Romesh. (n.d.). *Business Anthropology: New Direction of Research in India*. (Manuscript 2016).

Van Marrewijk, Alfons. 2010. European Developments in Business Anthropology. *International Journal of Business Anthropology*. 1(1).

Preface

The socio-cultural milieu in India is inimitable; its peculiarities shape the personalities of the management practitioner and the influence of management practices. One of the salient features of Indian management is the emphasis on the personalities of the top leaders in the organization. As found by various studies, the expectations of the employees are more favourably inclined towards a paternalistic management style. The essential requisite for paternalism appears to be unity in the leadership and a single identifiable source of power and patronage. The line of succession – if not clear – leads to lobbying and in the process subtly divides the organization into cliques. Another unique feature of Indian management is the familial feeling perceived by the employees because of the parental attitude adopted by the senior or top management, which in turn gives a sense of security and belongingness to employees. It has been found that among the organizations studied, harmony is easier to achieve when difference is attributed to familiarities, seniority and age.

In the Indian context, globalization has thrown open tremendous opportunities for Indians. The recent success of software companies is just a beginning in this direction. Similarly, communication revolution such as advent of Internet tilted the business – econometrics – to incorporate multicultural variables. It is no longer usual for Indian companies to set up offices across the globe; for example, Indian companies like Infosys, Wipro and Mahindra Satyam have operations running in various locations across the globe. This means Indians will be increasingly managing people with different work values, attitudes and behaviour and vice versa. Therefore, it is important for us to recognize that managers within the organizations hold particular sets of assumptions, ideas and beliefs about how to manage their human resources, which are strongly influenced by the sociocultural background specific to the host country or region where the organization is operating. This requires proper adaptability and flexibility in dealing with different cultures. However, literature survey indicates that there has been very little exploratory or basic research undertaken to identify cultural variables, which have a bearing on corporate and non-corporate management in India.

On the basis of this study, it is understood that organizational culture has a positive impact on performance. The study further shows that strong organizational culture is very helpful for new employees to adapt to the organization's culture and gain competitive advantage. Earlier studies had shown that employee's commitment and group efficiency play a crucial role in their efforts towards adopting the organizational values and principles and enhancing the performance of the organization. It also shows that organizational culture is good only if it fits the industry or the firm's strategy. Finally, an organization with a culture that encourages confidence and risk-taking among employees, has leadership that initiates and drives change, and focuses on the changing needs of customers will in all likelihood achieve success and be able to sustain its growth. Effective socialization also helps in enhancing employee performance, job satisfaction, intention to stay with the organization, low levels of distress symptoms and high level of employee commitment.

This book attempts to examine the impact of societal culture (Indian culture) on the management of corporate organizations in India. In the context of Indian management, ownership and management are not differentiated; almost invariably, these overlap. All of these are centred around the one who is the head of the organization, the chief executive of an organization and the head of the institution in the contemporary time or even in non-business structures or units with hierarchies, such as family, religious groups or factions, or kingdom. Obviously Indian management is known for its traditional style of decision-making. Hierarchy is key to management coordination. Horizontal peer-level coordination, so typical of Japanese society, is almost absent in the Indian scene. Presumably, members of an Indian organization look for top-down guidance and places emphasis on lifelong employment and job security (Sinha, 1991). There is a societal assumption that membership in a family, caste and corporate group has to be permanent. Although security and lifelong employment have been traditionally valued in India, in contemporary management there is much debate about their efficacy. Indian management is overconcerned with job identity. An Indian derives his or her identity from the social group to which he or she belongs, his or her occupation, and the job he or she performs. These are interlinked so much that a new employee typically first attempts to establish a reference group and job identity. It is the centralization of power and authority and the decentralization of activities. This has emerged from the belief that the chief has a *Mana* and is the storehouse of energy, authority and power. Even in organizations which have decentralized authority, one finds that people do not exercise their delegated authority and power. There is strong conviction in Indian society that power and authority flow from the fountainhead – the chief executive, the centre of the organization (Kakkar, 1974).

Indian management values loyalty, sometimes unquestioned loyalty – to the king, chief, head of the family and chief executive. There is often confusion between loyalty to the king or the country and loyalty to the chief or the organization. The assumption is that the king and country, and thus the chief executive and organization, are synonymous. This is a matter of great debate. Some researchers have commented that Indian society fosters dependency, and thus, necessitates demonstration of loyalty and fellowship and playing to the tune of the supervisors or any authority figure (Sinha, 1986). Indian management values individual excellence. It recognizes individuals who make distinguished contributions in any field of endeavour. In Indian society, one does not look for the same qualities in every man. Rather, one recognizes individual differences and respects excellence in whatever field one distinguishes themselves. It is believed that in a team not all members are alike. In fact, they should not be alike, but be as five fingers, with different lengths and shapes, bound together in one hand. Collective wisdom is valued in Indian society. Teamwork always commands attention. The story of a blind man and the lame man joining hands together to compensate for each other's deficiencies is a household tale. An effective team consists of people with different views, values, perspectives, professions, skills and wisdom working for a common goal so that together they convert energy into synergy and the competence of individual is translated into excellence through teamwork.

Many features of Indian management identified by earlier studies are found in the present study also, with little modification and variation. However, it largely depends on nature of the organizations, whether they are small or large, public or private, traditional or modern. It has been noticed that not all these characteristics are desirable for Indian managers to practice and pursue. In fact, there is an unending debate about the desirability of these characteristics; that is, whether (a) ownership and management should be differentiated, (b) chief executives should have so much authority, (c) hierarchy should play a major role in management coordination, (d) paternalistic/directed/nurturing leadership is most appropriate for an Indian organization, (e) one should accept the fact that Indian managers do their best flying solo and do not show interest in team work and (f) organization behaviour needs a change and if so what kind. These are burning issues for Indian management professionals and require in-depth studies to assess their effects across the organization and in the larger society.

During the course of this research work, I have received generous help from different quarters. Now the time has come for me to express my heartfelt thanks for all the help I had received. First and foremost, I would like to thank University Grant Commission (UGC), New Delhi, for selecting me for the Research Award (2012–2014) and Raman Postdoctoral Fellow (2015–2016), which enabled me to carry out this study and publish my findings in this book. I deeply appreciate the opportunity given to me and will remain grateful to UGC for their trust and support.

I am extremely grateful to the employees of the four organizations for their kind cooperation and help throughout data collection and also the hospitality provided to me and my students during the fieldwork. Especially I am greatly indebted to the respondents who had been a constant source of help and many a kindness shown throughout my fieldwork. I express my sincere thanks to Professor Ann T. Jordan (Business Anthropologist) for not only accepting to write Foreword to my book despite her busy academic schedule but also enriching my academic insight during my stay in the University of North Texas.

I am indebted to Professor Pankaj Jain, Department of Anthropology, University of North Texas, for hosting me in his department as visiting scholar for one year and his constant encouragement in my academic endeavour. I also thank all the faculty members and supporting staff of Anthropology Department, UNT, for all the help and support.

I express my sincere gratitude to (Late) Professor Dharni Sinha and (Late) Mrs Purnima Sinha, whose guidance, encouragement, suggestions and very constructive criticism have contributed immensely to the evolution of my ideas on this project. They are the ones who inspired me to start teaching business anthropology in my university.

I also express my heartfelt thanks to my senior colleagues, friends and staff in the Department of Anthropology, University of Hyderabad, for their constant support and encouragement.

I want to thank my wife, Usharani, who supported and encouraged me in spite of my work demands that kept me away from the family. It was a long and difficult journey for her. I am also thankful to my two wonderful kids Rushil and Ruthwik for making my life more beautiful and meaningful.

I would like to thank Mr Pranit Rawat for enabling me to publish this book.

M Romesh Singh

1

Introduction

With the globalization of economies and increasing competition, corporate enterprises worldwide are under tremendous pressure to ameliorate their performance. The concepts of planning, organizing, staffing, controlling, and coordinating are there in any culture, but then they do specifically vary from one culture to another. Western management theories are being tried out, adopted, reconciled and even being imposed on non-western management contexts which may have different logics, priorities and patterns of behaviour from those cultures within which these theories were developed.

In this context, the compatibility and reconciliation of Western and non-western management techniques across cultures is an issue and needs to be addressed through developing an insight into how people and change are managed in the organizational frame of reference. In India too, down the ages, the Indian thinking on management and administration has acquired a global touch. The difference between global and local practices arises from the norms and expectations of the community and people that came into being and were voiced at various points in time.

The development of Western management concepts is indeed an evolutionary process. It first evolved when management was a proprietary activity and the owner-managers had the prerogative and responsibility to plan, organize, direct and control the activities of their enterprises. However, over the years the ownership pattern changed from proprietary to public, and various interest groups within and outside the organization emerged and began acting as countervailing forces. Trade union, statutory audits, accountability to shareholders, consumer forums, governmental norms, and national and international regulations like World Trade Organization (WTO) influenced the managerial process. There is a strong view in Western management that organizational and managerial change in an organization has to be driven by the men at the top. Examples have been quoted that some of the most successful managers or top executives were responsible for bringing in substantive change and making the organization healthy and vibrant during their tenure. However, many such organizations collapsed when men at the top who initiated and managed changes left the organizations. Thus, the model organization, as widely believed and seen in the West and in India too, was run by one man who ran a spectacular show while he was there, only to see it crumble after his exit. However, in the Far East the success of Japanese methods of management and failure of Western management practices in Japanese companies have led to the thinking that culture directly affects management process and any management must align itself to the local context in order to succeed (Putti, 1991). In India, we have not so far witnessed the evolution of a management system that is attuned to Indian culture and values. Instead, what was done was the most convenient thing to do and less time-consuming too. Just like everything else on the technology front, we chose to adopt Western management principles and practices. As a result of this adaptation, we have been left with highly Westernized management thinking that works only partially. Therefore, understanding cultural characteristics of organizations has become more crucial than ever. In this project, an attempt has been made to examine the impact of culture on corporate organizations in India.

Many human resource management (HRM) and cross-cultural researchers have identified and discussed the importance of culture and its impact on HRM. Yet a common understanding and agreement on the definition of culture (including variations of culture) has not yet been reached. There are a number of studies done by many eminent scholars on culture and management. Some of the studies on the topic are reviewed to understand the culture of organizations in different contexts and the impact of culture specifically on management. The available literatures on culture and management have been categorized into five themes:

1. Culture concept, organizational culture and performance
2. Dimensions of national culture
3. Models/frameworks for understanding the dimensions of national culture
4. National culture and management practices (cross-cultural practices)
5. Organization culture and management in India.

Culture Concept, Organizational Culture and Performance

Anthropologists were the first to create a construct of societal culture. E.B. Tyler (1871) defined culture as a complex phenomenon which included knowledge, belief, art, morals, custom and any other capabilities and habits acquired by a person as a member of society. Years later, Ralph Linton (1945) described culture as 'a configuration of learned behavior . . . shared and promoted by the members of a particular society'. In his classic work, *Culture: A Critical Review of Concepts and Definitions*, Kluckhohn (1952) arrived at the thesis that culture is an individual's behaviour as well as shared behaviour within a group of people who share common purpose and values of life. Two things stand out: (a) culture is the way of life of an identified group of people and (b) culture is learned behaviour; culture is transmitted from one generation to another through idioms, rituals, besides formal and informal learning. The processes of enculturation mould the members to follow the shared norms and traditions which in turn influence their behaviour. Culture has its theoretical and practical elements, and culture is essentially the product of human creativeness. We will avoid the extremes of the positivistic and normative fallacies on one hand, and the metaphysical, naturalistic and culturalistic fallacies on the other. Culture, we maintain, is a historical creation of man and depends for its continuity upon free, conscious transmission and invention. Since culture is in part the cultivation of a person in relation to the physical environment, it is necessarily subject to the laws and limitations of human nature as well as of nature as a whole. Similarly, cultural ideals and practices, when assimilated and conformed to, do influence or condition the course of human development. But neither natural forces nor cultural achievements taken separately or combined can serve to explain the emergence and evolution of cultural life (Bidney, 1953). Today, instead of studying societies and tribes, researchers are more interested in social interactions. These researchers are studying behaviours at work, interactions with employing organizations, and customs and procedures within organizations.

Culture can also be examined at the corporate level. This is known as 'organizational culture'. A great deal of emphasis is being placed on examining organizations as units, with their own cultures within larger socialite cultures (Dyer, 1984). Organizational culture has been described as the glue that holds organizations together by providing cohesiveness and coherence among its parts (Schnieder, 1980). It refers to a system of shared meanings held by members that distinguish the organization from other organizations (Robbins, 1995). In other words, organizational culture represents the key elements of the work environment in which employees perform their jobs and also corresponds to a unique set of features that the organization values. An organization's culture is determined by a variety of elements, including business environment, values, rites and rituals, cultural networks, and ideas and skills possessed by its employees (Hardesty, 1988).

Mahadevan (2012) views culture as a collective of identities from an interpretative, sense-making perspective. He analyses religion-based cross-cultural conflict through the example of two ethnographic studies of multicultural high-tech organizations undergoing change. Connolly's (2010) study also provides a short history of ritual studies in anthropology and argues that business rituals can be investigated as a critical event, or conversely, a critical event can be analysed as a type of ritual. Studies of corporate rituals as condensed public drama can delve directly into the actual cognitive, emotive and neurological processes of meaning creation by various stakeholders and can capture multilevel enactments of organizational descent, power and hierarchical order as well as shifting images of future possibilities.

Smircich (1983) examines the significance of the concept of culture for organizational analysis. The intersection of culture theory and organization theory is evident in five current research themes: comparative management, corporate culture, organizational cognition, organizational symbolism, and unconscious processes and organization.

Contrary to currently popular notions of organizational culture, they claim that local organizational cultures that are distinct from more generally shared background cultures come into play relatively infrequently at the level of the whole organization. With respect to organizational performance, researchers are of the view that particular properties of local organizational culture are more important than others and that local organizational culture will be more critical to performance in one range of organizations than in others. They conclude by applying their point of view to the problem of changing organizational cultures and hold that organizational culture is more adaptive than what people generally think (Wilkins & Ouchi, 1983).

Weiss and Delbecq (1987) extend the concept of corporate culture to industrial culture and examine regional influences on management practices in Silicon Valley and Route 128. Results indicated that these high-technology cultures and related management practices differ significantly and are influenced by particular regional characteristics. Conceptual and consulting implications are also highlighted.

Organizational Culture and Performance

The literature on organizational culture is rich and diverse. Much of its richness is founded on the claim that culture is linked to organizational performance. Even though there are some theorists who questioned the culture–performance link, sufficient evidence exists to suggest that organizational culture is associated with organizational performance (Ogbonna & Harris, 2000). One of the earliest quantitative studies on the culture–performance link was conducted by Denison (1984), who used data from 34 American firms on cultural performance over a period of five years and scrutinized the characteristics of organizational culture and tracked the performance over time in these firms. Reichers and Schneider (1990) stated that although researchers studying culture have conducted various studies to develop definitions of culture, relatively few have contributed to research focusing on the link between culture and performance. The only reason for doing this was the complexity in the operational implications of the culture construct. Kotter and Heskett (1992) investigated the relationship between long-term organizational performance and economic performance across more than 200 organizations. Moreover, being one of the most important and most conscientious research efforts on this subject, their study has made three vital contributions. First, the relationship between culture and performance as established in their research is forceful. Second, the writers give an important combination from a theoretical point of view regarding the nature and scope of culture. Third, they sketch strong associations between culture, management practices and performance.

The claim that organizational culture is attached to performance is based on the apparent role that culture can play in creating a competitive advantage. Rousseau's (1990) study attempted to overcome some of the limitations in measuring the culture of organization. At the end, the results show that there are no positive correlations between culture and employees' performance. After critically reviewing the methodologies and findings of recent researches, it is assumed that there is a link between culture and performance (Lim, 1995). Theorists also argue that sustainable competitive advantage arises from the formation of organizational competencies which are both superior and nearly inimitable by competitors (Saa-Pe're & Garcia-Falcon, 2002). Practitioners and academics suggested that the performance of an organization is dependent on the degree to which the values of the culture are comprehensively shared (Denison, 1990).

Knowledge about different management styles and fresh demands in the work environment is at some level up to date in the case of relatively young organizations, which could lead us to assume that older firms have less cultural orientation towards learning. If older organizations made organizational learning culture, do the hard work to alter their culture, then it is not a very easy task; it is not a linear or quick process. At the same level, it not anything better than quoting an ironic expression (Schein, 1997). According to Saffold (1998), first, culture can give a shape to the organizational processes which again help to create and modify culture. Second, it is likely that culture's contribution to performance is significantly less undemanding than conducting many studies. Most writers and successful managers suggest that strong organizational culture is very essential for business because of three important functions:

First, organizational culture is extremely fixed with the social control that may cause to make an influence on the employee's decisions and behaviour. Second, organizational culture works as social glue to bond the employees together and make them feel a strong part of the corporate experience, which is useful to attract new staff and retain the best performers. Third, organizational culture is very useful to assist the sense-making process and helps the employees to understand the organizational events and objectives, which enhance the efficiency and effectiveness of the employees. Strong culture has almost been considered as a driving force to improve the performance of the employees. It enhances self-confidence and commitment of employees, reduces job stress and improves the ethical behaviour of the employees (Saffold, 1998). Further, he states that most studies on culture tend to emphasize on a single organizational culture. But in Deal and Kennedy's (1982) point of view, both strong and weak cultures have a great impact on the organizational behaviour, but in the strong culture employee's goals side with the goal of management and help to increase the overall organizational performance. According to Barney (1991), organizational culture provides sustainable aggressive advantage. He introduced three conditions; first, he suggests that culture must be viable; second, the culture must be rare and have attributes; and third, culture must be imperfectly imitable. These can provide assistance to superior organizational performance that can be temporary or continue for long term. Long-term increase in organizational performance may cause to get the competitive advantage under long run. Kotter and Heskett (1992) conducted a study and found that organizational performance increasing culture or strong culture raised the income of the organizations by 76.5% between 1977 and 1988, and only 1% increase in the same period of time for firms without performance-enhancing culture (Gallagher, 2008).

Marcoulides and Heck (1993) analysed the relationship between organizational culture and performance using data collected from 26 organizations. The authors proposed a model in which organizational culture was measured using several latent variables (organizational structure, organizational values, task organization, climate, and individual values and beliefs) and organizational performance was measured using capital, market and financial indicators. The results of this study showed that all of the latent variables used to measure organizational culture had some effect on performance with workers' attitudes and task organization activities being the most significant variables.

The cultural and behavioural characteristics of organizations have a measurable effect on a company's performance. Organizations with a participative culture not only perform better than those without such a culture but also have a margin of difference that widens over time, suggesting a possible cause-and-effect relationship between culture and performance. Organizations that have strong cultures with the required attributes can obtain sustained superior financial performance from their cultures (Daniel, 1984; Barney, 1986; Jesper, 2002; Shahzad et al., 2012).

Gordon (1992) investigates the relationships of culture strength and two substantive cultural values with corporate performance. Culture strength is measured by the consistency of responses to survey items across people and the two cultural values are measured by items on the survey that relate to either adaptability or stability. Denison and Mishra (1993) developed a model of organizational culture and effectiveness based on four traits of organizational cultures: involvement, consistency, adaptability and mission. Further, they highlight that culture can be studied as an integral part of the adaptation process of organizations and those specific culture traits may be useful predictors of performance and effectiveness. Study of Smart and John (1996) hypothesized that the linkage between organizational culture and effectiveness has focused on the differential effectiveness of organizations depending on their dominant culture type and their culture strength. Diagnosing and changing organizational culture provides a framework, a sense-making tool, a set of systematic steps and a methodology for helping managers and their organizations carefully analyse and alter their fundamental culture. Cameron and Quinn focus on the methods and mechanisms that are available to help managers and change agents transform the most fundamental elements of their organizations. Further, they provide instruments to help individuals guide the change process at the most basic level – culture. Diagnosing and changing organizational culture offers a systematic strategy for internal or external change agents to facilitate foundational change that in turn makes it possible to support and supplement other kinds of change initiatives (Cameron et al., 2005).

Mendonca et al. (1999) emphasize the need to understand the precise way in which culture influences the effectiveness of the organization's HRM practices. For this purpose, their study first describes the findings of a series of conceptual and empirical studies that 'explain why a set of HRM practices might be effective in one societal culture and not in another'. Their study explores the practical implications of these findings for the design of performance management – a most critical activity in managing human resources. It proposes practical strategies to tailor this activity to fit the societal and work cultures of most of the countries with emerging markets.

Daulatram (2003) examines the impact of organizational culture types on job satisfaction in a survey of marketing professionals in a cross-section of firms in the United States. Cameron and Freeman's (1991) model of organizational cultures comprising of clan, adhocracy, hierarchy and market was utilized as the conceptual framework for analysis. The results indicate that job satisfaction levels varied across corporate cultural typology. Within the study's conceptual framework, job satisfaction invoked an alignment of cultures on the vertical axis that represents a continuum of organic processes (with an emphasis on flexibility and spontaneity) to mechanistic processes (which emphasize control, stability and order). Job satisfaction was positively related to clan and adhocracy cultures and negatively related to market and hierarchy cultures. John (2003) highlights the extent to which community college faculty and administrators' perceptions of the organizational effectiveness of their institutions was related to their perceptions of the cognitive and behavioural complexity of the organizational cultures and the leadership roles performed by senior campus officials of their institutions. The findings show a strong relationship between perceptions of the organizational effectiveness of the institutions and the level of complexity in their campus cultures and the leadership behaviours of senior campus officials. Christophe and Vas (2009) study how the organizational culture influences the effectiveness of business schools. Similar assessments were carried out to study organizational culture in the medicine sector, focusing on nursing staff's job satisfaction and their turnover intention (Park & Kim, 2009). Study done by Peter (2004) examines the effects of organizational culture and leadership styles on job satisfaction and organizational commitment in samples comprising Hong Kong and Australian managers. Sharma and Aditi Sharma (2010) also examine the relationship between organizational culture and leadership.

Amah (2012) examines the effect of corporate culture on organizational effectiveness in the banking industry. The findings indicate that adaptability positively influences organizational profitability and market share. There is no significant relationship between adaptability and organizational productivity. Shared mission, employee involvement and shared values (consistency) are positively related to profitability, productivity and market share. Corporate culture has a significant influence on organizational effectiveness. An effective culture must be aligned with employee values and be consistent with the environment in which the organization operates. While it is best to establish a positive culture with which employees can identify during an organization's infancy, it is possible to change an existing culture. Such change is best accomplished by modelling desired behaviour at all levels of management and by planning events that foster frequent interaction among cross-functional employees. Another set of studies concluded that a positive culture can provide a significant competitive advantage (Sadri & Lee, 2001; Tiang et al., 2012).

MacNab et al. (2007) examine the relationship of culture to the propensity for, and potential effectiveness of, both internal reporting and whistleblowing as ethical management tools within a North American context. Samples from a total of 10 regions in the United States, Canada and Mexico increased the accuracy and meaningfulness of the findings. Hofstede's cultural dimensions such as uncertainty avoidance and power distance had the most consistent and significant relationship to propensity for both whistleblowing and internal reporting, while collectivism was not found to be significantly related to either of the ethics management tools. Managers who better understand the cultural links to ethics management are more likely to craft the most effective organizational ethics strategies. Bercovitch and Foulkes (2012) highlight that culture has become more important in the current environment, where much conflict takes place not just between states, but mostly between groups, divided along cultural or religious lines, within a state. They examine how culture affects the process and effectiveness of international mediation and develop a theoretical framework to examine culture, its dimensions and how these may impact mediation.

Shenkar (2001) explains that cultural distance is a widely used construct in international business, where it has been applied to foreign investment expansion, entry mode choice and the performance of foreign-invested affiliates, among others. He further presented a critical review of the cultural distance construct, outlining its hidden assumptions and challenging its theoretical and methodological properties. A comprehensive framework for the treatment of the construct is developed and concrete steps aimed at enhancing rigor are delineated.

Tran and Martin (2002) provide the results of an exploratory survey of construction industry managers in Singapore to isolate some of the common effects of national and organizational culture, together with the personal characteristics of managers, on the efficacy of project communication. By examination of significant correlation coefficients, the various types of influences are identified. The results of the research suggest that the managers' attitude and behaviours towards communication may be guided to a large extent by their level of competence. The study also provides evidence to suggest that the individuals' understanding of the communication process and its barriers, the way they behave with other individuals and expect to be treated, varies according to national cultures.

Currie and Kerrin (2004) examine the issues of epistemology, power and culture with respect to their impact upon the use of information and communication technology (ICT) to manage knowledge within an organization. They utilized an empirical case study of a global pharmaceutical company, in which the implementation of an intranet failed to meet aspirations of the chief executive: employees should be able to freely share knowledge. Study illustrates that "technical fixes" to knowledge management issues merely harden existing practices and routines, rather than open up new directions. In particular, broader organizational issues of power and culture may mean that employees are unwilling or unable to share knowledge and, beyond the epistemological problem, this is likely to further inhibit the contribution of ICT to the management of knowledge.

Mohe (2008) shows that the phenomenon of management consulting is culturally determined to a significant extent. At the same time, it will become clear that consultancies have a strong influence on clients as well as on countries and societies. On the other hand, Singh (2007) argued that the construct of culture has not improved the understanding of firm strategy or performance. This leads to the general argument that culture has limited relevance for strategy.

Dominic (2012) shows that studies on the management of cross-cultural conflict in organizations are put into an analytically structured synoptic model that helps to reveal a wide range of forms and of the extent of the assumed influence of culture on social interaction in organizational settings. Evaluations of competent conflict management strategies derived from these theories will differ, respectively. Furthermore, the model may illustrate clusters of contemporary research versus idle approaches of research that may hide some potential for future studies.

Costas (2012) explores normative control in a culture of friendship. In-depth qualitative data gathered at a management consultancy firm reveal how management seeks to foster informal, intimate and apparently egalitarian relationships with employees. This is conceptualized as a culture of friendship, indicative of broader trends towards individuality, choice and anti-authoritarianism. It begins by comparing with the culture prevalent in a family and further develops by referring to the culture of friendship. Despite the emphasis on freedom, openness and spontaneity, normative control is accentuated and extended, involving certain paradoxes and reinforcing control circles. Lumby (2011) argues that leadership must engage with culture as a key mediator of power within organizations. Four levels of cultural activity are suggested: the cultural context created by global phenomena, the cultures of local communities, the organizational culture and the sub- and counter-cultures within the organization.

Groeschi and Doherty (2000) review the way culture has been conceptualized by various writers. It concluded that two early definitions of culture, Kluckhohn and Strodtbeck's (1961) value orientations and Inkles and Levinson's (1969) predictions of common human problems, provide the foundation for more recent definitions of culture. The manifestation of culture is in terms of layers – behaviour (outermost), values (middle) and basic assumptions (inner).

Many researchers combine culture with another term to define its boundaries, such as national culture, industry culture, occupational culture, and corporate culture. The opinions differ when it comes to concluding about the degree of influence which national culture exerts on organizational cultures or the other way round.

Dimensions of National Culture

Few studies have focused on comparisons between the influence of national cultures and other levels of culture. This might be due to the thin and unclear borderlines between different levels of culture. Importance of understanding the barriers/cautions has been felt by Daun (1998), who further highlighted the barriers/cautions in describing the national culture:

Different sources of information present different material, which means that any national culture will appear differently on the particular sources which are used.

Differently framed questions generate different responses.

National culture presented is dependent on how intra-national variation is handled.

Generalizations about traits or values described as characteristic of a national culture have to be based on data in terms of statistical frequencies.

When comparing responses to the same question from different countries, possible culture-related differences in perceiving and interpreting the questions must be taken into account.

Given the fact that cultures continuously change, caution is necessary about data collected over a long period.

Situation is an important concept. Personality and individual values are modified by situations.

In a national culture many diverse phenomena are expected to carry the same message, since they are shaped by the same general environment. Nevertheless, there are always contradictions and exceptions that blur the systematic.

'Something' may be typical of a nation or significant to nationality. However, that does not mean that this 'something' is universally unique.

Self stereotypes that people hold about their own culture are themselves part of that national culture.

Surveys among individual subjects offer a highly differentiated (mixed) picture of national characteristic, in contrast to studies of institutions.

What might be called an essence of a national culture – or possibly described as several dominant factors – should mainly be labelled as a model that is an intellectual construction.

Even when research is pursued with objectivity as a scientific goal, the description of the culture will be perceived by an audience which is in itself biased by a culture.

Cummings and Schmidt (1972) examine the relative role of cultural background and degree of industrialization in the managerial beliefs of a sample of Greek managers. Adle's (1983) study delineates six approaches to researching cross-cultural management issues: parochial, ethnocentric, polycentric, comparative, geocentric and synergistic. For each approach, assumptions are discussed concerning the similarity and difference across cultures and the extent to which management phenomena are or are not universal. The primary types of management questions which can be addressed using each approach are clarified.

Chee (1992) focuses on cultural behaviour and organizational management behaviour in the context of Malay culture and argued that they relate to each other in subtle and intricate ways. The tasks of management teaching are inter alia to ascertain their modes of relationship, on the one hand, and, on the other, to explain how one may enhance the other.

Hofstede's (1983) work summarizes a large research project, involving 116,000 questionnaires, about the work-related value patterns of matched samples of industrial employees in 50 countries and 3 regions at 2 points in time. Half of the variance in the countries' mean scores can be explained by four basic dimensions, here labelled as power distance, uncertainty avoidance, individualism versus collectivism, and masculinity versus femininity. These dimensions are offered as a framework for developing hypotheses in cross-cultural organization studies. Index scores of the countries on the four dimensions correlate significantly with the outcomes of about 40 existing comparative studies. The four dimensions considered here relate to very fundamental problems which are faced by any human society. Different societies have found different solutions to these problems. They are used to explain (a) different ways of structuring organizations, (b) differentiations of people within organizations and (c) different issues people and organizations face within society. On the basis of combined scores, the countries studied can be grouped by cultural clusters. The data also allow some conclusions about trends in value shifts over time.

Bruce and Harbir (1988) discuss that characteristics of national cultures have frequently been claimed to influence the selection of entry mode by developing a theoretical argument for the reasons culture should influence the choice of entry. Two hypotheses are derived which relate culture to entry mode choice, one focusing on the cultural distance between countries, the other on attitudes towards uncertainty avoidance. Using a multinomial logic model and controlling for other effects, the hypotheses are tested by analysing data on 228 entries into the United States market by acquisition, wholly owned by greenfield, and joint venture. Empirical support for the effect of national culture on entry choice is found.

Chow et al. (1991) show that the increasing dominance of Asian manufacturing firms in the global economy has raised an important issue: whether these firms' superior manufacturing performance is caused by their management control systems, the national culture of their employees, or the interaction of these two factors. This experimental study provides a direct test of the effects of national culture and management control system on manufacturing performance. The dimension of national culture studied was individualism (versus collectivism) because this work-related attribute has been noted as a major difference between Asian and Western cultures. In turn, the focus on cultural individualism motivated a study of two aspects of management controls: work flow interdependence and pay interdependence. The results are consistent with cultural individualism and management controls having independent, but not interactive, effects on manufacturing performance. Later, various studies proved that there is impact of national culture on organizational behaviour and reviewed whether national culture, as determined by the nationality-based work values, beliefs and orientations of the owners and managers of organizations, influences the values, orientations and practices of organizations (Smith, 1996; Awasthi et al., 1998; Chui, 2002; Bruce & Roberto, 2004; Parboteeah & Bronson, 2005; Bhaskaran & Sukumaran, 2007).

Adriana and Hilal's (2006) study looks into the organizational culture of a Brazilian company, concentrating on its main Brazilian branches as well as on its European, Latin American, Central American, North American and Asian branches, making a total sample of 36 cities and 1,742 respondents. Results indicate the influence of national culture on organizational culture, as the dimensions found clearly reflect the ambiguity and double-edged ethic characteristics of Brazilian culture. This study also shows the importance of hierarchy and relational networks, which stresses the relevance of the cultural element in organizational structure and functioning. In brief, understanding the double-edged ethic that governs Brazilian culture helps us understand apparently different, ambiguous, or even contradictory behaviours reflected in the organizational culture practices of a Brazilian company with international operations.

Myloni et al. (2004) investigate that whether HRM in Greece is maintaining its national character or whether it is converging towards a model that potentially clashes with the country's traditional societal values. This issue fits in the wider convergence–divergence debate that has been the concern of many cross-cultural researchers. Using data collected from Greek firms and subsidiaries of multinationals companies (MNCs) located in Greece, we compare the two groups on specific HRM practices. The aim is to show how HRM practices of Greek firms differ from those of MNCs' subsidiaries and examine the extent and the way these HRM practices reflect Greek national culture. Our empirical results indicate that HRM practices in Greek firms reflect national culture to a great extent. Moreover, they imply that in some areas MNC subsidiaries have realized a considerable degree of adaptation, embracing practices that are in line with the Greek cultural environment.

Veser (2004) offers a theoretical framework for stakeholder management in an international and multicultural environment. Through the use of an extensive qualitative case study analysis, a methodological approach was developed for analysing stakeholder dialogue data for cultural differences. Based on the empirical data it was possible to show specific ways in which cultural dimensions affect the international diffusion of stakeholder-related policies. These findings contribute to the field's knowledge on internal stakeholder management implementation, by addressing the complexity of embedding stakeholder management principles and practices within various international subsidiaries of the same multinational organization.

Hewett et al. (2006) examine whether national culture directly moderates the link between buyer and seller relationship strength and repurchase intentions in industrial markets, as well as whether it indirectly moderates the same link through its influence on corporate culture. Barinaga (2007) argues that cultural differences are given explanatory authority, cultural diversity acquiring a positivist status and group members being treated as 'dopes of their culture'. An alternative approach is to conceive 'cultural diversity' and 'national culture' as discursive resources used by group members in everyday group life.

Gerhart (2008) opines that national culture is widely viewed as a constraint on management practice. However, that view is increasingly inconsistent with available empirical evidence. Chevrier's (2009) article advocates that national cultures should be considered even in the global economic context. First, analysis on the national scale makes sense when it is grounded in a political approach to culture. Second, the relevance of the national level is illustrated by the case of Switzerland. Even though at first sight it appears that Switzerland is a country with multiple internal cultures and borders, a closer analysis shows that the Swiss people share a common political culture based upon attachment to local communities and institutions, to government through consensus and to conflict solving by resorting to arbitration and pragmatism. In the Swiss case, the article shows that management practices are embedded in national political cultures. Heijes (2011) examines the role of power and power differences in cross-cultural perception and demonstrate how cross-cultural perception between two specific ethnic groups, European Dutch and African Curaçaoans, changes depending on the amount of power imbalance in the various organizational and national contexts. The study highlights the need for research on the impact of power dynamics on cross-cultural perception, an approach that goes beyond the traditional, dimensional approach that is prevalent in organization literature. Cross-cultural conflict and its management in a multicultural work environment are affected by teamwork paradoxes as perceived and experienced by multicultural team members working in project and management teams. The multicultural team paradoxes and their managerial implications are explained in terms of cross-cultural conflict management on multiple levels (Plessis, 2011).

D'Iribarne (2009) discusses that the idea of a national culture is generally challenged by those using an interpretative approach. It is stated that, within a given society, one comes across rival definitions of reality. But it is possible to present a theory enabling us to take into consideration what is diverse and changing as well as what is shared and stable. There is emerging evidence that shows national culture influences visitor behaviour and moderates the relationship between managers and impact of national culture on CEO compensation and salary gaps between CEOs and manufacturing workers (Hofstede, 1980; Reisinger & Crotts, 2010; Grenness, 2011; Smith et al., 2011).

Smith (2011) presents that national cultures may be distinguished in terms of prevalent styles of communication, as exemplified by survey response styles. A distinction is made between the average communication style within a given nation and the nation-level dispersion of communication styles. Peretz and Rosenblatt (2011) discuss the role of cultural practices on the level of organizational investment in training, with the added effect of key organizational background characteristics (size and technological level). Secondary analysis was conducted on the data of project GLOBE (Global Leadership and Organizational Effectiveness) and of CRANET (Cross-Country Human Resource Management Research), covering 5991 organizations and 21 countries. Controlled for organization size and technology level, as well as economic strength (GNI), cultural practices such as low power distance, high future orientation and high uncertainty avoidance explained increased investment in training, supporting the study hypotheses. Organizational characteristics were also related to investment in training: larger size and high (vs. low) technology predicted increased investment. The two organizational background characteristics interacted with national values, so the above effects of uncertainty avoidance and future orientation were higher, respectively, for larger organizations and high-tech organizations. Implications are particularly relevant for diverse organizations, which encourage the employment of a diverse workforce, and for international organizations, which tend to emphasize a global organizational culture and standard organizational practices while underestimating local cultural values.

Minkov and Hofstede (2012) state that many cross-cultural studies have used nations as the units of analysis; the concept of national culture has been challenged on various grounds. One objection is that there may be significant cultural diversity within some countries and similarities across national borders, compromising the concept of national culture. This objection has little empirical support. They used latest World Values Survey data and found that 299 in-country regions from 28 countries in East and Southeast Asia, sub-Saharan Africa, Latin America, and the Anglo world overwhelmingly cluster along national lines on basic cultural values, cross-border inter-mixtures being relatively rare. This is true even of countries like Malaysia and Indonesia, or Mexico and Guatemala, despite their shared official languages, religions, ethnic groups, historical experiences and various traditions. Even the regions of neighbouring African nations, such as Ghana, Burkina Faso and Mali, do not intermingle much when they are clustered on the basis of cultural values.

Witte (2012) argues that isolating culture within organizational analysis and extracting cultural lessons from managerial situations have generated cross-national categories of culture and competing paradigms for studying the cultural, inter-cultural and cross-cultural influences of economic and social life. As organizations around the world combine different cultural diversities, and the use of individual, national and political aggregates of study do not necessarily transpose well onto many business situations (especially in atypical examples such as those presented in nongovernmental organizations [NGOs], clubs, associations and public agencies), the use of nation profiles and dimensions as analytical terms for culture in organizations has become questionable. Further, Witte (2012) explores options for integrating the cultural credibility among the explanatory tools of contractual human organization and for innovating on the methods, designs and formats of cultural research for management studies.

Models/Frameworks for Understanding Dimensions of National Culture

Some scholars have developed models/frameworks for understanding dimensions of national culture by providing different perspectives. Trompenaars (1994) identified seven dimensions by which culture can be distinguished from each other. Every culture distinguishes itself from others by the specific solutions it chooses to certain problems. It is convenient to look at these problems under three headings: those that arise from our relationships with other people, those that come with the passage of time and those that relate to the environment. From the solutions different cultures have chosen to these universal problems, seven fundamental dimensions of culture can be identified.

Relationships with People

There are five orientations encapsulating the ways in which human beings deal with each other:

Universalism versus Particularism

The Universalist approach can be summed up approximately as 'what is good and right can be defined and always applies.' In particularistic cultures far greater attention is given to the obligations of relationships and unique circumstances. For example, instead of assuming that the one good way must always be followed, the particularistic reasoning is that friendship has special obligations and hence may come first.

Individualism versus Collectivism

Do people regard themselves primarily as individuals or primarily as part of a group? Furthermore, is it more important to focus on individuals so that they can contribute to the collective as and if they wish, or is it more important to consider the collective first since that is shared by many individuals?

Neutral or Emotional

Should the nature of our interactions be objective and detached, or is expressing emotion acceptable? In North America and North-West Europe business relationships are typically instrumental and all about achieving objectives. The brain checks emotions because these are believed to confuse the issues. But further south and in many other cultures, business is a human affair and the whole gamut of emotions is deemed appropriate. Laughing louder, banging your fist on the table, or leaving a conference room in anger during a negotiation is all part of business.

Specific versus Diffuse

In specific-oriented cultures a manager segregates out the task relationship he or she has with a subordinate and insulates this from other dealings. Each area in which the two encounter each other is considered apart from the other, a specific case. But in diffusion-oriented cultures, every life space and every level of personality tends to permeate all others.

Achievement versus Ascription

Achievement means that you are judged on what you have recently accomplished and have on your record. Ascription means that status is attributed to you, not only by birth, kinship, gender or age but also by your connections (who you know) and your educational record. In an achievement culture, the first question is likely to be 'What did you study?,' while in a more ascriptive culture the question will more likely be 'Where did you study?' Only if it was a lousy university or one they do not recognize will ascriptive people ask what did you study and that will be to enable you to save face.

Attitudes to Time

The way in which societies look at time also differs, in terms of the relative importance given to the past, present and future. In some societies what somebody has achieved in the past is not that important. It is more important to know what plan they have developed for the future. In other societies you can make more of an impression with your past accomplishments than those of today. These are cultural differences that greatly influence corporate activities.

Attitudes to the Environment

Some cultures see the major focus affecting their lives and the origins of vice and virtue as residing within the person. Here, motivations and values are derived from within. Other cultures see the world as more powerful than individuals. They see nature as something to be feared or emulated.

Effective management strives towards reconciling the above dilemmas. You can only prosper if as many particulars as possible are covered by rules, yet exceptions are seen and noted. You can only think effectively if both the specifics and diffuse wholes and the segments and the integrations are covered. Whether you are at heart an individualist or a collectivist, your individuals must be capable of organizing themselves and your collectivities are only as good as the health, wealth and wisdom of each member. It is crucial to give status to achievers, but equally crucial to back strategies, projects and new initiatives from people who have not yet achieved anything, in other words to ascribe status to these in order to facilitate success. It is both true that time is a passing sequence of events and a moment of truth, a 'now' in which past, present and future are given new meanings. We need to accept influences both from the depth of our inner convictions and from the world around us.

In the final analysis, culture is the manner in which these dilemmas are reconciled, since every nation seeks a different and winding path to its own ideals of integrity. Business will succeed to the extent that this reconciliation occurs.

Hofstede (1994) made significant contribution towards understanding of national culture and characterized national culture as follows:

Four Dimensions of National Culture

National culture can be defined as the collective programming of the mind acquired by growing up in a particular country. Hofstede (1974) surveyed employees who worked in the local subsidiaries of IBM, in over 50 countries in the world. He found that from one country to another, they represent almost perfectly matched samples; they are similar in all respects except nationality, which makes the effect of nationality differences in their answers stand out unusually clearly. His findings supported theory of Inkeles and Levinson (1954) empirically, and he named four dimensions of national culture. They are power distance, collectivism versus individualism, femininity versus masculinity, and uncertainty avoidance. Later, he added the fifth dimension, named short-term versus long-term orientation (Confucianism).

Power distance can be defined as the extent to which the less powerful members of institution and organization within a country expect and accept that power is distributed unequally.

Individualism pertains to societies in which the ties between individuals are loose; everyone is expected to look after himself or herself and his or her family, whereas collectivism pertains to societies in which people from birth onwards are integrated into strong, cohesive in-groups, which throughout people's lifetime continue to protect them in exchange for unquestioning loyalty.

Masculinity pertains to societies in which social gender roles are clearly distinct (e.g., men are supposed to be assertive, tough and focused on material success whereas women are supposed to be more modest, tender and concerned with the quality of life). Femininity pertains to societies in which social gender roles overlap (e.g., both men and women are supposed to be modest, tender and concerned with quality of life).

Uncertainty avoidance refers to the extent to which the members of a culture feel threatened by uncertain or unknown situations. These feelings are expressed through nervous stress and in a need for predictability, for example, a need for written and unwritten rules.

Six Dimensions of Organization Culture

While the IBM studies led to the identification of four dimensions of national cultures, a cross-organizational study referred to in Hofstede's book found six different dimensions for organizational cultures. Whereas the study on the national cultures focused on values, the research leading to the dimensions of organizational culture dealt more with practices. The research analysis produced six clear factors reflecting dimensions of practices, and these were labelled the following:

Process Oriented versus Resulted Oriented

The dimension opposed a concern with means (process oriented) to a concern with goals (result oriented). In process-oriented cultures people perceive themselves as avoiding risks and making only a limited effort in their job, while each day is mostly the same. In results-oriented cultures people perceive themselves as comfortable in unfamiliar situations and put in maximal effort, while each day is felt to bring new challenges. Hofstede argues that for this dimension it is not difficult to label process-oriented cultures as bad and results-oriented cultures as good. However, sometimes and in certain industries it is necessary to have a single-minded focus on the process.

Employee Oriented versus Job Oriented

This dimension opposes a concern for people (employee oriented) to a concern for completing a job (job oriented). In employee-oriented cultures people feel their personal problems are taken into account that the organization takes a responsibility for employee welfare and that important decisions are usually made by groups of committees. On the other hand, people in the job-oriented cultures experience a strong pressure to complete the job; they perceive the organization as only interested in the work employees do and not in their personal and family welfare, and important decisions tend to be made by individuals. The study showed that while individuals may be both employee and job oriented at the same time, organizational cultures are likely to favour one or another.

Parochial versus Professional

This dimension distinguishes organizations whose employees have their identity largely from the organization (parochial) to organizations in which people identify with their type of job (professional). Results from the study show that members of parochial cultures feel the organization's norms cover their behaviour at home as well as on the job. Moreover, they feel that in hiring employees, the company takes their social and family background into account as much as their job competence. Also, these people do not look far into the future, and perhaps this is due to the assumption of the organization doing this for them. Members of professional cultures consider their private lives their own business; they feel the organization hires on the basis of job competence only, and they do think far ahead. In addition, professional organizations tend to have employees with more education than parochial organizations.

Open System versus Closed System

This dimension is really describing the communication climate and opposes open and closed systems. Members of an open system consider both the organization and its people open to newcomers and outsiders; almost anyone would fit into the organization, and new employees need to spend only a few days to feel at home. In closed systems, the organization and its people are felt to be closed and secretive, even among insiders. Only very special people fit into the closed organization and new employees need more than a year to feel at home.

Lose Control versus Tight Control

The dimension refers to the amount of internal structuring in the organization and whether the control is loose or tight. People in loose-control organizations feel that no one thinks of cost, meeting times are only kept approximately and jokes about the company and the job are frequent. People in tight-control organizations have a very cost-conscious working environment, meeting times are kept punctually and jokes about the company or the job are rare.

Normative versus Pragmatic

This dimension deals with the popular notion of 'customer orientation'. Pragmatic organizations are market driven, while normative organizations view their task towards the outside world as the implementation of inviolable rules. In normative organizations the emphasis is on correctly following the organizational procedures, which are more important than results. Also, the organization's standards are high in matters of business ethics and honesty. In the pragmatic organizations, there is major stress and weight on meeting the customer's needs, results are more important than correct procedures and a pragmatic rather than a dogmatic attitude in matters of business ethics prevails.

National Culture and Management Practices (Cross-cultural Research)

In recent times, cross-cultural research has occupied an important space in the management studies and it is widely accepted that understanding of cross-cultural practices helps in making business successful across the world. Smith (1992) examines the degree to which organizational behaviour is found to vary between national cultures, by reviewing findings and prior studies, relating organizational structure, effective leader styles, HRM policies and negotiation to variations in national culture. The implications of the differences found between multicultural management, training and career development are explored. The framework provided by Hofstede is used to interpret the variations found; for example, Aston hypotheses are not so strongly supported in non-western data. Further, none of the non-western countries in Aston's sample score above the midpoint for collectivism in Hofstede's study (Donaldson, 1986). A comparison of Japanese, Hong Kong and British Firms of similar sizes (Redding & Pugh, 1986) showed that formalization was highest in Japan, followed by Britain and Hong Kong. Structures put in place may be similar, but they will only be put to use in ways that are culturally compatible. Tayeb (1988) found that though firms were structurally similar, British managers tended to consult their subordinates before reaching decision, while Indian managers did not. In the case of United States it was shown that there was no empirical support for one 'best way to lead'; in collectivistic countries (Japan, Taiwan, Iran, Brazil and India) the notion of a single effective leader style has received much stronger support (Smith & Tayeb, 1988) – high task + high relationship.

With regards to HRM policies, a comparison of United States, Japanese and European firms (Kanungo, 1985) showed that Japanese firms reported flatter hierarchies, less precise job descriptions, longer-term performance evaluation, control systems based upon self-discipline and more promotion from within. Child's (1981) study of British versus German companies showed that British firms demonstrated more internal promotion and more concern for employees' rewards and benefits and development of young executives. With regards to level of directness employed by negotiators, Graham (1985) showed that Brazilians took much longer, spoke more frequently, and said 'no' 10 times and touched or made physical contact with one another from time to time. Japanese were more modest during the initial bids, looked at each other less, said 'no' less often, and remained silent most of the times. Americans expressed and made forceful demands in the earlier part of the negotiation and intermediate on other criteria. Other aspects of negotiation where differences exist include: pace of negotiations, short-term versus long-term focus and desirability of explicit contract.

Triandis (2001) reviews the extent literature under three headings – Theory, Method and Applications – and gives suggestions for future research in cross-cultural management.

Theory: 'In future, we should have much better theories about what culture really is, what aspects of management phenomena are universal and what aspects are culture-specific, and ways in which we can integrate what is specific to one culture into a theoretical framework that deals with all cultures.'

We must examine more dimensions of culture and refine existing dimensions (e.g., Triandis, 2001). Also the inter-linkages among the various dimensions must be studied. Further, how do these dimensions emerge in different ecologies and how do historical factors shape them?

We must develop ways to describe specific phenomena, such as effective leadership, by using these dimensions as parameters.

Method: Three methodological perspectives are important: (a) the anthropological perspective, (b) the indigenous perspective and (c) the cross-cultural perspective. Triandis (1999) argues that ideally we should use all three approaches with multi-method measurements and look for convergence among the approaches.

Applications: Most important is how to deal with differences in subjective culture when people work together.

Tayeb (2001) focuses on six issues of concern: dimension of national culture, treatment of non-cultural factors in cross-cultural studies, disentanglement of national culture from organizational culture, parity of meaning of concepts across cultural boundaries with special emphasis on HRM, research tools, and researcher's cultural bias.

Dimension of culture, while facilitating comparisons across boundaries, simplifies a complex and dynamic construct and diminishes the accuracy and therefore reliability of research findings along the way. In addition, breaking down culture to a handful of bi-polar dimensions ignores the fact that the two opposing poles of each of these dimensions may exist in the same culture.

Non-cultural factors are still not taken as seriously in many cross-cultural studies as they should be. They could be either studied alongside the cultural factors in order to arrive at a fuller picture of what actually influences workplace values and actions or, alternatively, design them out of the equation by comparing like with like – through matching samples in different countries on non-critical factors.

The issue of separation of organizational culture from the national culture has always been a problem. One can, to some extent, hold organizational culture constant by studying a single MNC across a number of nations, but even this does not fully disentangle the two cultures completely or satisfactorily.

Parity of meaning across cultures is another problem. For example, the term HRM may seem familiar to everyone, but in reality, people assign widely different meanings to it depending on where they come from. The different cultural backgrounds of both the researcher and the researched create an environment ripe for misunderstanding, frustration, prejudice and even hurt.

Morden (1995) examines the process of international cultural interpretation and adaptation in relation to (a) motivation theories, (b) leadership concepts and (c) management by objectives.

Motivation Theories

In societies that are individualistic, masculine and display low uncertainty avoidance (United States), there is a primacy of achievement needs implying self-advancement and the attaining of self-satisfaction through increased material rewards, increased status and personal 'self-actualization'.

In societies where masculinity, low power distance and high uncertainty avoidance (Germany and Austria) prevail, work motivation is a function of the need to relieve tension and stress.

Performance-based systems of remuneration work in masculine societies, in which emphasis is placed on individual performance. However, in societies that are feminine, though highly individualistic (Scandinavia, Netherlands), which stress interpersonal cooperation and de-emphasize interpersonal competition, such systems may be seen as inappropriate or even counterproductive.

Theory Z will be difficult to achieve in cultures characterized by large power distance, strong individualism, aggressive masculinity, strong uncertainty avoidance and a strong attachment to hierarchies. Ideally, Theory Z appears to support collectivistic societies, wherein exists a small power distance culture.

Leadership Concepts

In general, issues of leadership will be more relevant to cultures, which are characterized by large power distance, masculinity and strong uncertainty avoidance. Management style will tend towards Theory X, the exploitative-authoritative or the benevolent-authoritative and/or the paternalistic.

Leadership may be perceived to be less of an issue in collectivist or communitarian cultures or those cultures characterized by low power distance, femininity and weak uncertainty avoidance. Management style may tend towards Theory Y, the consultative or the participative group, or Theory Z.

Management by Objectives (MBO)

MBO is likely to succeed in societies characterized by low power distance, high masculinity and weak uncertainty avoidance.

Hofstede (1983) argues that the native assumption that management is the same or is becoming same around the world is not tenable, in view of the demonstrated differences in national cultures across four dimensions, namely, individualism versus collectivism, large or small power distance, strong or weak uncertainty avoidance, and masculinity versus femininity.

The consequences of national culture differences for management theory and practice are then brought out. Further, Hofstede stated that national and regional differences are not disappearing; they are here to stay. In fact these differences may become one of the most crucial problems for management, in particular for the management of multinational, multicultural organizations.

Schneider and Meyer (1991) encountered that perceptions of environmental uncertainty and organizational control influence strategic behaviour, which could be broadly categorized as either proactive or reactive. As national culture influences these perceptions, strategic behaviour is likely to be influenced by national culture. Given a case describing an issue concerning deregulation of the US banking industry, managers completed questionnaires rating interpretations and responses to issues raised in those questionnaires. National culture was found to influence the interpretation and responses. In particular, Latin-European managers compared with other managers were more likely to interpret the issue as a crisis and as a threat. Latin-Europeans were also more likely to recommend proactive behaviour.

Gilbert and Lorange (1994) state that strategic management is viewed as consisting of two major tasks: (a) strategy formulation, which focuses on business opportunity seeking and (b) strategy implementation, which focuses on mobilizing the firm's resources to go after the identified opportunities. Further, strategy formulation is assumed to be impacted by the cognitive style of managers, while strategy implementation is assumed to be influenced by the nature of the social contact. And national differences result in quite different cognitive approaches to strategic management's tenability. Cognitive styles can vary from the normative (France) at one extreme to the experiential (United States) at the other, with a mix of the two (Japan) as a possibility. Similarly, the nature of social contact can vary from individualistic (United States) at one extreme to societal (Japan) at the other, with a middle-way 'corporatism' (France).

Groeschi's (2003) work delineates the appraisal process into its component stages and attempts to explain how cultural differences could impact each stage. The stages/functions of the appraisal process are as follows:

- Focus of assessment
- Individualist– more performance oriented

- Collectivist – more emphasis on personal relationships, harmony and organizational integration
- Assessment methods
- Could vary in the degree of participation and openness, and cultural preferences could vary based on the extent of participation/openness
- Assessment criteria
- Competencies identified could be contingent on the national/organizational culture
- High-masculine – leadership, independence, challenge and recognition
- Low-masculine – cooperation, group decisions, implementation of appraisal systems
- High individualistic, high uncertainty avoidance – formal systems high collectivism, low uncertainty avoidance – informal systems, choice of appraiser
- High power distance – immediate supervisors low power distance – multisource assessment (360 degree feedback), reviewing past performance
- High level of control over environment, high uncertainty avoidance – performance feedback has a positive effect
- Low level of control over environment, low uncertainty avoidance – performance feedback may not have expected positive effect
- Temporal focus
- No attention to the past – feedback process negatively affected
- No attention to the future – career planning and setting financial/non-financial goals and objectives not given any importance

Mendonca and Kanungo (1996) highlight the sociocultural environment of the developing countries, compared to the developed countries, as one marked by a relatively high uncertainty avoidance and power distance and relatively low individualism and masculinity. One of the important conditions for effectively managing subordinate's performance is to involve them in setting of challenging and difficult goals. Because high uncertainty avoidance discourages risk taking, it becomes a severe constraint on effective performance management.

Newman and Nollen's (1996) study showed that the financial performance of European and Asian work units of one MNC was examined as a function of the congruence between management practices and national culture. Using Hofstede's five national culture dimensions and analogous management practices, it was found that work unit performance was higher when management practices in the unit were congruent with the national culture.

Jaeger and Kanungo (1990) point out that the value configuration of the developing countries is clearly very different from that of the developed countries.

Dimensions	Developed countries	Developing countries
Uncertainty avoidance	Relatively low	Relatively high
Individualism–collectivism	Relatively high individualism	Relatively low individualism
Power distance	Relatively low	Relatively high
Masculinity–femininity	Relatively high masculinity	Relatively low masculinity
Abstractive–associative thinking	Relatively high abstractive/ relatively low associative thinking	Relatively high associative/ relatively low abstractive thinking

There is a wide gap between the culture values of developing countries and the values underlying most American management techniques and practices:

- Planning (career planning, strategic planning and MBO)
- Leadership and decision-making (leadership models, theory X, Y, brainstorming and decision-making models)
- Organizing and controlling (decentralization, delegation, bureaucracy, adhocracy, matrix structure)
- Organizational change (organizational development)

Thus, one should not be surprised if these techniques and practices are not well received and if they do not work. An exception to this is 'bureaucracy', which is quite congruent with the values found in developing countries.

Pizam et al. (1997) has taken up a study among 192 hotel managers in Hong Kong, Japan and Korea for determining (a) whether national cultures, as defined by Hofstede, have a greater effect on the managerial behaviour of hotel managers than the culture of the hotel industry and (b) whether personal work-related values have a determining effect on managerial behaviour. The results demonstrated more differences than similarities between the managerial practices of hotel managers from Hong Kong, Japan and Korea, indicating therefore that nationality cultures have a stronger effect on managerial behaviour than the culture of the hotel industry. The findings also show that to a large extent there was a positive relationship between work values and managerial behaviour. Therefore, it was possible to conclude that as hypothesized y Hofstede and others, values affect attitudes, which in turn affects behaviour.

According to Hofstede:

	Power distance	Uncertainty avoidance	Individualism	Masculinity
Hong Kong	High	Low	Low	High
Korea	Moderate	High	Low	Fairly low
Japan	Fairly high	High	Low	High

Out of a total of 29 managerial practices studied, only seven showed no significant differences across the three countries, indicating therefore that there was some commonality among hotel managers regardless of the country in which they operated. However, in the majority of the practices they were significantly different across the three countries, indicating that nationality cultures have a strong effect on managerial practices.

Chang (2002) brings out, using the six cultural dimensions drawn from the Kluckhohn–Strodtbek Framework, the extent to which national culture exerts influence on the way managers and employees make decisions and interpret their roles. The six dimensions are relationship with the environment, time orientation, nature of people, activity orientation, focus of responsibility, and conception of space. The determinants of culture are social structure, religion, language, education, economic philosophy and political philosophy.

Black (1999) examines the relationship between national culture and high commitment management (HCM), HCM practices include:

- Employee involvement and participation through team working, team briefs and quality circles
- Employee autonomy achieved through job design for responsibility and flexibility
- Job security
- Opportunities for advancement in the workplace
- Recruitment practices aimed at employee commitment and development
- Good relationship between management and employees
- Performance-related pay

The results were as follows:

Practice 1. measured by the percentage of respondents saying that they have at least some involvement in designing or planning their daily work, was found to be highest in Israel, Norway, the Netherlands and the United States and lowest in Germany, Austria and Ireland.

Practice 2. indicated by the percentage of respondents saying that they can work independently, was found to be most prevalent in Norway (87%) but less prevalent in Israel (48%) and Italy (43%).

Practice 3. was found to be quite prevalent in Germany, Austria and the United States. It was less widespread in Norway, Italy and the United Kingdom.

Practice 4. was found to be widely prevalent in the United States and Israel and relatively rare in Norway and Italy.

Practice 5. was found to be very/quite good in Israel, Germany and Ireland compared to the Netherlands, Italy, the United Kingdom and the United States.

Ogbor (2000) challenges the conventional idea that transfer and application of cross-cultural management and organizational practice results in either the existing traditional (non-western) practices being displaced by Western ones or a situation of incompatibility of norms leading to a total rejection of Western norms in a non-western organizational context. This study investigates the experience of a Nigerian corporation, Hayibo, in adopting modern (Western) authority and leadership norms in order to make the organization more effective and efficient in achieving its stated objectives. Interestingly, it was found that Western bureaucratic norms in the Hayibo organization sometimes served traditional purposes, while traditional norms served the purpose of the Western bureaucratic organization. The analysis provided in this study points out that the synthesis of Western and non-western norms of organizational behaviour and authority relationships brings forth consciousness that in certain contexts of cross-cultural transfer of organizational practices a conflict of existing and novel arrangements might not arise. This is because a given element of alien organizational practice might in fact coincide with indigenous norms. The possibility that organizational norms of radically different sociocultural origins may constructively coexist is conspicuously absent in the ideas expressed in the convergence, divergence and even cross-convergence theses.

Hope and Muhlemann (2001) developed a structure for issues in Production and Operation Management (POM), in order to make it amenable to study the impact of cultural dimensions on the implementation of best practices in POM. Twenty aspects of POM were identified and then grouped into six broad areas as follows:

- Product/service design
- Product/service process design
- Planning of operations
- Facilities management and planning
- Operations strategy
- People issues in POM

The nine cultural dimensions used in the study are drawn from Hofstede (1980) and Kluckhohn and Strodtbeck (1961). The study attempts to establish conceptually which aspects of 'best practice' are most likely to be influenced by differences in national cultures.

Guss (2002) explains how individualistic and collectivistic value orientations influence decision-making. People with individualistic value orientations try to prevent friction by controlling the situation through deep exploration and information gathering (Strohschneider & Guss, 1998). They are achievement oriented (Triandis, 1994) and are willing to take risks, resulting in an expansive decisive strategy. Cross-cultural comparisons showed that people in individualistic cultures prefer active, assertive and confrontational strategies for resolving conflicts (Ohbuchi et al., 1999), have more confidence in their personal decisions (Mann et al., 1998) and might therefore be more decisive and risk-taking than people in collectivist cultures in their decisions. People with collectivist values pay much more attention to the social aspects of problems (Triandis, 1994) and search especially contextual information in uncertain and complex situations (Strohschneider & Guss, 1999). They are sensitive to social consequences of their actions and follow a more defensive incremental strategy (Guss et al., 2000). They value security, are more risk avoiding and follow passive, collaborative and avoiding strategies (Ohbuchi et al., 1999).

Schuler and Rogowsky (1998) explore the relationships between the cultural dimensions suggested by Hofstede and specific compensation practices. The results suggest that national culture provides an important explanation for the variance in the utilization of different compensation practices in different countries.

Sparrow and Budhawar's (1997) study attempts to position HRM practices in India against the HRM practices of 12 other countries, utilizing the IBM/Towers Perrin World Wide Survey (1991) and the data collected from India. The total set of 38 core HR practices surveyed were reduced to nine factors.

The findings revealed that India is a cultural island in HRM terms and the thinking of its HRM practitioners does not relate significantly to that in any of the other 12 countries. However, if forced to decide which country's business model is closest to India, it is safe to say the Japanese business model shares many features with the Indian business model. Both countries have low 'structural empowerment', low 'accelerated resource development', high 'corporate responsibility' and high 'long termism'. India differs from Japan by having a lower level of 'efficiency emphasis'.

Chow et al. (1999) investigate the effect of national culture on the design of and employee's preference for management controls. Their findings are consistent with the fact that national culture affects these firms' design of and employees' preference for the seven management controls, though there are also anomalies. These findings are combined with prior research for identifying desirable improvements in research design and method, variable measurement and selection, and, most important, the theoretical foundation for culture-based research on management controls.

Gonzalez (2008) presented an approach based on cultural studies to conceive of and pursue cultural inquiry in international management by developing a genealogical framework for understanding how the international management literature has engaged with culture over the past 40 years. This framework focuses on decisions that international management scholars have made as they attempt to address culture in their research. It also focuses on the consequences of these decisions, which have skewed the field towards certain intellectual positions and have maintained culture as a problematic concept. Further, they highlighted an alternative approach situated within cultural studies to address the problem of culture in international management scholarship.

Myers et al. (1995) carried out rigorous factors analysis of the data collected from about 2500 respondents and identifies four types of top management styles:

- Consensus (typical of Swedish and Finnish top managers)
- Towards a common goal (German and Austrian)
- Managing from a distance (French)
- Leading from the front (British, Spanish and Irish)

The top management leadership style complements national cultures more strongly for the French, German and Austrian respondents. Greater variance in styles of top management is exemplified by the respondents from the other countries.

Kirkman and Shapiro's (1996) paper identifies two potential sources of resistance to SMWTs – resistance to self-management and resistance to teams – and predicts how aspects of national culture might affect one or both sources of resistance. Specifically, the propositions developed are:

The more an individual is high in power distance, the more he or she will resist self-management.

People who have a dominant being orientation will resist self-management more than people with a dominant doing orientation.

People who have a dominant determinism orientation will resist self-management more than people with a dominant free will orientation.

The more an employee values individualism, the more he or she will resist teams.

The more an employee values individualism, the more he or she will perceive SMWT pay as distributively fair if the pay is allocated equitably rather than equally; the more an employee values collectivism, the more he or she will perceive SMWT pay as distributively fair if the pay is allocated equally rather than equitably.

Ouchi and Jaeger (1978) compare aspects of the 'ideal types' of American (Type A) and Japanese (Type J) forms of organization and relate them to their sociocultural roots. They then present a hybrid organizational 'ideal type' (Type Z), which is particularly appropriate in today's American society.

Type A is usually followed in a society characterized by high rates of individual mobility being an integral part of its culture, which supports norms of independence, self-reliance and individual responsibility. In contrast, Type J prevails in a society in which individual mobility has been low in its culture shaped by norms of collectivism.

Two familiar organizational ideals: Type A and J and the emerging Type Z

Type A (American)	Type J (Japanese)	Type Z (modified American)
Short-term employment	Lifetime employment	Long-term employment
Individual decision-making	Consensual decision-making	Individual responsibility
Rapid evaluation and promotion	Slow evaluation and promotion	Slow evaluation and promotion
Explicit, formalized control	Implicit, informal control	Implicit, informal control with explicit formalized measures
Specialized career path	Non-specialized career	Moderately specialized career path
Segmented concern	Holistic concern	Holistic concern, including family

Axel (1995) argues that the Japanese management system is shaped essentially by the features of Japanese culture. These features can in turn be traced back to the family system and child-rearing pattern in Japan.

Three features make up the core of the Japanese management system: (a) lifetime employment, (b) the principle of seniority and (c) company-based labour unions and or an understanding of the enterprises as a community. The basic features of Japanese culture are (a) maintenance of permanent vertical emotional human bonds/ningen/kankei, (b) group orientation/groupism/aidagara and (c) emphasis on harmony/wa. The three core features of Japanese culture are directly linked to the Japanese method of child rearing and the Japanese family system.

Herbig and Jacobs (1998) provide a detailed description of Japanese culture and attempts to link it to innovation. Hofstede's (1984) scores on culture dimensions for Japan reveal above-average ratings for uncertainty avoidance, masculinity and Confucian dynamics. Between the United States and Japan, four differences can be identified: individualism is higher for the United States while uncertainty avoidance, masculinity and Confucian dynamics are higher for Japan than for the United States.

The key Japanese culture attributes identified are collectivism, Wa (harmony), mutual dependence, Kata (prescribed behaviour), hierarchy (status m, seniority, acceptance of authority) coexisting with consultation of subordinates and consensual decision-making, uncertainty avoidance (conservative and risk-averse) and non-confrontational behaviour, strict role separation between men and women, and adherence to Confucian values.

While the study initially states that it would explain Japanese superiority in process innovation but their relative inferiority in radical innovation, through Japanese cultural attributes, this linkage has not been clearly brought out.

Ford and Earl (1992) bring out the basic national cultural differences between Japan and the United States. The cultural differences identified are:

In Japan, the actual process often becomes more important than the end result.

In Japan, conformity to the norms of the community is vital, as opposed to individual autonomy (entrepreneurship).

The Japanese society is highly structured (well-defined hierarchy) and this gets reflected in the language spoken.

Japanese are committed to long-term survival rather than short-term results.

The implications in the context of the above cultural differences for the Americans intending to do business with the Japanese are:

- Be tolerant and patient of the Japanese process.
- Don't push for a decision before appropriate time has been allowed for the group to reach one.

In Japan, there is a well-defined chain of command. Always adhere to proper channels.

When strategies, decisions are made, the Japanese firm will be totally committed to have a chance for success, and the American firm should approach with the same level of commitment.

Organization Culture and Management in India

As mentioned earlier, debate on the understanding of societal culture and its impact on management of organizations in India has been going on for many decades without arriving at a concrete agenda on this issue. However, many scholars have highlighted the importance of culture on effective management of organizations in India. Some of the scholars' view points and their findings are discussed in the following.

The differences between the internal work culture of public and private sector organizations in India. The model of culture fit postulates that the sociocultural environment affects the internal work culture, which in turn influences HRM practices. This model was tested by two independent cross-cultural studies comparing Indian and Canadian managers and employees. In both studies, India scored higher than Canada on paternalism, power distance and uncertainty avoidance, loyalty towards community, reactivity, and futuristic orientation. Indian employees reported having less enriched jobs than did Canadian employees. Mediated multiple regression analyses supported the model of culture fit. Results suggest that the paternalism, self-reliance and employee participation constructs merit further exploration, as does participant methodology (Mathur et al., 1999)

Amba Rao et al. (2000) show the culture-based analyses indicating homogeneity in Indian management practices; this empirical study compares performance appraisal practices and management values in India by firm ownership. Differences in Indian private investor corporations, public sector enterprises, foreign/joint ventures and private family businesses are examined to assist managers to adapt selectively to firms in the changing Indian economy.

Arora (2005) observes that successful entry and continuous growth in a foreign market, effective communication with the unfamiliar partner, and adaptation to culture is important. Globalization requires cross-cultural literacy and successful management of diversity. Though not much empirical evidence is available on the impact of cross-cultural literacy on the cost of doing business in foreign markets, it is fair to assume that cross-cultural literacy reduces the total costs of operating in foreign markets. Multinational companies (MNCs) with worldwide subsidiaries need to recognize the impact of sociocultural values on local organizational behaviour to be able to successfully transfer the know-how to various local units. Further analysed is the experience of MNCs in India, with a particular emphasis on the sociocultural aspects of HRM. The main purpose is to help expatriates in understanding the complex sociocultural aspects of Indian work culture and management practices and improving their effectiveness.

Sinha (2005) mentions that under pressure of globalization, Indian work organizations tend to move from being culturally embedded to market-driven and strategically-oriented entities, often retaining parts of the old ways of working and superimposing on them the new organizational demands. He briefly explained how the primordial Hindu worldview enfolded alien influences and got itself broadened into indigenous societal culture, the inroads of the global management culture, the opposite modes of expressing them, and finally, he described Indians' cultural competence to keep aligning their cultural frames to the demands of organizational culture. Global management culture has not replaced the Indian societal culture. Indians possess a complex repertoire of both sets of cultural beliefs, preferences and practices. They smoothly shift their cultural frame one to another depending on the nature of the context, organizational cultures, quality of work and non-work relationships. He further suggested that key to turn this shifting cultural frame into organizational competency is to synchronize it with long-term strategic framework of doing business in India and cultivating an enabling organizational culture.

Bhal and Debnath (2006) argue that researchers in the field of cross-cultural research have highlighted the need to study one culture in depth particularly to understand the complex causes of behaviours those managers belonging to a culture manifest. This study reports the conceptualization and measurement of the Indian personality construct of Gunas; a possible predictor of ethics of Indian managers. The Indian scripture, the Gita, identifies three personality constructs, collectively referred to as Gunas that are considered relevant for understanding ethical behaviour. The article reports the development of a scale to measure three

Gunas – illumination, passion and dullness – through a four-step process. In the first step, construct definitions and items of the three Gunas are generated. The second, third and fourth steps report empirical studies conducted on different samples to assess the factor stability, reliability, discriminant validity and other validities of the scale. The scale is used to predict spirituality, ethical frameworks and acts of software piracy in organizations.

Punia (2006) observes that recent times have evinced a very high degree of diversity and uncertainty in the business environment. Workplace of today witnesses the coexistence of employees from various sociocultural backgrounds making the corporate culture a completely diverse one. The progressive companies of today look for diverse workforce which can bring and help in managing diverse talents, interests and viewpoints and that too in the continuously changing business environment. This diverse corporate culture has further affected the employment relations by not keeping them confined to traditional issues but extend them to address areas like empowerment, effectiveness, retention, development, managing cross-cultural diversity, management of gender issues, organizational learning, change management which have emerged as contemporary challenges leading to new paradigms in corporate culture.

Som (2008) discussed that the Indian economy was forced to adopt a structural adjustment programme at the beginning of 1991. The structural adjustment programme or liberalization initiated the process of the opening up of an otherwise closed economy of India. Liberalization created a hypercompetitive environment, and to respond to this turbulence Indian organizations adopted innovative changes in their HRM practices. Current research shows that HRM practices are important for enhanced corporate performance, but little has been reported on the effect of HRM practices and corporate performance in the context of economic liberalization of India. This study tries to understand the role of innovative HRM practices and specifically questions how HRM practices, such as the role of HR department, recruitment, retraining and redeployment, performance appraisal and compensation, enhance corporate performance during the change process. A multiple-respondent survey of 69 Indian organizations was undertaken to study the impact of innovative HRM practices on firm performance. The survey found that the innovative recruitment and compensation practices have a positive significant relationship with firm performance. It was observed that recruitment, the role of the HR department and compensation practices seem to be significantly changing within the Indian firms in the context of India's economic liberalization. The synergy between innovative HRM practices was not significant in enhancing corporate performance during the liberalization process.

Shah and Bhaskar (2000) highlight that in recent times there have been scores of corporate failures all over the world due to moral turpitude, lack of good governance and erosion of values. The need for a change in corporate's approach towards stakeholder management is greater now than ever before. Though the term 'stakeholder' was first used in the West in the 1930s, this concept has been highlighted in the ancient Indian scriptures written centuries ago. These highlight the methodologies the kings used to ensure the welfare of all their stakeholders. The kings of yore, who considered themselves as trustees of their kingdom, can be compared to the top management in corporates of this era. Thus, the concepts highlighted in these ancient scriptures find relevance and applicability even in today's times. This chapter takes a brief look at few of the studies undertaken in this area and also highlights excerpts from the ancient Indian scriptures to prove that the concept of stakeholder management owes its origin to India.

Nazir and Lone (2008), taking cue from the recent surge in organizational culture and effectiveness studies mainly in Western countries, investigated the link between these two constructs using Denison's Organizational Culture Survey (DOCS) in the Indian context. The results, besides finding a strong support for the DOCS model, indicated that of the four cultural traits studied – involvement, adaptability, mission and consistency – mission was found to be the single most cultural trait responsible for a number of bottom-line performance indicators.

Srivastava (2009) opines that organizational culture has become a widely researched topic and efforts to understand the phenomena surrounding managerial motivation have been even more widespread. The most important reason for this is that employee motivation continues to be a big problem and organizational culture plays an important role in determining employee motivation. Organizational culture is a deeply rooted phenomena, which is the end-product of several variables, most of them being the offshoots of HR policies and practices. Ravikumar (2005) emphasizes that success of a nation or society is significantly determined by the degree to which its practices emanate from its culture. He argued that while India can boast of its rich cultural heritage, it has not paid enough attention to understand its application to management of organizations. He further pointed out some of the age-old tenets or *sutras* that can be of value in providing more meaningful alternative in management practice, such as understanding and managing self, managing truth, interpersonal relations, managing collectivity, and leadership.

Pandey and Wali (2010) observe that the lacunae of Theory X and Y compounded with insufficient research evidence in favour of these theories resulted in the proposition of Theory Z. It is a beautiful amalgamation of both Theory X and Y and has enough empirical evidence to support it. It is easily deduced that most of the successful firms share some common characteristics, which are untouched by geographical boundaries of nations. Theory Z has great relevance in the Indian scenario, as it is a culmination of both American and Japanese cultures. India interestingly has a national culture, which is also a blend of both types of characteristics. This study draws from ethics-related literature from ancient Indian scriptures to demonstrate the points of convergence and divergence between Theory Z and the Indian management approach. It also tries to emphasize the applicability of the old phenomenon in the light of new changes in the corporate world. Indian culture is an elusive concept. It has many meanings. Metaphors for Indian culture are plenty, such as rainbow culture, confluence culture, mixture culture, Indian blend, from street to stock market, holy culture, democratic *kutumb* (family), materialism, and spiritualism culture. These manifestations of varying forms are seen in different parts of India. The future of Indian management depends upon a new social vision in the era of globalization; the ancient vision of vedic seers and sages in terms of balancing of Dharma, Artha and Moksha needs to be reformulated in terms of a new vision of sacro-civic society (Sharma, 2005).

Nigam and Su (2011) opine that many Indian MNCs have started operating in more developed countries. This raises questions about which culture they ought to follow in subsidiaries in developed countries. The Indian management culture may be seen through the multinational's HRM practices. The management culture may not necessarily have the same effect or hold similar values in the subsidiaries of Indian

MNCs located in developed countries because of the many cultural and institutional differences. Several studies have been conducted from the point of view of developed countries' MNCs and their management but scarcely any from the Indian perspective. In view of the opening up of the Indian economy, it becomes extremely important to make an inquiry. Jain and Premkumar (2011) show that in the wake of globalization, liberalization and privatization on the economic front, organizations are expected to make an objective assessment of existing status of their HRD system and processes in order to evolve need-based pragmatic HRD agenda for the future. This study gives a concrete base and direction as it provides the empirical evidence as regards to the current status of HRD subsystems and facilitators in relation to HR productivity with reference to Indian private sector and public sector organizations.

Shrivastava and Sangya (2012) highlight that since early 1991 India has experienced a significant growth in FDI inflows. This has contributed to the growing presence of foreign companies in India and created an urgent need for a better understanding of India's work culture and management practices. This chapter sought to fulfill two main aims. First, analysing the adaptation experience of expatriates in India. Second, highlighting the peculiarities in Indian organizational behaviour and management culture. The ultimate goal was to help MNCs improve their understanding of India's business world and reduce the psychic distance between the investing country and India.

Madhu Bala et al. (2012) attempt to provide an integrated discussion of culture through both universal and indigenous approaches: etic and emic. Both universal and indigenous points of views are very important in understanding specific culture and how it fares and what sets it apart from other cultures. Methodological concerns of both, however, have resulted in valuable yet incomplete explanation of the concept of culture. Intricacies of using both in culture research have been explained in the article. They use these two lenses to Indian context vis-à-vis other cultures in order to come up with unique aspects of Indian organizations. This way it offers a comprehensive look at culture as a concept, providing different approaches to capture the unique features of culture in the Indian organizational context. It also discusses the challenges of culture research in the multicultural environment of India.

Gertsen and Zølner (2012) analyse the recontextualization of the corporate values of a MNC in one of its subsidiaries. This study draws upon qualitative material from a case study of a company of Danish origin and its endeavours to implement its corporate values in an Indian subsidiary in Bangalore and shows how these values take on new meanings when interpreted by local employees. On one hand, their understandings are shaped by the prevailing meaning system, including leadership ideals, and on the other, by their resources and strategies. To further their understanding of the recontextualization, they point out that it is important to go beyond the system of signification shared within a national culture and include social agency conceived in Bourdieusian terms.

Kakkar (1971) states that authority is a relationship between two individuals, namely, the superior and the subordinate. Further, the relationship depends not just on the individuals but also on the positions they occupy in the formal hierarchy of the work organization. In view of the cultural and historical patterns of authority in India, it was expected that high affiliation of the superior and, more important, a high degree of control exercised over task performance, would tend to have a positive relationship with subordinate performance and satisfaction in work. However, the findings of the study did not support these expectations.

Panda and Gupta (2005) explore the effects of societal culture on prevailing organizational culture in a cross-societal perspective based on a study conducted in a public sector bank in Gujarat and Orissa. They argue that task orientation, control and bureaucratic approach characterize the general prevailing work culture of the branches in Orissa whereas relationship orientation, customer orientation and future orientation characterize the general work culture of the branches in Gujarat. They further highlighted that the societal culture influences the general work culture, leadership style and employees' attitudes in the organizations located therein. In societies marked by higher degree of social capital, organizations enjoy work culture that elicits commitment, whereas organizations located in society marked with weak social capital should contend with control-oriented work culture. There is a need to develop an institutionalized mechanism of bringing about changes in the organizational policies so that the changes are not based on the whims of individual personalities but are subject to certain checks and balances at the top so that the organizations do not face upheavals and continue to function on the basis of long-term objectives. Indian management is capable of absorbing principles alien to it, but to develop a positive performance culture all such principles have to be tailored to suit Indian conditions. If such a blending is not done then the dualism in Indian management could flare into conflicts and the compromises in the implementation of policies and principles may lead to organizational failure (Virmani, 2005).

Few scholars have identified the basic characteristics of Indian organizations. Tan and Khoo (2002) identify India's culture-related factors and its implications for the Rajiv Gandhi National Quality Award criteria (1, 2, 3, 6, 7 and 8) for TQ.

India's culture-related factors in this context are as given below:

- Highly religious/spiritual
- Highly status conscious (fear of losing face)
- Desire protection/guidance from superior
- Respond favourably to hierarchical forms of management (respect for powerful figures)
- Collectivist society (individuals not behaving according to group norms are ostracized)
- Desire ethical work environment
- Need clear job instructions
- Avoid uncertainties and extremes
- Respect for nature and natural life forces

The selected RGNQA criteria are as follows:

- Leadership
- Policies and strategies
- Human resource management
- Customer/consumer satisfaction
- Employee satisfaction
- Impact on environment and society

Sinha (1990) observes that culture reflects the way of life of people, their traditions, heritage, design for living and so on; culture determines everything that people do, feel and think. 'Human Behavior, therefore, is determined by culture' (White, 1948: 244).

Indian Social Milieu

Hierarchical Social Structures and Relations

> An essential element in any analysis of Hindu social organizations, relationships, and psychological make-up is the concept of hierarchy or ranked status relationship. Hierarchy pervades Hindu society and culture and those hierarchical relationships as governed by Hindu ideology and culture are essentially different from Western relationships and patterns that are more contractual and egalitarian, even when hierarchical. (Roland, 1980: 1)

Indians feel comfortable in the superior–subordinate framework. Hence peer group relationships induce anxiety till peers are ranked on some real or imaginary dimensions and thereby the relationship manifest equally is transformed into some kind of hierarchy.

Once a hierarchy is established, juniors yield to seniors on every conceivable occasion. The senior must protect and take care of those who are inferior to him or her and maintain deference and respectful compliance with his or her superiors (called 'affective reciprocity', Roland, 1984).

Social Networking through Own–Other Dichotomy

Affective reciprocity is not extended indiscriminately to all members of the society. Rather, it is limited to those who are considered to be own and personal, that is, members of the in-group. However, people are found to shift their allegiance from one type of in-group to another rather easily.

Sneh–Shradha (Affection–Deference) Relationships within In-groups

While in-group relationships are mutually supportive, the members within such relationships do not constitute an egalitarian homogeneous group. Rather, they reflect a hierarchy saturated with 'affective reciprocity'. 'Nurturance' is the preferred attitude of the superior towards his or her subordinates and juniors. Superiors tend to opt for it and subordinates are bound to relish it. Similarly, dependency is one of the culturally fostered relationships in India. Indians seek attention, support, advice and help even in situations where they are fully capable of taking decisions on their own.

Preference for Personalized Relationship over Contractual Relationship

In contrast to the contractual relationship, where work is the basis of relating to each other, Indians tend to relate with each other directly, and if the relationship turns out to be positive, work behaviour as part of the relationship is automatically facilitated. A competent person who confines him or herself to a job-specific relationship may be respected but is not included in an in-group. Hence, he or she is mistrusted, ignored or isolated.

Power Play

Indians are reported to be high on power need. Quite often the in-groups are more manifest than real and the superiors show pseudo nurturance and the subordinates reciprocate with pseudo dependency. The superiors, when they give more, demand more in return. Subordinates overtly show submissiveness and use tactics for ingratiation. This results in manipulative behaviour from both superiors and subordinates.

Sinha (1996) identifies the basic ingredients of Indian management and stated that ownership and management are undifferentiated and overlapping; there is power and paternalism in the model of leadership; consultative decision-making is valued; hierarchy is the key to management coordination; emphasis is given to security and lifelong employment; preference is given to learning on the job; orientation is short term; identity and job specificity are valued; existence of dual information systems: there is value for both informal grapevine and formal data flow (hierarchy based); unconditional loyalty to chief executive and dependency; performance is extracted using mild pressure; centralization of power and decentralization of activities; open door policy – CEO/management is accessible to all, not only to immediate subordinates, and both individual excellence and interdependence and team work are valued. Sinha further brought out a few salient values of Indian society on leadership, such as model of selflessness, consultative process, and encouraging leaders to develop commitment to task and organization, not to themselves. In fact, Japanese demonstrated that they could blend indigenous culture with managerial imperatives. Their success has underlined the thesis that culture and management need to be blended and integrated to Indian management merits an immediate inquiry to explore this in the Indian context.

Observations from the Review of Literature

From the review of literature the following observations can be made regarding the culture and its impact on management of the organization:

Scholars provided different views on the concept of culture and understood that it is learned behaviour, transmitted from one generation to another through idioms, rituals, besides formal and informal learning. The processes of enculturation mould the members to acquire shared norms and traditions which in turn influence their behaviour.

Emphasis is being placed on examining organizations as units having their own cultures within larger socialite cultures. Organizational culture represents the key elements of the work environment in which employees perform their jobs and also corresponds to a unique set of features that the organization values. An organization's culture is determined by a variety of elements, including business environment, values, rites and rituals, cultural networks, and ideas and skills possessed by its employees.

Many of the studies reflected that management is culture-bound and emphasize the need to understand the precise way in which culture influences the effectiveness of the organization's HRM practices.

The cultural and behavioural characteristics of organizations have a measurable effect on a company's performance and highlight the impact of organizational culture on job satisfaction, leadership, commitment and performance.

Some scholars focus on cultural behaviour and organizational management behaviour in the context of cross-cultural management by taking up studies from various countries and bring out the influence of national cultures on organizational culture and thus bring out the basic national cultural differences between various countries.

Many cross-cultural studies have used nations as the unit of analysis; the concept of national culture has been challenged on various grounds. One objection is that there may be significant cultural diversity within some countries and similarities across national borders, questioning the credibility of the concept of national culture.

Few opine that national culture is widely viewed as a constraint on management practice.

Provide Important Models/Frameworks for Understanding the Dimensions of National Culture

Examines the degree to which organizational behaviour is found to vary between national cultures, by reviewing findings and prior studies relating organizational structure, effective leader styles, HRM policies and negotiation to variations in national culture.

Theory, Method and Applications and Suggestions for Future Research in Cross-cultural Management

The conventional idea that transfer and application of cross-cultural management and organizational practice results in either existing traditional (non-western) practices being displaced by Western ones or a situation of incompatibility of norms leading to a total rejection of Western norms in a non-western organizational context.

In addition to the above observations, a few more can be made from studies in Indian context.

Culture-based Analyses Indicates Homogeneity in Indian Management Practices

There is a need for understanding the complex sociocultural aspects of Indian work culture and management practices and improving their effectiveness. It is emphasized that success of a nation or society is significantly determined by the degree to which its practices emanate from its culture.

The future of Indian management depends upon a new social vision in the era of globalization; the ancient vision of vedic seers and sages in terms of balancing of Dharma, Artha and Moksha needs to be reformulated in terms of a new vision of sacro-civic society.

Identify the Basic Ingredients of Indian Management

Japanese demonstrated that they could blend indigenous culture with managerial imperatives. Their success has underlined the thesis that culture and management need to be blended and integrated into Indian management merits an immediate inquiry to explore further their relevance in the Indian context.

On the whole, it is clear that many scholars and cross-cultural researchers have identified and discussed the importance of culture and its impact on HRM. Yet a common understanding and agreement on the definition of culture (including variations of culture) has not yet been reached. However, it is also true that the cultural characteristics of organizations have a measurable effect on organizational effectiveness. Organizations with a participative culture perform better than those without such a culture, but the margin of difference that widens over time suggests a possible cause-and-effect relationship between culture and performance. There is an urgent need to conduct more research to substantiate these findings.

Purpose of the Study

The sociocultural environment in India is unique; its peculiarities mould the personalities of the management practitioner and influence management practices. One of the salient features of the Indian management is the emphasis on the personalities of the top leaders in the organization. One study (Virmani, 2002) indicates that Indian employees are more favourably inclined towards having a paternalistic management. The essential requisite for paternalism appears to be unity in the leadership, and a single, identifiable source of power and patronage. The line of succession – if not clear – leads to people lobbying in the position, which in the process subtly divides the organization into cliques. Another unique feature of Indian management is the familial feeling perceived by the employees because of the parental attitude adopted by the superior and the colleagues which creates a sense of security and belongingness among the employees. It is found that among the organizations studied, harmony is easier to achieve when difference is given to familiarities, seniority and age.

Due to increased mobility in the global labour market and the internationalization of business, many organizations are confronted with the challenges of managing an increasingly culturally diverse workforce. In the Indian context, globalization has thrown open tremendous opportunities for Indians. The recent success of software companies is just the tip of the iceberg. Similarly, communication revolutions, such as advent of Internet, tilted the business econometrics to incorporate multicultural variables. The mushrooming of business process outsourcing (BPO) units and call centres and medical transcriptions centres are good examples for how globalization is affecting Indian middle class. The fact that Indian companies like Infosys, Wipro and Seacom Pvt Ltd are opening offices in various part of the world is not new. This means Indians will not only be increasingly managing people with different work values, attitudes and behaviour but also be managed by such people. Therefore, to manage human resources, it is important for managers to hold particular sets of assumptions, ideas and beliefs, which are strongly influenced by the sociocultural background of those resources. To deal with such multicultural environments, one requires proper adaptability and flexibility. However, literature survey indicates that there has been very little exploratory or basic research undertaken to identify cultural variables, which have a bearing on corporate and non-corporate management in India. In this context, the present study is to explore, identify and understand the impact of culture on Indian management.

Objectives of the Study

Based on the above views and expressions, the present study is going to examine the following objectives:

- Understand the culture of Indian management and its attributes, variables and constraints
- Understand the ways of doing ethnography in business organizations
- Understand variations in organizational culture in India through case studies
- Examine the impact of societal culture and its bearing on management processes and practices

Methodology

The entire project work has been carried out based on the following broad phases which include:

- A comprehensive secondary research on the subject of the study
- In-depth ethnographic case studies of corporate organizations from various sectors.

A comprehensive literature survey has been carried out, spanning both Indian and international journals and books, and material available on the internet. To make the literature survey systematic and amenable for better treatment, it was broken down into the following categories:

- Conceptualizing culture
- Dimensions of national culture
- National culture and management practices (cross-cultural research)
- Linking a nation's culture to its management practices
- Indian culture and management

In the background of the above comprehensive literature survey undertaken in different parts of the world, this study first attempted to identify key cultural parameters in Indian corporates and then carried out in-depth ethnographic study of four high-performing Indian organizations. A preliminary survey was undertaken on the basis of dimensions adopted from the works of Hofstede, Trompenaars and Fukuyuma.

In-depth ethnographic case studies of four organizations from various sectors were conducted between March 2012 and September 2013. The organizations selected for the study include Scientific Organization, Seacom Pvt Ltd, Heavy Electrical Company, and Telcom Product Company. In the present study, name of the organizations have been changed to protect their identity.

All these organizations are based in Hyderabad. The basic criteria for selecting these organizations include age and size of the company and coverage of diverse sectors such as research, manufacturing and IT services. Besides, these organizations are unquestioned leaders in their respective fields and they have registered phenomenal growth during the decades besides earning a brand image indicating quality and contribution to society.

Difficulties in Conducting Field Work

Conducting an ethnographic study in corporate organizations was not an easy task to capture authentic information. Initially, I and my assistances were not able to extract the required data or information as the informants were not convinced about the importance of the project work. As a result, they did not show much interest to provide information about their experience in the organization as well as about the organization. Moreover, the majority of the employees were very busy with their respective assignments. First three weeks were spent on introducing the research project and casual discussions with the employees. Later on, it helped in collecting in-depth information about the organizations and individual employees. Despite many constraints, I have managed to collect the required information from all the organizations.

Tools and Techniques

All together social research tools are used for collecting data from various sources. These are mainly survey questionnaire, observation, participant observation, interviews both formal and informal, which helped to prepare a detailed checklist which includes IT industries strategy and planning, vision and mission, organization structure, operating schedules, delivery, staff recruitment, benefits and welfare, organizational values and beliefs, communication system, leadership, decision-making processes, performance management and so on.

Besides, data from secondary sources are gathered from newsletters, magazines, annual reports, press reports, job profiling processes and appraisal processes.

Observation is an important method in eliciting facts for management research. Through participant observation it is aimed to get a better understanding of the prevailing cultural aspects in the management of organizations. Some of the basic information like how people dress, how they greet each other, day-to-day interactions within company/across company, how freely information flows, levels of cooperation/conflict, rituals/ceremonies/rite of passage (e.g., promotion, retirement, get-together, socialization of newly recruited person, norms of behaviour, leadership behaviour towards subordinates, peer relationships and so on) were collected with the help of observation. Throughout the field study researcher used observation methods for finer details and verification of data collected through the use of other techniques of data collection. In addition, it made possible to check the disparity between what people say and what people actually do.

Interviews – both formal and informal interviews – were conducted using all the details of the checklist regarding employees' views on the company and their relationships with others, job preference, training, orientation programmes for employees, what happens when problems come up, facilities provided by the company and level of satisfaction with the work/career and so on. Apart from this, focus group discussions were conducted with some of the key informants in the company with regard to planning strategy, future vision and its changing paradigms.

Besides these techniques, secondary information have been collected from different sources like university library, newsletters and reports from the organizations, and so on.

Chapterization of the Report

The present report is presented in eight chapters. The first chapter introduces the topic and throws light on the contributions of different scholars in the field of culture and management research. An introduction is given about the present study in which the purpose and the objectives of the study and organization of the chapters have been discussed.

The second chapter provides a brief review on doing ethnography in business organization and also highlights the changing trend in ethnography. The third chapter discusses about the historical perspective of Indian management. The fourth chapter presents the case study of the scientific organization. The fifth chapter presents the case study of Seacom Computer Pvt Ltd. The sixth chapter presents the case study of Telcom Company Pvt Ltd. The seventh chapter presents the case study of heavy electrical company. In the final chapter, summary and conclusions are presented.

2

Doing Ethnography in Business Organization

This chapter highlights the meaning and nature of ethnography and its origins and changing trends in the present-day research. To begin with, ethnography is the systematic, organized and detailed description of a particular culture and includes the procedures through which such information is collected. In other words, the term ethnography refers to both the research procedures and the descriptive results and thus encompasses both the means and the ends. With its focus on understanding the culture underlying any given community, ethnography emphasizes viewing the culture from its *members' points of view.* An ethnographic description must 'represent its host culture with fidelity' and 'closely resemble the original cultural reality' (Werner & Schoepfle, 1987: 24). Ethnography thus aims at providing an 'insider's picture' of the community under study. On the other hand, *ethnography* is a term commonly used to describe intensive and lengthy field projects that seek to understand 'natives' in their own cultural context. It is the scientific study of human social, cultural, economic phenomena and communities, through the means of anthropological fieldwork. As such, it is considered a branch of cultural anthropology which focuses on the study of human societies and cultures. In the literature, ethnography, fieldwork and participant observation are frequently used interchangeably and are typically meant to represent qualitative research involving long periods of time watching people, conversing with them about what they are doing, thinking and saying, all in an attempt to see how they understand their world.

In the anthropological discipline, ethnography is often used to refer to either the fundamental research methods of cultural anthropology or the written text produced to report ethnographic research results. As a research method, ethnography seeks to answer central anthropological questions concerning the ways human beings live. Generally speaking, ethnographic questions concern the link between culture and behavior and/or how cultural processes develop over time. The database for ethnographies is usually an extensive description of the details of social life or cultural phenomena in a small number of cases.

Trends of Ethnography

The origins of ethnography can be traced to cultural anthropology, from which it derives its conceptual and methodological bearings. Cultural anthropology is the study of the patterns of thought, behavior and artefacts of a given culture. Initially, ethnography was limited to the study of 'primitive', small-scale societies. However, this shortcoming is being overcome rapidly by the increasing number of ethnographic studies of modern, Western social groupings of varied natures. Ethnographic inquiry is becoming widespread in the study of urban, social conglomerations.

One can trace the development in ethnography, not only from the studies of primitive tribes to modern settings but also in the advanced and detailed use of tools. Present-day ethnography can involve sophisticated technologies such as audio and video recording and cinematography. Business ethnographic research, engaging in any type of business studies, should begin with the selection of a topic and a review of the literature pertaining to that topic. For example, if a business anthropologist is interested in studying a specific consumer group, he or she should begin with a review of all literature on that group; doing so helps with identifying variables that are important to the group's members that in turn influence their consumption behavior. Typically, ethnography is accomplished by living with the people who are study subjects, watching them work and play, thinking carefully about what is seen, interpreting it, and talking to the actors to check the emerging interpretations (Tiang, 2013).

In traditional anthropological fieldwork, researchers are totally immersed in the culture under study, maintaining continuous contact for an extensive period of time, often done by living as a member of the cultural system throughout the duration of the study. Conversely, observational research in an organizational context is based on a more partial immersion, often translating into significant blocks of time dedicated to observing and participating in work activity during normal business hours. The ethnographer's role involves a range of data collection activities and can be placed somewhere along a continuum stretching from the passive observer at one end to the active participant-observer at the other. At the extreme ends of this continuum, there can be too much or too little interaction with a culture, either of which can significantly undermine the data collection effort.

An ethnographic understanding of a culture or a community or a business organization is developed through close exploration of several sources of data. Using these data sources as a base, the ethnographer relies on a cultural frame of analysis to fulfill the task. Participant observation is the primary source of ethnographic data. The term *participant observation* represents the dual role of the ethnographer: to gain a real understanding of what is going on in a particular setting the researcher must not only become a participant in the target setting or milieu but also maintain a distance as an observer, someone who can describe the experience with an objective perspective.

It is clear that the term *participant observation* does not mean actual participation but rather involves a level of immersion that allows the researcher to be able to internalize what is seen and write about it convincingly. To develop a strong familiarity with the culture being studied, ethnographers must unravel different clusters of meaning by engaging in a level of interaction that allows them to test their insights about a setting. Ultimately, ethnography is an inductive process where data are produced by repeated and prolonged contact between a researcher and informant, often with considerable mutual involvement in the personal lives of native participants. Participant observation allows the researcher to share in the life of the culture being observed, so that he or she not only observes and studies the group but experiences his or her own life as a part of it. The benefit of participant observation is that the researcher gains an insider's understanding of the experience that he later communicates to outsiders.

Interview is another important method for ethnographers to collect data. Interviews ensure what might be called 'targeted' data collection by asking specific but open-ended questions. There are various styles of interview to choose from and each ethnographer brings his or her own unique approach to the process. No matter which approach is adopted, the key point is allowing the person(s) being interviewed to answer questions without being limited by predefined choices, which clearly differentiates such interviews as qualitative methods from more quantitative or demographic surveys. In most cases, an ethnographic interview looks and feels little different than an everyday conversation, and indeed in the course of long-term participant-observation most conversations are in fact purely spontaneous and without any specific agenda. In doing ethnographic researches, business anthropologists need to collect other sources of data which depend on the specific nature of the field setting. This may take the form of representative artefacts that embody characteristics of the topic of interest, government reports, informants' business records, individuals' diaries and letters, and newspaper and magazine articles. Although often not tied to the site of study, secondary academic sources are utilized to 'locate' the specific study within an existing body of literature. In doing his ethnographic research about Chinese refugees in Canada, Robert Tiang, for instance, collected about 100 personal letters and many dairies from his informants; he also collected considerable number of articles and reports about Chinese immigrants from the local Chinese newspapers. He also reviewed several family business records and collected important information for his analysis of ethnic resources for immigrants' economical adaptation (Tiang, 2013: 234).

Importance of Emic and Etic Perspectives

Since ethnographic research believes that emic and etic perspectives complement each other, it relies on both. Emic seeks to understand mental processes that cannot be empirically, rigorously and objectively examined. Etic research focuses upon categories, information, research designs and so on that centre around the researcher. Just as phonetics is based upon empirical evidence that can be directly observed, etic centres on patterns of behavior of mankind and society that researchers can detect rigorously. Hence, much social research needs to be emic and not etic.

As the qualitative and humanistic methods were favoured by most anthropologists, they reflect the emic style of investigation, and later on anthropologists began to use the etic-emic dichotomy to justify their qualitative and humanistic methods. This line of reasoning, however, gave rise to a major methodological debate within anthropology. For some ethnographers, the starting point for collecting data is the emic perspective, also known as the insider's or native's perspective of reality. Cultivating close informal relationships with the natives helps to ensure authenticity to the ethnographer's interpretation of local events and practices. Alternatively, other ethnographers prefer to place their data strictly in an etic or socio-scientific perspective of reality. This is achieved by interpreting important events in the context of the materialist and positivist philosophical end of the ethnographic spectrum. According to Fetterman, most ethnographers start collecting data from the emic perspective and then try to make sense of what they have collected in terms of both the native's view and their own scientific analysis.

Combination of these two approaches provides the maximum level of cultural familiarity, allowing them to develop a conceptual understanding of the culture being studied and an experiential familiarity that can be readily conveyed in their writing. As indicated above, ethnographic research has its own special characteristics. When considering using this method for solutions to business problems we must be aware of how the ethnographic process works and the implications of choosing this strategy of investigation.

It is very important to know that ethnography, as a qualitative research method and product, differs from the other three major ways of investigating and writing: quantitative research, public policy research and journalism. The nature of guiding questions addressed through these three kinds of research is significantly dissimilar from those that can be ethnographically addressed. Quantitative research usually arrives at percentages (of people who believe certain premise or do a certain thing) or otherwise counts of instances of a phenomenon, which is less descriptive with a larger number of cases than pure ethnography could be. One of its main methods is widely distributed surveys or questionnaires. Public policy research is generally geared towards providing information that helps policymakers decide how a certain phenomenon might be perceived in terms of better or worse social outcomes. It is worth knowing that public policy research might be performed either qualitatively or quantitatively or both. Journalism attempts to provide objective (not interpretive) outsider news information in a quick, timely manner, often against a deadline. Journalists write for the audience the newspaper, magazine or other publication target to reach and usually does not consider the general question regarding culture as crucial to the endeavour as would be the case for ethnographers.

Hymes' classification (1978) is based on the aim of specific ethnographies. He identifies three types of ethnographies:

1. *Comprehensive ethnography seeks to document the total way of life.* The ethnographer doing comprehensive ethnography tries to describe a wide range of practices, relationships and artefacts through participant observation, aiming at covering most areas of the community before completing the study.
2. *Topic-oriented ethnography* emphasizes one or more aspects of life known to exist in a community. For example, an ethnography of leadership patterns in an organization would be a topic-oriented ethnography.
3. *Hypothesis-oriented ethnography* is closely linked with both the types mentioned above. In this the ethnographer seeks to generate specific hypotheses about a community. Hypotheses can be raised only when one's knowledge of the community is almost complete.

Steps in Doing Ethnography

Research questions provide the primary objective behind the location selection and the choice of people to be studied. For example, a research project might require a particular time (the third shift), place (the shop floor) or event (a shift handover), depending on the focal point of the investigation. One of the more challenging tasks comes with negotiating access to a site, which can sometimes be met with resistance. Sara Delamont (2012) identified three golden rules when making these initial encounters:

1. Every aspect of the process needs to be meticulously recorded because vital features of the setting are made visible during the access stages.

2. Failed access attempts are 'data', just as successful ones are.
5. The harder it is to gain access, the more likely the work will be rewarding once 'inside' and vice versa.

To get acquainted and accepted to the groups, culture or setting being studied, enabling the researcher to immerse him or herself in the culture is the first step for doing the fieldwork. To gain admission, it is important that the researcher should make his or her research goals clear to members of the community or group being studied and gain their consent in advance to participate in the study. The length of an ethnographer's immersion depends on the setting and the group or culture being studied. Some ethnographers studying foreign cultures have lived for months or even years among members of the group they study.

One tactic to enhance the likelihood of an ethnographer's admission or acceptance is to allow to be introduced by an intermediary or facilitator who has some credibility with site members. Not only does this avoid the potential chilling effect on ethnographic research, an introduction from a trusted source is likely to strengthen the field worker's capacity to work at the site and generate a higher quality of data. Upon gaining acceptance to a site, the ethnographer is likely to warm up to some people more than others and participants may come to view the researcher as a friend. This may lead to a temptation on the part of the researcher to cross over and 'go native', abandoning the researcher perspective and adopting the views of the study audience/site members. Nonetheless, the fieldworker must remain focused on the primary objective, namely, the discovery and accurate depiction of the phenomenological reality as experienced by both the outsider and the insider.

Data Collection and Analysis

According to Fetterman (1998), an ethnographer functions as a human instrument that must discriminate among different types of data and analyse the relative worth of one path over another at every turn, which should be well before any formalized analysis takes place. In light of the dynamic nature of the data collection effort, research does not proceed in a straight line, as the researcher is often called to reflect upon, and even revisit, earlier steps. Ethnography can therefore become physically, emotionally and mentally exhausting.

As discussed above, ethnography involves a combination of both structured and regularly improvised data collection techniques. In some instances, systematic measurement may be necessary to design meaningful, fair and objective scales and classification systems to guarantee that their application is consistent and reliable. For the most part, however, ethnographic studies are qualitative in nature and require a researcher to collect information on a huge range of interactions and events. As such, how to select what to record represents a major challenge and must be approached in a systematic way. Thinking through which of the possible locations, times and people one should focus on is an important task and central to good field work. The more organized the ethnographer, the easier will be his or her task of making sense of the mountains of data.

Using a metaphor of the *life cycle* (infancy, childhood and adolescence; young adulthood, mature adulthood and old age), Mariampolski (2006) describes the ethnographic process in terms of a developmental sequence of five predictable stages. It is believed that adherence to these stages helps to ensure a smooth process and is important for establishing a level of rapport necessary for obtaining good disclosure from participants. These five stages include:

1. *Stage 1: The introductory stage (infancy)*. This stage includes introductions, greeting informants, explanation of roles, communication of ground rules and a general orientation session (questions, clarifications, consent forms etc.)
2. *Stage 2: The role-taking and rapport-building stage (childhood and adolescence)*. Following the introductory stage, the main objective is to set an appropriate tone for the project, by establishing rapport and gain the confidence of participants. Researchers and informants begin a dialogue by disclosing a little personal information about themselves.
3. *Stage 3: The general questions stage (young adulthood)*. Researchers begin to probe with general questions to gain a basic understanding of factual matters and insight into broad informant perspectives. General observations of visible manifestations of culture are made.
4. *Stage 4: The specific questions and activities stage (mature adulthood)*. This stage of the research process includes direct observation of individual behavior, more pointed and direct questioning of

informants, and a deeper examination of subjects' feelings and emotions. Of the five stages, this stage of the site visit is the longest in duration.

5. *Stage 5: Closing (old age).* At this stage, a research team gathers any remaining information, reviews and summarizes its findings and validates perceptions that have emerged. The researcher thanks the informants for their contribution and breaks off the relationship in a positive and constructive manner.

In short, data analysis and reporting of findings are the final stages of the ethnographic research projects, with qualitative data collected from interviews, observations and all kinds of documents that are available. To ethnographers analysis means bringing order to the data by organizing them into patterns or categories. To do so ethnographers often need to carefully read and reread their fieldwork notes and documents in order to search for key themes and patterns. Then, they need to carefully interpret these materials, finding meaning and significance in the observed patterns. Business solutions often emerge from the participant observation and analysis that the researcher conducts.

Ethical Issues and Concerns

In this section, we will discuss the problems and ethical issues in doing ethnographic research projects. Although qualitatively based ethnographic methods are widely applied in the real world to solve various social, cultural, economic and business problems, the problems of reliability and validity of ethnographic researches continue to remain a contentious subject for scholars over many years. The ethnographic research report tends to centre around a specific point of time or a specific event, which might be fictional or extrapolated from the past, known as the 'ethnographic present'. Apparently, the ethnographic present tends to describe the social situation being studied in a manner that does not focus upon change or internal tensions within the organizations or communities under examination. Business anthropologists often present their ethnographic analyses in such a static manner to demonstrate how a business system functions and how various aspects of business fit together in a holistic manner. There is no doubt that this kind of presentations distort the real business world because all human organizations or groups are in a constant state of flux and rivalries invariably exist.

Although a powerful tool, the ethnographic method is filled with pitfalls; a good discussion of these problems is presented by Fine in his 'Ten Lies of Ethnography'. Fine points out that while qualitative researchers often celebrate the rigorous nature of their method, significant shortcomings actually exist. Fine, for example, debunks what he calls the myths of the 'precise ethnographer', the 'observant ethnographer' and the 'unobtrusive ethnographer'. For instance, ethnographers often present their findings as exactly what happened and their detailed notes as unerring evidence of human behavior that was carefully observed. Thus, the assertion is made that what is described in the ethnography is precisely what took place. Fine believes that, in reality, ethnographers often take loose and almost fictionalized accounts of social situation and present them as complete and unadulterated truth. Ethnographers, Fine argues, can never truly capture 'reality'; this inability needs to be acknowledged.

An open mind on the part of an ethnographer does not imply a lack of rigor. Given that the observations of native cultures are regarded as data for scientific study, it is essential to view them with detachment and objectivity. To that end, ethnographers should enter the field with as few preconceptions as possible, suspending their own prejudices and partialities as they seek to understand how people in a cultural system think or behave. This requires an ethnographer to adopt a non-judgmental orientation, suspending any personal appraisal in order to allow a more complete picture to unfold. Therefore, rather than immediately dispelling an obviously illogical or unbelievable set off circumstances an ethnographer should give them sufficient consideration. After all, these observations may eventually invalidate past theories and help to construct new models about events in the field.

Ethnographers typically present themselves as unobtrusive, just like a 'fly on the wallpaper', that observes but does not impact what is going on. In reality, of course, many qualitative researchers take an active part of the social settings they are observing and, as a result, they may be impacting the data they gather to a degree that clouds reality. The level of impact and the ability to account for the resulting distortions will differ in various situations. The skill and experience of the researcher also needs to be taken into account. The validity of information collected by the ethnographers can be greatly impacted by their own biases. Accurate description requires the ethnographer to be very objective in describing the visible artefacts of a culture and very empathic in describing shared assumptions that are experienced by insiders. Switching back and forth between the insiders' view and that of an analyst is a difficult challenge and requires an ethnographer to be aware of his or her presumptions.

Objective, accurate field observations call for an ethnographer to transcend his or her biases and suspend his or her reliance on judgmental heuristics. Full recognition of the biases that are brought to the situation help to give assurances that field observations are not what the ethnographer wanted to see but what is really out there. Informants can bring another source of bias. When interpreting results, researchers should consider asking how, why and under what conditions a particular set of data was collected. Informants often want to help researchers, by showing and telling what they think investigators want to see and hear. Attempts to exaggerate or embellish their claims represent a subject's attempt at impression management. Conversely, informants may try to hide things or tell lies, to protect themselves or for privacy reasons. Ultimately, every piece of information collected in the field could be viewed with some degree of scepticism. How can a researcher be sure that his or her data represent an accurate depiction of a cultural system? Lofland and Lofland (2006) proposed some basic questions that can be used to evaluate the accuracy of field observations:

- *Directness of the report*. Is this account based on direct perception, or does it come second-, third- or fourth-hand? If latter is the case, is it therefore to be treated with caution towards stated facts, even if it is as accurate as image?
- *Spatial location of the reporter*. Even if first-hand, what was my (or my reporter's) spatial location such that this perception might be accurate in some respects but still skewed or partial?
- *Social locational skewing of reported opinion*. With regard to reports of opinion, what might there be about the relationship between myself and the reporter that might lead her or him to lie, distort, omit, falsely elaborate or otherwise be less then accurate?

- *Self-serving error and bias concerning reports.* From what I know on other grounds about my own or the reporter's commitments, values and announced biases, are there reasons to be suspicious of the content of this report? Does it fit all too conveniently with what I want to believe or what the reporter might want to believe, about people and events, that is self-serving and therefore to be regarded with caution?
- *Previous plain error in reports.* From what is known about my or the reporter's previous perceptions, am I an accurate observer/ listener? Have I or the reporter made errors in the past, even though they are not self-serving errors?
- *Internal consistency of the report.* Is this report consistent with itself? Are there spatial-temporal facts stated at one point that contradict spatial-temporal assertions made at another? Were the events of this report possible within the time and space constraints given in the report or known about on other grounds? Do the people involved unaccountably contradict themselves with this report?
- *External consistency. Agreement among independent reports.* Is this account consistent with other accounts of the same events or experiences? Have I assembled enough independent accounts, subjected them to the above questions and then compared them for degree of agreement? On points of remaining disagreement, have I made sufficient effort to speak with more participants in the event or persons involved in the experience – persons who are otherwise qualified reporters – in order to arrive at a truthful account?

To minimize the impact of any potential bias, triangulation is one validation technique ethnographers use to try to protect themselves. To use this procedure, an ethnographer would test one source of information against another to strip away alternative explanations, thereby enabling them to strengthen their assertions.

Use of Ethnographic Methods in Organizational Research

In the West, ethnographic studies of research laboratories have a history of over a decade. A pioneering investigation, which took an anthropological approach to the study of a research laboratory, is Latour and Woolgar's work, *Laboratory Life* (1979). Allen (1977) conducted an extensive study of communication in engineering firm. Dubinskas (1988) reveals his understanding of the cultural contrast and conflict in such a firm and of the roots of this conflict as being in the contrasting images of selfhood within each group (scientists and engineers). He argues that differences within organizations can shape organizational life more powerfully than some blanket 'corporate culture'.

Knorr-Cetina and Mulkay (1983) discuss various analytical perspectives in *Social Studies of Science*. These include the ethno-methodological study of scientific practice, the discourse analysis of scientists' talk and writing, and the ethnography of scientific work. The authors describe four themes that correspond to different analytical positions. The first is a concern to include the technical content of science within the scope of sociological analysis. The second theme is the choice between an internalist and an externalist methodology in the study of science. The third is the 'linguistic turn' underlying several of these perspectives, and the fourth theme is the rejection of traditional distinctions such as that between the social and the scientific.

Lambright and Teich (1981) focus on the organizational context of scientific research, which they describe as an activity that uses systematic procedures to test, modify and expand knowledge. They explore key issues regarding sponsor–performer relationships. The performer may be either an individual scientist or a team of scientists within a sponsoring organization (as in the case of a company laboratory) or wholly outside a sponsoring organization (e.g., when a government agency contracts with a university).

Lambright and Teich begin by describing the characteristics of scientists as organizational members. They then review how various organizations can accommodate or exacerbate the tensions that arise from research. They consider those organizations which have sponsored research and those organizations or subunits which perform research. The authors look at the operating norms of each and how they interact. They deal with the consequences of research for the environments of organizations. They then discuss how organizations attempt to use research to alter their environments. Finally, they suggest ways in which organizational designs might contribute better to both the performance and the utilization of research.

Change in Ethnographic Research

The origins of the present-day paradigms in ethnography may be traced back to the cultural anthropologist Franz Boas. The early focus was on the historical reconstruction of cultures. Later the emphasis shifted to the description and interpretation of cultures as patterns of integrated themes or principles termed *configurations*. The principal exponents of this paradigm were Ruth Benedict and Margaret Mead. According to this school of thought, 'each culture selects or chooses from the infinite variety of behavioral possibilities, a limited portion that sometimes conforms to a configuration' (Sanday, 1979: 530).

As opposed to Benedict and Mead, Radcliffe-Brown and Malinowski were not interested in characterizing the cultural whole but in how each cultural trait functions in the cultural complex of which it is a part. They differed in their definition of function. Malinowski's paradigm is termed *functionalist* since he defined function in relation to the seven biological needs of individual human beings. Radcliffe-Brown's paradigm is termed *structural-functionalist* since according to him the function of a cultural custom or institution should be defined in terms of the contribution it makes to the maintenance of social structure.

Burrell and Morgan (1979) state that with reference to organizational analysis, the structural-functionalist perspective is criticized for being unduly committed to positivism and a naive empiricism. Another criticism is that this paradigm is characterized by a complete disregard for the nature of the phenomena under investigation. The research of social systems theorists and objectivists, who are the principal proponents of this paradigm, is criticized as being dubious since it reflects too strong a commitment to the models and methods of the natural sciences as a basis for organizational analysis. Yet another charge levelled at social systems theory and objectivism is that it is ideologically biased in favour of a managerial organizations' view of organizations; in other words, it is about which manger's attribute to organizations is seen as being given undue prominence especially in relation to the meanings and orientations of other organizational actors. This is despite the fact that much of organizational activity may be accounted for by non-managerial interests. Social systems theorists are also criticized for their unitary conceptualization of organizations and for their disregard of power as an organizational variable.

All the paradigms described above regard culture as an integrated whole. However, in the semiotic approach culture is regarded either as a system of shared meanings which the carriers of the culture use to make sense of their world or as a system of shared knowledge which they use for perceiving, believing, evaluating or acting. Geertz (1973, as quoted by Sanday, 1979: 532) writes that 'the whole point of a semiotic approach to culture is to aid us in gaining access to the conceptual world in which our subjects live so that we can, in some extended sense of the term, converse with them.' In the semiotic approach, the main task of the ethnographer is to adopt an informant's mode of thought while retaining his or her own critical faculties.

In closing, drawing from Burrell and Morgan (1979), we briefly review the hermeneutic and phenomenological traditions in ethnographic research. Hermeneutics is concerned with interpreting and understanding the products of the human mind which characterize the social and cultural world. The ontological standpoint adopted by its proponents is an 'objective-idealist' view of the sociocultural environment, seeing it as a humanly constructed phenomenon. That is to say, in the course of life human beings externalize the internal processes of their minds through the creation of cultural artefacts which attain an objective character. Examples of this process of objectification include institutions, works of art, literature, languages, religions and so on. Such objectifications of the human mind are the subject of study of hermeneutics. From the perspective of sociology, the hermeneutic tradition has received relatively little attention within the context of the interpretive paradigm.

In phenomenological sociology, human behavior is viewed as a product of how people interpret their world. Based on this principle a phenomenologist attempts to see things from a person's point of you and seeks to graph the meaning of that person's behavior. Burrell and Morgan identify two traditions in phenomenological sociology. The first, ethno-methodology, is grounded in the detailed study of the world of everyday life. It is concerned about learning the ways in which people order and make sense of their everyday activities and the ways in which they make them accountable to others in the sense of being observable and reportable. In the second tradition, symbolic interactionism, people are regarded as being constantly in a process of interpretation and definition as they move from one situation to another. While people may act within the framework of an organization, it is the interpretation and not the organization which determines action. Social roles, norms, values and goals may set conditions and consequences for action but do not determine what a person will do.

Over the past few decades paradigms from cultural anthropology have been used to study culture even in organizations. We discuss these briefly, drawing from Sanday (1979), Gregory (1983) and Smircich (1983).

In Kuhn's classic definition, paradigms are 'the source of the methods, problem-field and standards of solution accepted by any mature scientific field at any given time' (1962: 103). Similarly, following Gregory (1983), we use the word 'paradigm' to denote the conceptual perspective of a researcher from which his or her research questions, methods and presentation of findings follow.

Elaborating on Sanday's earlier classification of ethnographic paradigms that have been in vogue in cultural anthropology, Gregory (1983) identifies three dimensions of contrast: holistic-particulate, concerns about ontological perspectives of culture; on one hand, culture is viewed as an integrated whole and, on the other, culture is viewed as a collection of traits that bear no relation to, and may be studied in isolation from, each other. The second dimension, termed *explanatory-interpretive*, concerns the focus of research; here the emphasis may vary from the detection of cause–effect relationships and co-varying patterns to description and interpretation. The third dimension, termed *native view-external view*, concerns the interpretive framework used by the researcher in his or her study; in a native-view paradigm, the cultural researcher strives to adopt an insider's or 'native' standpoint, whereas with the external view researcher interprets what he or she observes using a framework that is his or her own.

We now discuss some important strands of research in organizational culture. The human relations school (examples include Mayo, 1933, and Richardson & Walker, 1948) was a major strand of management research that recognized the importance of informal social structure in industrial organizations. Researchers in this school applied the metaphor of a small, stable, homogeneous society to study organizations, thereby viewing them as robust units of cultural analysis. Consequently, their descriptions of 'organizational cultures' de-emphasized intra-cultural variations. Applying a structural-functionalist paradigm, these studies described cultures in terms of 'routines, patterns, regularities, layout, methods of keeping records, and symbols' (Holzberg & Giovannini, 1981: 328) and charted the formal and informal social structures in organizations.

The human relations school has been criticized for studying organizations in and of themselves with a static, non-contextual orientation. Gregory labels the paradigm of this school as holistic-explanatory. Since this school of researchers interpreted behavioural aspects of lower-ranking personnel as 'irrational' with reference to the 'rational manager' model, it adopted an external-view, pro-management, interpretive framework. The holistic approach towards organizational culture also formed the basis for the recent wave of studies on corporate culture. Compared to the human relations school, however, there was a greater emphasis on characterizing organizations as configurations of values in terms of distinct personality-like patterns of integrated themes. In anthropology, this approach to culture dates back to Ruth Benedict who applied this perspective to the study of three cultures and found two dominant types. One corresponds to the Appollonian distrust of excess and orgy and the other to the Dionysian cultivation of emotional and psychic excesses. This configurationalist and typologizing approach towards culture is manifested in studies on corporate culture conducted since the 1980s. Ouchi (1981) compared the sets of values of Japanese companies to those of some American companies and was able to delineate three configurations that he called 'A' (American), 'J' (Japanese) and 'Z' (an American type with several Japanese-like features). Pascale and Athos (1981) amplified Ourchi's typology.

Although Gregory labels the cultural paradigm of corporate culture studies as holistic-interpretive, many researchers on corporate culture are not content merely with characterizing cultural configurations in organizations but also relate them to organizational success. Such researchers usually adopt a systems theory framework which conceptualizes organizations like organisms, as ones struggling for survival in a changing environment. Culture here is usually defined as the social or normative glue that holds an organization together (Siehl & Martin, 1981). It expresses the values or social ideals and beliefs that members of the organization come to share. Culture is seen as a subjectivist but critical organizational variable which in some manner contributes to the overall systemic balance of the organization and to its effectiveness. Therefore, considerable emphasis is given to articulating contingent relationships that will be useful to those trying to manage organizations. As Smircich (1983: 346) observes, the broad research agenda that arises from such a perspective on culture is 'how to mould and share culture in particular ways and how to change culture, consistent with managerial purposes'.

Thus, several authors (e.g., Deal & Kennedy, 1982; Peters & Waterman, 1982) argue that organizations with 'strong' cultures are apt to be more successful. Baker (1980: 8) states that 'some successful corporations have especially distinctive cultures that they actively cultivate and manage, and that contribute significantly to their success.' He cites the example of IBM whose culture he characterizes by such shared beliefs as: (a) all employees should be respected and treated with dignity; (b) the company should aim at accomplishing every task in a superior way; and (c) the customer should be given the best service possible. Baker remarks that the style of top management of the 1980s was largely due to this culture that had been created by the management. In a survey-based study of the relationship of corporate culture to performance, Gordon (1985) reported that high-performing firms scored considerably higher than low-performing firms on a dimension of corporate culture entitled 'openness in dealing with conflicts and criticisms'. A managerial implication of such a finding is that top-level management must openly confront conflict with and criticisms from subordinates if the organization is to be successful.

Like Gordon (1985), Amsa (1986), Hosfstede et al. (1990) and Reynolds (1986) have developed instruments to measure organizational culture. Amsa studied the organizational cultures of a number of textile manufacturing plants from both public and private sectors in Ahmedabad. Methods of observation and informal, open-ended interviews were used to identify elements and/or dimensions of organizational culture, which were subsequently measured through structured interviews with loom-shed workers. Loitering was measured by the work sampling method. Amsa found a definite relationship between culture and loitering and difference between the public and private sectors in manufacturing mills.

Hofstede et al. (1990) studied organizational cultures in 20 units from different organizations in Denmark and the Netherlands. Their main finding shares that perceptions of daily practices are the core of an organization's culture. They also found that the values of founders and key leaders undoubtedly shape organizational cultures but that the way these cultures affect ordinary members is through shared practices. Data were obtained through in-depth interviews of selected informants and through a questionnaire survey of a stratified random sample of organizational members.

While researchers of corporate culture tend to adopt pro-management orientations, those who use semiotic approaches to the study of culture in organizations strive to eschew any such biases and assume a cultural relativist posture which denies the superiority to any cultural perspective. Their objective is to discover and describe the 'native' view points of the subjects of their study. This goal is driven by the conception of an organization as a social world that is constructed, interpreted and modified by its members in the course of their interactions. Hence in this approach culture is a 'root metaphor' for organizations (Smirich, 1983).

Gregory (1983) makes a case for native-view cultural paradigms in organizational studies by arguing that the corporate culture approach confuses organizational integration with cultural integration. However, an organization that lacks integration may actually comprise multiple cultures that are internally consistent but externally conflicting. The multiculturalist nature of organizations has been noted by many researchers. Consequently, by studying culture in an organization presuming it is shared by the members, key organizational processes that result from cultural diversity and cross-cultural interaction might be obscured. Native-view paradigms attempt to circumvent this problem by not starting with an assumption of shared culture.

With the emergence of business anthropology as a new subfield of anthropology, application of ethnography methods in business organization becomes an important tool for researchers across the world and it has been widely recognized by the business world. There has been a wide range of techniques to study the problems in the real world and to provide solutions to resolve these real-world problems. Business anthropology is best known in the business world for its qualitative and subjective strategies of investigation represented by its unique method of ethnography. In other words, without doing ethnography in the business world the works by business anthropologists might not be valued that much by the business firms as they are valued now. Traditionally, those seeking careers in anthropology are typically required to engage in a significant ethnographic research project as a professional rite of passage. In addition, their research contributes to the growing number of accounts of human behavior that are available to the profession and to other interested people. In our view, to learn how to do good business ethnographies is a key factor in one's endeavours to be a good business anthropologist.

3

Management Culture in India: A Historical Perspective

This chapter examines Indian management in its historical context. It has evolved from two different routes: one can be traced to the origins and development of the Indian civilization; the other could be attributed to the Western influence originating from the industrial revolution of the eighteenth century. It is necessary to understand these two streams of influence to appreciate the dilemmas, complexities and concerns of the contemporary Indian management. Indian civilization goes back to the third millennium BC. Its growth, based on internal evolution and tempered by external influences and their ultimate absorption, has led to a cultural mosaic that is India today. Its great tradition binds many little traditions, which are spotted across the subcontinent (Redfield, 1955; Singer, 1968). Some of the social characteristics which have survived through time are:

- Solidarity of the joint family and the kinship groups
- Stratification based on the caste groups, irrespective of religious affiliation
- Specialization and interdependence of occupational groups
- Language and territory as symbols of regional identity
- Religion and state transcending all of these.

Management is an approach to organized corporate activities and institutions. In Indian history, there are accounts of corporate activities in the field of economy, education and religion and polity (Altekar, 1949; Majumdar, 1969).

Historically, Indian organizations started with the family and then possibly extended to the clan/tribe headed by the king. For thousands of years in India, the head of the family or the tribe or the king had played a dominant role in the decision-making process.

However, there is also evidence indicating the tradition of consultation by the head and certain checks and balances to ensure justice. For example, during the Vedic period (1700–1200 AD) there was a strict written code of conduct enumerated in the Vedas where duties of the king, heads, as well as the subject were earmarked and any deviation from them was deemed as sinful. The advent of modern organizations started with the development of guilds. Artisans of one trade or similar trades organized themselves into a common guild and selected their own head who was endowed with special qualities. The king also regulated the functioning of the guilds to ensure that no member is exploited. There was a code governing the wage payment systems besides incentives, rewards and punishments for breach of contracts. One striking feature of the Indian management drawn from the ancient philosophy was the system of blood relationship or extended family, where there was incentive, reward and punishment and a certain amount of built-in security ensured for the members (Virmani, 2007).

However, another peculiar feature was that independent of security, the members of the family/guild were expected to obey the authority of the head. The uniqueness of the Indian system was that, though it provided security, it demanded unconditional obedience to authority which to a great extent was linked with age and seniority. There were times when both these principles were tampered with, especially when foreign invaders came to India and tried to establish their rule. But the deviations could not last long because of the deep-rooted attachment to traditional values.

During the ancient period, Chanakya the author of *Arthasastra,* advised King Chandragupta Maurya on how to develop a system of mistrust so that nobody can rebel against the king. One of the reasons for Chanakya's advice to Chandragupta was to evolve a system whereby kingship is secure and that any rebellion is nipped in the bud as Chandragupta himself had usurped the throne.

Chanakya therefore suggested a very vigorous system of control, reward and punishment. However, his whole treatise was an ideal advice to the king on how to rule. There is little evidence of whether his advice was really followed. On the contrary, the history of the guilds suggests that the traditional system of security and respect for age and authority was duly maintained which was not necessarily linked to efficiency as we understand it today.

Another peculiar feature in ancient India was that the king rarely interfered in the grass-root functioning of the village or even of the guilds unless his own personal interest was involved. The main reason was not that they did not want to interfere, but that the various small states in India were constantly engaged in fights. Therefore, in spite of various controls, systems and so on the grass-root operations remained the same. For example, the administration at the village and district levels rarely changed. Even during the medieval and Mughal periods, there was change only in the nomenclature used to describe functions or positions, and the functionaries by and large remained the same. During the medieval period the guild system, barring exceptions, gradually strengthened.

The unconditional obedience to the head remained a cardinal principle. Consequently, those who could get closer to the head or were in a position to influence him always took advantage. This also to an extent, created an exploitative society by the intermediaries or middlemen. They were able to influence the head or the king and get orders issued. This held good during the ancient and medieval periods.

Another interesting feature is that whenever there was interference in the normal functioning of certain institutions like guilds, there was disorganization. However, when they were left to themselves, they did try to evolve certain criteria of selecting the heads, rules and norms, based on the social values prevalent at that time. Since the kings were extremely busy with the political affairs, in many cases their interference was much less and the administrative institutions functioned better and more democratically. Another factor which affected the administration was a short-term view of the organizations. It was again the unstable political environment which prevented them from taking a long-term view. However, where the interference was less, the traditional practices continued without change, and in certain instances there were even long-term perspectives such as in the village administration by the panchayats.

A peculiar historical factor in the Indian management was a greater reliance on family/blood relationship. Outsiders, no matter how efficient they were, were always mistrusted. Therefore, no external person or agency was allowed. But at the same time, internally, there was in-fighting among the members of the family. This is there even in today's organizations, and if this concept is extended to the enterprise or national level, the same holds good.

During the British period, many of the British companies started setting up manufacturing units in India. These mainly related to jute and textiles and later to mining of coal. They were located in London and established an institution of managing agency system in India to manage the enterprises on behalf of the parent company. This also helped later in creating a class of professional managers who were experienced in managing the enterprises.

Gradually, some of the enterprises were taken over by Indians who initially were traders and took over as managing agents. Whenever they brought in their system (of management based on personal loyalty, caste etc.), family loyalties and family conflicts crept into the Indian enterprises. One managing agency could manage a number of enterprises. Sometimes they would own one company and still have managing agencies within the family. Later on, the Government of India abolished the managing agency system, but these family entrepreneurs continued to manage the enterprises by holding sometimes the minimum number of shares, even minority shares, to retain substantial control in the company.

One of the strengths of the East India Company and the British rule in India was that they did not try to enforce their system. On the contrary, even while administering the law, they went by the traditional Indian practices of the various communities involved. The Britishers, by and large, tried to behave like Indian kings with centralized control. However, there were periods when they tried to bring improvements and impose the British system. For example, the separation of the executive and the judiciary at the district level. But whenever they tried to decentralize, it created problems and they reverted to centralized controls. It happened in the case of district administration as well as in the management of enterprises. A unique feature of the British system was that they tried to institutionalize the decision-making process by bringing in rules and regulations and formalize the administration of justice by developing elaborate judicial machinery based on specific Indian practices.

Another feature of the Indian administration was mistrust of the people which started right from the ancient days and continued during the British period. In many cases, the system got reinforced after 1857 when there was a large-scale rebellion in Indian administration against the British rule.

Therefore, the British introduced a very elaborate system of rules and regulations to curb the dissident tendency among the native employees. There was too much emphasis on the rules, signatures, seals, secrecy in administration, and even annual confidential reporting system on employees, and all these are based on mistrust. Though the British have left, the same approach and systems continue even today.

In the Indian administration, the availability of the head to whom people or the employees can go for redressel of their grievance was dominant. For example, the administrator combined in himself all the functions and was considered as *'Ma-baap'* by the people of the district. However, when effort was made, especially during the British period, to separate the functions it created more confusion and as a result the British government had to revert back to centralized control under one administrative head. Besides, in the Indian management system, there has always been an effort to have a direct approach to the head for resolving one's grievances rather than going through various procedures. This has both advantages and disadvantages. The advantage is that the employees can go directly to one person and get their grievances resolved without delay. The disadvantage is that such a practice could be misused by the middlemen and could also delay remedial measures.

The concept of open-door policy or *'Darbar'* has been prevalent in India from time immemorial and is still preferred. However, the advocates of modern management do not subscribe to it. The organizations which claim better results also attribute their achievements to the open-door policy. The British rule, by and large, continued the *'Darbar'* system with all its drawbacks as well as strengths.

After the British left the country, many managers and academicians thought of professionalizing management. In that context, professionalization meant Western approach of management which comprises scientific management in the Taylor context; accent on formal systems, rules and regulations; and behavioural science approach to management of human resources and so on. Later, some of the concepts like management by objectives, organization development and so on have also gained ground at least in theory. Collective bargaining became an important means of regulating employer–employee relations. With the advocacy of these modern concepts, there was further confusion especially when their application was sudden into a society which was very much traditional and had not changed substantially for thousands of years. Therefore, we ended up with a dilemma in our management practices, that is, one set of practices which were on paper based on the modern concepts and the other which was actually followed based on the traditional concepts.

This resulted in dissatisfaction among the employers as well as employees. The employers blamed the employees for not accepting the modern professional management concepts while the employees blamed the employers for ad hoc decisions and not following the stated policies. Therefore, on paper we have perfectly laid down policies and norms but hardly any of those are followed properly in practice. Changes and evolution in Indian management/administration through the ages are illustrated in the following table.

Chronology of management evolution in India

Vedic period (1700–1200 BC)	Emergence of administrative machinery Largely patriarchal administration Administration based on caste system *(Varna)* Gradual emergence of Office of Collector of Revenue Existence of barter system
1200–600 BC	Development of system of taxation and revenue administration Extension and specialization in administration Beginnings of provisional government
600–300 BC	Prescribed wage system in place Wages paid in cash and kind Development of bureaucracy Rise of class of high officials for general affairs, justice, army and so onBeginning of the formation of guilds
Maryann period (1700–1200 BC)	Reward, punishment and wage system codified Qualifications and responsibilities of each official laid down Quasi-democratic administrative machinery Strengthening and centralization of bureaucracy, with delegation of authority
200–300 BC	Decline of centralized bureaucracy Declining importance of hierarchies due to repeated invasions and political instability Division and ranking of labour Emergence of artisan clans and guilds

Chronology of management evolution in India

Gupta period AD 325–500	Close contact between rulers and the common people Disappearance of non-monarchial system Relatively decentralized but hierarchical administration Re-emergence of bureaucracy Highly organized and evolved administrative and labour policies Development of autonomous regulatory mechanisms in administration Timely payment of wages regulated by contract and state Development of autonomous guilds – origin of rudimentary factory/ production system
Medieval period AD 1175–1526	Invasions, regicide and rebellion were frequent Wide gulf between rulers and ruled Traditional administration at village level continued largely unaffected Military strength rather than democracy ruled Judicial, legislative, administrative and military powers highly centralized Taxes and duties on trade and commerce were levied at central and provincial level Industrial organization achieved through guilds
Mughal period AD 1526–1707	Centralization of authority Disappearance of bureaucracy in government administration, replaced by military strength Absence of hereditary aristocracy (among *nawabs*, *omrahs*) Strengthening of guild system in business and trade More emphasis on arts and crafts, not industry
British period AD 1707–1947	Trade turned into administration Constant changes in arrangements for discharge of revenue, magisterial and judicial functions Growth of professional and trained judicial hierarchy and importance of law Growth of bureaucracy and emphasis on formal education for middle-level administrative posts System of budgeting introduced Bleeding of Indian industry led to its collapse Regrowth was slow Emergence of proprietary industry, resulting in the exploitation of labour After 1857, paternal and authoritarian rule was restored in the local representative of the government Racial basis introduced in selection Elaborate rules and regulations laid down for administration and industry Managing agency methods introduced, which became hereditary Industrial development financed by foreign capital

Chronology of management evolution in India

AD 1947–56	Patriarchal system continued High degree of patronage, inadequate delegation of responsibility, especially in managing agency system Managing agency system reformed to Board of Directors, who continued to be representatives of managing agents

Adapted from Virmani (2007: 88–89)

Modern Context of Indian Management

The aforesaid management practices and processes, which continued with minor adjustments throughout the centuries, were subjected to major influences with the coming of the British in the eighteenth century. They imported systems into the country. Large corporations evolved, production processes were centralized, managing agencies were created, and a new distinction was made between those who owned enterprises and those who worked for them. Between them a new class of professionals – non-owning managers – emerged. The corporate sector fitted in well with the Indian stratified society. However, the trust which characterized the traditional relationship between stratified social groups slowly faded away. Decentralized economic activities were replaced by impersonal and contractual relationships along with centralized economy and controls.

Also the industrial revolution in Britain, which gave rise to formalized authority and control, a division between policy and executive roles, and elaborate systems and procedures to create efficiency, found its way into Indian organizations. Soon technology, systems and procedures became the determining variables in business corporations and profit at by the word.

Indian management took easily to the import of technology and systems. During the second half of this century, India built infrastructure and manufacturing facilities for all possible goods and services – from making pins to planes, mining to manufacturing and transportation to satellite communication. Indian management has also attempted to follow Western systems of management, particularly techniques in production planning, maintenance scheduling, inventory management market research, forecasting, long-range planning, management information systems and computer applications, and finance and control, and transferred them successfully to their work places. But these have generated the following illusions:

- That sensible decision can be made through these techniques; that automation, computers and the whole gamut of modern production techniques will increase productivity and employees satisfaction.
- That business problems can be solved by a formalized planning process. This has made Indian management systems to follow Western management processes and human resource management.
- The above have been in variance with the Indian management and with the Indian ethos and are yet to be integrated with the traditional systems of management, particularly where management of human resource in organization is concerned. Ownership and control, centralization and decentralization, relationship, formal or informal systems of work, styles of management, and decision-making processes have caused much of soul searching and concern in Indian management today.

Features of Indian Management

Viewed in this context, one may describe the following as the basic ingredients of Indian management (adapted from Sinha, 1991).

First, in Indian management, ownership and management are not differentiated; almost invariably these overlap. This is primarily an extension of the agrarian and artisan base in the Indian society where the farmers own and till the land, and artisans own the equipment and manufacture pots, pans, baskets, clothes, furniture and carvings. The nature of traditional economic enterprise is such that differentiation between ownership and management is unnecessary. In spite of the recent attempts to change this, one finds an extension of these practices in the contemporary large corporate sector in this country. Whether it is right or wrong, an effective or ineffective practice in management is desirable but it is there.

The second characteristic feature of Indian management is that it is centred around the chief, family head, religious head, the king, the chief executive of an organization, and the head of the institution in the contemporary times. The chief in the Indian society has the *Mana* – a benevolent spirit, an insight which makes him all powerful. He is considered pure and sacred. He is the custodian of what is good and what is desirable and he must be a nurturant leader (Sinha, 1980). Leadership in Indian society is an important concept for human resource development.

The third hallmark of Indian management is rooted in its traditional style of decision-making. While it is the head who is the unquestioned chief, a respected chief is one who manages with the consent of those who depend on him. The consent, traditionally in the subcontinent, is obtained through consultation. However, this consultation is not a consensus-building process. It is an information gathering system whereby the chief collects points and counterpoints and incorporates them in his own thinking and decision-making. Sometimes, this consultative process is seen as a ritualistic exercise. At times, it is perceived as a pragmatic way of pooling ideas and involving those who may be affected by the decision, providing an opportunity for catharsis, and paving the way for implementation of the decision. It is also true that in Indian management arriving at a collective decision or building a consensus in the Western sense of the term is an alien concept. One finds that, in a situation where most of the members converge on a decision, at least one will oppose it, sometimes with a 'convenient' logic and consideration.

Fourth, in Indian management, hierarchy is key to management coordination. Horizontal peer-level coordination, so typical of Japanese society, is almost absent in the Indian scene. Presumably, members of an Indian organization look for top-down guidance.

The fifth characteristic of Indian management is its emphasis on lifelong employment and job security. There is a societal assumption that membership in a family, caste and corporate group has to be permanent. Although security and lifelong employment have been traditionally valued in India, in contemporary management there is much debate about its efficacy.

The sixth characteristic is the widespread belief that there is no substitute for learning on the job. Nowhere in Indian history does one find any account of administrators receiving professional training. Being a manager means learning on the job. There is a definite preference for job experience against job knowledge.

The seventh characteristic of Indian management is its short-term orientation. The past is past, and the future is uncertain; therefore, the present is the most important matter the manager has to deal with. Because of seasonal fluctuations and floods and famines, the farmers and artisans in traditional India had to focus on the present and the immediate. Coping with uncertain demand and markets made long-range economic planning difficult. It is interesting that in Indian society where values and beliefs revolve around past deeds and future achievements, the framework of reference for economic activity has always been short and seasonal.

The eighth hallmark of Indian management is its overconcern with job identity. An Indian derives his or her identity from the social group to which he or she belongs, his or her occupation and the job he or she performs. These are so interlinked that in his or her work organization his or her first attempt is invariably to establish a reference group and job identity.

The ninth characteristic of Indian management is the centralization of power and authority and the decentralization of activities. This has emerged from the powerful belief that the chief has a *Manna* and is the storehouse of energy, authority and power. Even in organizations which have decentralized authority, one finds that people do not exercise their delegated authority and power. There is strong conviction in Indian society that power and authority flow from the fountainhead – the chief executive, the centre of the organization (Kakkar, 1974).

Indian management values loyalty, sometimes unquestioned loyalty – to the king, chief, head of the family, and the chief executive. There is often confusion between loyalty to the king or the country, and loyalty to the chief or the organization. The assumption is that the king and the country and the chief executive and the organization are synonymous. This is a matter of great debate. Some researchers have commented that Indian society fosters dependency thus calling for loyalty and fellowship and playing to the tune of the supervisors or authority figure (Sinha, 1986).

In Indian management, there is a preference for an open-door policy. The king must be accessible, the head of the joint family must listen, and the chief executive must be approachable, not only to those who are close to him but to anyone in his organization. His doors should be always ajar, although there would neither plethora of complaints nor long lines of people seeking audience if the doors opened only occasionally. In an open-door organization, those who really need to approach the chief reach him; others are satisfied with the thought that he could be reached if occasion demanded. There are many stories of exemplary kings in the Indian history who ran an open-door policy. The poor could share their anxieties with the king and problems and receive instant help.

Indian management characteristically has two parallel information systems – the formal, which is structured either top-down or bottom-up, and the informal, which is unstructured and criss-crosses the organization hierarchy like a grapevine. The former is slow; the latter is faster. The skills of shifting information from one system to another and using them effectively are considered important assets for successful managers.

Performance in Indian management requires pressure and persuasion. Deadlines, targets and crises are great motivators and challenges in the Indian society. Work is cyclical – long rest, short activity. This is primarily an agrarian characteristic which seems to have pervaded other spheres of economic activity. In most Indian organizations, one finds that the last quarter of the year always has higher productivity than the average of the other three quarters. The pressure to meet deadlines works so well in Indian management.

Last, Indian management values individual excellence. It recognizes individuals who make distinguished contributions in whatever field of endeavour they are. In Indian society, one does not look for the same qualities in every person. Rather, one recognizes individual differences and respects excellence in whatever field one distinguishes him or herself. It is believed that in a team, not all members are alike. In fact, they should not be alike, but be like five fingers, with different lengths and shapes, bound together in one hand.

Collective wisdom is valued in Indian society. Teamwork always commands attention. The story of a Blind Man and the Lame Man joining hands together to compensate for each other's deficiencies is a household word. An effective team consists of people with different views, values, perceptions, professions, skills and wisdom, working for a common goal so that together they convert energy into synergy and the competence of individual is translated into excellence through teamwork.

It is true that business and management culture in India has always been a reflection of the complexity and diversity which characterize the country as a whole. The basic features of Indian management also reflect contemporary process of social and economic change that is now reshaping the very 'idea' and image of India.

In recent times, Indian management systems are moving towards a new global orientation and operational context. Family-dominated business conglomerates and large public sector enterprises continue to dominate the Indian economy, but these are beginning to give way to innovative, globally oriented, corporate players, especially within the booming Information Technology (IT) industry (Samir & Mark, 2005). Many scholars highlighted that several traditional characteristics of management in India remain in place – notions of authority and hierarchy, role of familial networks, indigenous ethical-philosophical framework and community boundaries; the importance of continuity and stability in institutional and institutional norms and practices; and, finally, a general acceptance of ambiguity.

The degree to which these typical features of Indian management systems are likely to be transformed by a new global context is, in some respects, the crux of contemporary debate about the evolution of Indian management systems. As suggested by the broad range of arguments and perspectives presented by management scholars, it has been proven that it is possible and plausible to suggest that India is moving towards developing a unique 'hybrid' form of management that seeks to remain grounded in selected practice of global management systems.

Transitional Trends of Managerial Culture in India

Understanding Indian culture and the values and social norms it entails is crucial in a rapidly globalizing context. Managers in India retain a strong orientation towards the cultural legacy of an ancient country with a continuously living and evolving civilization. However, superimposed on this legacy is the impact of changing technological and organizational systems. In India, cultural factors deeply influence many aspects of organizational, social, familial and religious life at the micro level, while at the macro level these culture systems are beginning to adjust to the unavoidable realities of economic reform, communication technology and globalization. In terms of their capacity to cope with these dramatic transformations, it is perhaps relevant that Indian management has been noted for its ability to tolerate high levels of uncertainty and ambiguity – as indicated by research that shows that India is one of the five countries with the lowest scores of 'uncertainty avoidance' out of an extensive sample of nations (Hofstede, 1991).

After decades of independence, a new generation has come into its own in India and has assumed a position of corporate and familial leadership. The worldview of this generation is much less ideology-driven than that of its predecessors, who were, typically, reared on stories of sacrifice and idealism of heroic figures from the Indian national movement. Several developments have caused a break with continuity, shifting values from selfless service and the pursuit of salvation to a 'here and how' approach, which is more focused upon individual self-interest and advancement (Chatterjee, 1998). In contrast with previous decades, entering a commercial profession is now seen to be the first rather than the last preference for many of India's 'best and brightest' graduates. In part, this is due to a widening gap between public and private sectors in terms of salary remuneration (Lawler et al., 1995). More generally, this change in perceptions is also due to a more general aspiration among the so-called great Indian middle class towards entrepreneurial success and conspicuous consumptions.

There has also been a discernible shift in India towards valuing professional/technical personnel and inputs within the workplace. Thus, even the oldest of 'family' conglomerates are now keen to stress that their business operations are driven by a dedicated team of specialized professionals who have obtained their positions through their technical or managerial expertise. This trend has been strengthened by the share market listing of corporations, meaning that professional, organizational and managerial structures and standards of corporate governance are subject to greater scrutiny of regulatory bodies and general public. It is important to note that Indian corporation and managers are starting to create synergetic links with the social networks of the so-called Indian diasporas living abroad. Overseas Indian and associated social networks have become increasingly important and influential contributors in today's setting. On the other hand, an increasing number of foreign business and MNCs are now establishing major operations in India. Again, their entry has introduced a new 'global' dynamic within Indian management culture as employees and local mangers learn to operate within the broader context of the unique corporate culture of these transnational business giants. Nonetheless, very often there is also an equivalent need for these corporations to adapt their marketing and management strategies to the local Indian context. Some prominent scholars of Indian management advocate that a paradigm shift in managerial values and assumptions does not necessarily imply a rejection of 'traditional' wisdom, ethical frameworks and values (Chakraborty, 1998). These scholars suggest that like that of Japanese Indian managerial values and goals need to arise out of deeply rooted social and ethical traditions. While 'tradition' is unmistakably observable in the daily lives of managers and employees across the country, work organizations appears to be at the crossroads. At least among senior-level Indian managers, there appears to be a parallel emergence of 'global' value paradigms (Chatterjee & Pearson, 2000a, 2000b).

Similarly, scholars of business culture have been debating theories of 'convergence' and 'divergence', as the influence of globalization takes hold. The convergence theorists argue that the emergence of a Western market-oriented economy inevitably leads to the adoption of values and culture associated with it (Webber, 1969; Child, 1981; Bond & King, 1985). In contrast, the divergence theorists argue that if the culture of the indigenous location is sufficiently powerful, it will retain its uniqueness in spite of the impact of broader, sweeping effects of homogenization (England & Lee, 1974; Laurent, 1983). In contrast, anthropological 'acculturation' theorists suggest that the dynamic interaction of all of these influences often allow for the emergence of 'hybrid' forms of culture (Beals, 1953). Several research surveys of Asian managers have also contended that these business leaders are able to maintain a duality of values; one field of value formation is drawn from their own cultural heritage, while the other impact on them through the wider forces of internationalization (Bedi, 1991). In the Indian context, it is thus possible to suggest that a hybrid set of values is creating neither convergence nor divergence but a unique Indian managerial value system.

On the whole, the basic contours of Indian management are drawn from the tenets of traditional culture of India. The proceeding chapters are going to examine the relevance of these arguments and perspectives by taking the case studies of four India-based corporate organizations in Hyderabad, India.

4

Case Study of Scientific Organization

First Section

The Scientific Organization is a pioneer in laboratories set up in India that are devoted to modern biology, with emphasis on basic research. It is a proud member of the Council of Scientific and Industrial Research (or CSIR) laboratories at national level. The CSIR is the premier multidisciplinary research and development organization of the Government of India.

The laboratory was established under the guidance of Pushpa Mittra Bhargava, who is a renowned scientist and the architect of modern biology in India. He conceived the idea of establishing the Scientific Organization and ensured that it was built, well-equipped and staffed with highly qualified research fellows without compromising on any standards.

The Scientific Organization is India's foremost research lab which shouldered the responsibility for onset of biotechnology revolution in the country and successfully demonstrated application of biology in various fields such as pharmaceuticals, agriculture and security. Its research contribution is being globally acknowledged consistently.

In the year 1977, the laboratory was set up as a semi-autonomous body within Regional Research Laboratory of Hyderabad and very soon achieved the status of a full-fledged national laboratory during the financial year 1981–1982. Subsequently, on 26 November 1987, it was dedicated to the nation by the then Prime Minister of India Late Shri Rajiv Gandhi. In the new millennium, the centre ushered in an era to continue its mission of conducting a high-quality basic research in chosen areas of biology, socially relevant research and application – oriented work towards commercialization.

The prime objective of the centre is to aid the development of biotechnology in India. It also offers training courses in advanced areas of biology. The goal is to promote centralized national facilities for new and modern techniques in the interdisciplinary areas of biology, simultaneously interacting with industry segments that are carrying out basic and applied work in the field of biotechnology and to collect, collate and disseminate information relevant to biological research.

Vision

Scientific Organization has been conceived, visualized and acclaimed as a centre for research in frontier areas of modern biology at par with those in Western countries. It has significantly fulfilled a long-felt need in the country for accelerating the necessary thrust in the field of molecular and cellular biology. Scientific Organization is the first institution in India devoted exclusively to research in frontier areas of modern biology and has played a key role in the development of biotechnology programme in the country.

The results of the care and attention to detail that founder director evinced at every step are clearly visible – both in the laboratories and in the beautiful green surroundings. His successful experiment in forging a novel framework for the sharing of all facilities, equipment and chemicals among the scientific group is unique in Indian setup. In effect, this means that the Scientific Organization functions as one integrated laboratory. He firmly believed that science and art are two facets of creative human activity as they go hand in hand. His penchant for aesthetics reflects at various places in the Scientific Organization campus. His continued association and support to Scientific Organization is a great help to maintain and thrive on these traditions.

Values

In Scientific Organization, scientists are strongly believed to have a common understanding among the scientific community and so are the achievements, new discoveries and innovations which made valuable contributions to the field they are researching in. Team work is also valued as scientists worked in coordination and operated as members of an egalitarian family extending help whenever required. Sharing knowledge and results, particularly instruments and ingredients for running experiments, is part of their daily regime.

Mission

The centre's mission statement is to aid the development of biotechnology in India and to continue its journey of conducting a high-quality basic research in chosen areas of biology with socially relevant research and application-oriented work with added commercial value.

Scientific Organization has also stepped into the field of research and development in many new areas, such as gene therapy, drug delivery system and the human genome using the advanced DNA technologies. It also has plans to acquire the 'DNA Chip Technology' and an advanced version of NMR imaging facility to study the images of experimental animals without having the need to kill them.

The laboratory is well abreast of the fast-changing R&D scenario, as the advances in biotechnology are bound to have a far-reaching impact on mankind. The mapping of human genome, for example, would enable us to define normal and abnormal human biology, and we can utilize this knowledge in detecting, predicting, preventing, counselling and possibly treating human diseases through the application of DNA technology by gene therapy.

With the onset of the new millennium, yet another exciting area in the field of biotechnology, the 'Gene Chip' technology, has opened up that would make it possible to look for subtle changes in any gene at a reasonable cost and subject any defective gene to therapeutic regimes to circumvent its limitation. This preventive therapy would enable majority of individuals to live a normal and healthy life without any diseases. Scientific Organization has come forward to shoulder this responsibility by adopting, modifying and developing these areas for the benefit of the country in general and biotechnology industry in particular.

Location and Staff of the Organization

The Scientific Organization building is stretched over 14 acres of land, which is close to several other prestigious research institutions like IICT, GSI and NGRI. The campus is situated on Uppal Road with an electrically operated automatic gate on main entrance. It is about 10 km away from the city airport. The entire campus of Scientific Organization has been designed keeping in view the functions that need to be performed in it. An attempt was made to anticipate as many requirements as possible and then to build for them. Other aspects like elegance, aesthetics and cost-effectiveness have also been taken care of. The Scientific Organization laboratory complex consists of the following buildings:

- Main laboratory building (central area/west/south/east wings)/ animal house/store and steel yard/workshop/canteen/guest house/pump house, sumps and overhead tank/substation building; HT yards/security lodges/administration building/ oxidation pond; incinerator shed/greenhouses/building for housing and fish and snakes/DA/BARC 32 P-labelled nucleotides facility/diesel tank/lecture halls/farm house/students hostel

It is well-equipped with a highly functional laboratory which meets international standards. It has all the major equipment used for research in various areas of modern biology. The organization has the following special facilities:

- DNA micro array, proteomics, confocal microscopy, automated DNA sequencing, flow cytometry, peptide synthesis, protein analysis, nucleic acid synthesis, electron micros copy, cell culture, laboratory animal facility, Pisciculture Laboratory, bio-informatics, digital imaging, Laboratory for the Conservation of Endangered Species (LACORNES), library, the Halden Collection.

As stated in recent annual report, the total strength of Scientific Organization is close to 906 employees. The institute is headed by a director who is assisted by the heads of various sections. Out of these members, about 407 belong to different scientific groups who are working in various laboratories. The groups include various grades such as group leader, senior scientist, technical officer, post-doctoral fellow (PDF), senior research fellow (SRF), junior research fellow (JRF), project assistant and lab assistant and so on. The group of scientists is drawn from across the country. About 38% of the workforce are women, working in various groups/sections of Scientific Organization at various levels and positions. The lower-grade employees are mostly drawn from Andhra Pradesh and Telangana, which contribute to about 90% of the total work force.

The group leader is the head of the laboratory and looks after all the administrative affairs of the laboratory. The other scientific staff members work under his supervision. Under group leader, there are senior scientists posted in each laboratory to help and assist research scholars and project assistants to carry out biological research in various areas. Each laboratory is engaged in various fields of modern biological research that is especially carried out by PDF, SRF, JRF and project assistants. Laboratory technician/assistant provides all the necessary support to the scientific staff members in their day-to-day experiments.

There are other support service groups as well who render full support and are instrumental in facilitating the research activities of Scientific Organization in high spirit. The following groups are the main support groups which help scientific community directly or indirectly to enhance their performance:

Instrumentation

There are 30 people working in this group under the supervision of Head of Instrumentation, Sekhar Ramachandran. This group is playing a major role in installing equipment intended for state-of-the-art-facilities in the Scientific Organization. These members are also responsible for the maintenance of instruments and also provide training to the research staff on the usage of these equipment. As a whole, this group looks after all the modern biological research instruments which are needed by researchers.

Fine Chemicals

This group consists of two officers, two assistant staff members and a technician. The group maintains a stock of about 5,000 types of biochemicals for ongoing research activities of the laboratory.

Animal House

A team of 15 staff members run this unit, out of which 11 are qualified animal caretakers. They have obtained specialized training in the care, breeding and management of laboratory animals. The animal house maintains 3 strains of rats, 13 strain mice, Syrian hamster, New Zealand white rabbits and guinea pigs in different rooms. The average number of animals in animal house at one time is close to 4000. A 12-hour light–dark cycle is maintained with an automatic timer.

Engineering Service

The organization complex has a number of modern facilities such as vacuum, compressed air and gas online, pre-treated water supply, liquid nitrogen, centralized air conditioning and provision for 1500 KVA of emergency power. Professional staff members in the engineering group (civil, electrical, mechanical etc.) run these facilities.

Horticulture and Experiment Farm

The horticulture group maintains the lush green surroundings of the Scientific Organization. An experimental farm is also being maintained by this staff to meet the requirements of the plant's genetic fingerprinting work. Green house facility is used for studies in plant molecular biology. In addition to this, coffee plants are reared for experimental purposes for the ongoing programme on coffee germplasm studies. The fodder for rabbits in the animal house is also grown in the campus.

Planning, Monitoring and Evaluation

The main responsibility of this group is to assist the director in the planning and execution of the various programmes and activities of the centre and act as a liaison between the director and the various research groups, CSIR headquarters and other organizations. This unit is responsible for the budget and manpower data, reports and seminars.

Director's technical staff: This segment was created by the director to render technical assistance in matters concerning the annual reports, documentation, communication, visitor liaison, media relations and host of other related functions. This segment also serves as a link between the director and various groups/sections in the Scientific Organization.

Photography

This group provides specialized and routine photographic services to members of the scientific staff. High-quality reproductions in the form of black and white prints, colour prints and slides are prepared for the purpose of publication, display or projection. This unit is equipped with the digital imaging facility.

Administration

The overall administration of the centre and the supervision of ancillary services such as transport and telecommunications are under the purview of the administration. In addition to this, secretarial assistance is also provided to the staff for maintenance of records and databases, preparation of reports, scientific manuscripts and other correspondence. The administration has created a Hindi cell to facilitate communication and other official transaction in Hindi.

Finance and Account

All financial matters pertaining to Scientific Organization, including budget planning, preparation and allocation, are taken care of by this section. It interacts with the CSIR Head Quarters and works in close coordination with the administration. This section handles all payments pertaining to local and other purchases, including disbursement of staff salaries.

Stores and Purchase

This unit consists of 9 purchase staff, 11 store staff and 2 officers. This section carries out the processing of purchase orders and the procurement of equipment and materials for the centre. The stores and purchase section maintains an exhaustive inventory and maintains supplies of inorganic chemicals, stationary, glassware, plastic ware and other items.

Guest House and Catering

Scientific Organization operates an international-style air-conditioned guest house which is fully furnished with internet connectivity in all the rooms. It also has a well-maintained catering facility for the staff with two dining halls for breakfast, lunch and dinner and a lounge as well as kiosk for tea and snacks. It serves special food on a large scale during meetings and conferences.

Security

The security services of the Scientific Organization operate round the clock supervised by four trained permanent security officers. It also has 7 ASO and 45 security guards hired on contract basis. All the security personnel are ex-servicemen from defence services background. They have expertise in dealing with security-related issues in the Scientific Organization campus.

Medical Services

Medical care is available round the clock for the staff and their families well attended by the physicians and the paramedical staff. Scientific Organization has in-campus medical facility of a clinic and a dispensary on shared basis with the neighbouring sister institution IICT.

This centre is operated by well-qualified medical and paramedical staff including four doctors, three nurses, three pharmacists, four technicians in pathology laboratory, three receptionists and four helpers. It is well-equipped for preliminary analytical and diagnostic tests. It regularly maintains medical records of the staff and their dependent family members as well.

All the above groups are headed by experts in their respective fields and supported by their subordinates. They have been providing effective support to the scientific staff.

High-performing Organization

Since its inception, Scientific Organization has published about 1200 research papers mainly in reputed international journals. The centre has the distinction of being one of the top three institutions in the country in terms of the impact factor, that is, an index of the number of times a research paper is referred by others in their publications.

Scientific Organization started filing patents way back in 1979 and has filed more than 14 patents so far, both at Indian and international levels. Few of the patents filed till now are as follows:

- DNA markers for assessing seed purity (patent filed with countries like Sri Lanka, Bangladesh, Indonesia, Malaysia, Nepal, Pakistan, Thailand and Vietnam)
- Creation, optimization and production of a Lipase, India

- In Vivo assay system for screening and validation of drugs and other substances, the United States
- Use of DNA encoding a promoter or promoters along with CIS regulatory elements and a novel process for producing polypeptides, Japan.

Scientific Organization has collaborated with various institutions for research and development purpose:

- *Universities*: A total of 16 universities have collaborated with Scientific Organization; few of the prestigious universities to mention here are: Jawaharlal Nehru University, University of Delhi, University of Pune, University of California (USA), University of Giessen (Germany) and University of Oxford (UK)
- *Research Institutes*: An array of research institutes like Agharkar Research Institute, Pune; Indian Institute of Science, Bangalore; Tata Institute of Fundamental Research, Mumbai; AISIN-COSMOS, Japan; Santa Fe Institute, USA; and Imperial Cancer Research Fund, UK
- *Medical Organizations*: A spectrum of 20 prestigious medical organizations like Nizam Institute of Medical Sciences, Hyderabad; Tata Memorial Centre, Mumbai; Regional Medical Research Centre, Port Blair; and Hemophilia Federation of India, Delhi
- *Industries*: A group of 22 industries like Biological E Ltd., Hyderabad; Dabur Research Foundation, Ghaziabad; Hindustan Lever Ltd, Bangalore; and Torrent Pharmaceutical Ltd, Hyderabad. Nine other organizations, including Anthropological Survey of India, Nagpur; Central Zoo Authority of India, Delhi; Indian Space Research Organization; and the Wildlife Institute, Dehradun.

Besides these, the Scientific Organization has also gained the stature of a truly international centre with short-term and long-term overseas visitors from countries like the United States, the United Kingdom, France, Germany, Japan, China, New Zealand, the Czech Republic, Mauritius, Cameroon and so on for research assignments in various laboratory groups.

About 50 ongoing projects are externally funded by various national agencies:

- Conservation of endangered wild animals, funded by Central Zoo Authority (CZO)
- An evaluation of the endemism of the amphibian assemblages from the Western Ghats using molecular markers, funded by Department of Biotechnology (DBT)
- Molecular characterization of genes causing primary open-angle glaucoma in the Indian population, funded by Department of Science and Technology (DST)
- NISSAT: Establishment of value-added patent information system in Scientific Organization, funded by Department of Scientific Industrial Research (DSIR)
- Molecular marker-assisted selection for bacterial leaf blight resistance in rice, funded by Indian Council Of Agriculture Research (ICAR)
- Genetic analysis of pancreatitis in Indian population, funded by Indian Council of Medical Research (ICMR)
- Eye Diseases, funded by LV Prasad Eye Institute; creation of Framework Linkage Map of Domestic Buffalo Genome, funded by national Dairy Development Board (NDDB)
- Conservation genetics of marine turtles, using mitochondrial DNA sequencing analysis and microsatellite analysis, funded by Wildlife Institute of India (WII).

About 15 international agencies projects are taken up by the Scientific Organization, such as optimization of capillary gel electrophoresis-based whole-genome expression profiling (and efficient recA enzyme) funded by AISIN-COSMOS; role of nuclear organization and ply comb in transcriptional and post-transcriptional gene silencing, funded by Human Frontier Science Program Organization (HFSP); modulation of embryonic cell migration and adhesion to the extracellular matrix by phospholipids and cholesterol, funded by Indo-French Centre for the Promotion of Advanced Research (IFCPASR) and molecular basis of cold adaptation; Antarctic cyan bacteria and bacteria as model systems, funded by Indo-Japanese Society for Promotion of Science (I-ISPS).

The Scientific Organization played a key role in the development of the country's first recombinant DNA-based Hepatitis B vaccine for human use, by Shantha Biotechnics (P) Ltd, Hyderabad; Scientific Organization has helped Dr Reddy's Research Foundation, Hyderabad through specific technology tie-ups; technology for RNasin – an enzyme-inhibitor – has been successfully transferred to M/s Bangalore Genei (P) Ltd, Bangalore; organization's scientists have also helped M/s EID Parry Ltd, Chennai, by developing a protocol for standardization of PCR-based markers to distinguish the parental and hybrid seed varieties of rice. It has also undertaken a collaborative research project with M/s Dabber Research Foundation and the IICT to develop a new therapeutic agent for the treatment of cancer. A collaborative research programme is on the anvil with M/s Biological Evans Ltd, Hyderabad, to provide rapid, accurate and reliable diagnostic service to cancer patients, based on modern molecular methods.

Awards and Honours

Over the years, the organization has received the following international/ national awards and honours:

1. UNESCO's Global Network of Molecular and Cell Biology have identified Scientific Organization as Centre of Excellence (1990).
2. In the past, it has received the Third World Academy of Sciences (TWAS) Award, Italy, and was also designated as a South Centre of Excellence in Research and Training (1992).
3. The probe developed at the organization for DNA fingerprinting won the CSIR Technology Award in Biological Sciences (1994).
4. It has been given the Federation of Indian Chambers of Commerce and Industry (FICCI) Award for Outstanding Achievement in Science and Technology (1998).
5. Organization is a Member of the ICICI Knowledge Park launched jointly by the Industrial Credit and Investment Corporation of India (ICICI) Ltd and the Govt. of Andhra Pradesh, Hyderabad (1998).
6. Scientific Organization is also a Member of AP Bio Net, an international website for the advancement of Bioinformatics (2001).

Distinctions

The organization has achieved major breakthroughs in various biological research programmes. A few of them are described here:

- Unique RNase from cobra snake venom: RNase cutting enzyme, which has specificity towards cytidylic acid, was isolated, purified and characterized from cobra venom. Such an enzyme was reported by the scientists for the first time at the Scientific Organization. The enzyme has potential to be used as a tool for sequencing RNAs and in their structural studies.
- Gene delivery system: Scientific Organization, in collaboration with its sister institute, the IICT, has successfully designed a formulation for efficient delivery of DNA into the cells. This patented formulation, based on the novel chemistry and DNA condensation process, has demonstrated higher transfection efficiency as compared to its commercial formulation.
- Microbes from Antarctica: Biodiversity and Cold Adaptation – scientists at the Scientific Organization have identified a number of cold-loving bacteria and yeasts, hitherto unknown from Antarctica. The cold-loving bacteria adapt to low temperature by their ability to modulate membrane fluidity through the regulation of the synthesis of fatty acids. A few cold-active and heat-labile enzymes from these micro-organisms have been characterized for the first time.
- Genetics of osmoregulation: The Scientific Organization team was one of the first to discover the gene ProU in E. coli, to decipher the genetic organization and to establish its role in osmoregulation. Functions of several other similar genes have also been established. As an offshoot, this work has led to the development in the production of genetically engineered polypeptide products.
- How does the protein fold? Protein folding is one of the major issues that are still unsolved in biology. Scientific Organization scientists have arrested the protein (RNase-A) under a certain set of conditions, in a state of partially folded active protein, known as molten globule initially. Failure of protein folding may lead to many diseases. It was established that one of the eye lens proteins called Crystalline has shown positive results in assisting for the process of protein folding and assembling – an ability similar to molecular chaperones. These studies have relevance in preparing the remedy for the treatment of the eye disease cataract.

- Peptides to fight bacterial invasion: Nature uses peptides to combat bacterial invasions. Taking this as an example, Scientific Organization scientists have designed peptides consisting of 11–15 amino acid residues, which possess selective antibacterial activity. Understanding of the structure–function relationship in antibacterial and membrane-active peptide toxins could be used in therapies in such a way that resistance would not be developed against these molecules.
- Protein from seminal plasma plays multifunctional role: A protein called seminal plasma, discovered at this centre is a potent microbial agent as well as an anti-HIV agent. It lyses dividing cells and shows inhibitory properties towards host of other biological functions, such as RNA-polymerases, reverse transcriptase's, sperm motility and in vitro fertilizing ability of spermatozoa.
- Regulation of cell division: A new model explaining the non-phenomenology of regulation of cell division and malignant transformation was proposed by scientists from this centre.
- A new universal probe for DNA fingerprinting: Scientific Organization developed a new probe derived from an Indian banded krait snake. This probe is being used for forensic investigations, paternity determination and seed stock verifications. Based on this probe, DNA fingerprinting evidence was presented in the court of law for the first time in the annals of Indian history and was accepted as infallible evidence. This indigenous probe was used in more than 600 cases such as paternity disputes, identification of missing children, identification of mutilated bodies, exchange of babies in maternity wards, cases of rape and murder and so on.
- Molecular basis of sex determination: Sex determination is one of the most important unsolved problems in modern biology. Isolation of highly conserved sex chromosome-specific satellite DNA, 'Bkm' from the female Indian branded krait snake has paved the way to our understanding of the molecular basis of sex determination. The contribution from the Scientific Organization is considered to be a major breakthrough in this field and has become the basis of our understanding of sex reversal in humans as well.

Due to above activities and achievements, Scientific Organization has been considered as a high-performing Organization in India.

Second Section

Enculturation: rite-de-passage

Every human being goes through different stages in life, and there are common rituals and practices when one attains certain stages like birth, marriage, death and so on. Such practices are quite common in most of the communities.

Like any other community, in any organization, enculturation is the process by which anyone can acquire membership and psychological ownership of that organization he or she becomes a part of. It is mostly informal where members learn the culturally accepted behavior through observation, imitation and mentoring. In Scientific Organization, new entrants learn the cultural ropes by observing the behavior of those who are already in the organization.

In any organization a member goes through various stages of work life such as entry, induction, training and development, performance evaluation and promotion from one level to the other, and separation or retirement that is marked by celebration.

Entry and Induction

Recruitment is crucial for every organization, since the quality of people and commitment of the employees bring credibility through their skilful work. Scientific Organization follows certain rules and regulations for recruiting competent person in respective branches. It is known for competent and dedicated staff in all areas since its inception. This organization follows rigorous selection processes to maintain the quality of institution.

Since, this organization is a wing of Council for Scientific Industrial Research (CSIR), it has to follow some basic rules and regulations like minimum qualifications and experience as prescribed by CSIR for recruitment of scientists. However, selection of senior scientists in the organization is done through various stages of screening by experts from inside as well as outside.

The candidates' resume is first circulated to all the group leaders (scientists) who are required to write brief comments on the candidates' profiles. After going through all the comments written by group leaders, few candidates are shortlisted for group discussion and interview. The selection committee, which consists of director, senior scientists and experts from CSIR, conducts the recruitment process.

All the candidates called for an interview are asked to present their earlier research work and findings to Scientific Organization scientists. This presentation is open to all the members in the organization. Generally, there are lots of questions raised on the candidates' presentation from scientific staff and also by the selection committee members. After this process, there is a brief interaction session between candidates and the selection committee. Through this process, the committee decides on the suitable and competent candidate required for the institution.

Transparency is maintained in the system of recruitment of senior scientists as well. As a result of such a rigorous procedure, there are many senior scientists in Scientific Organization who have wide exposure to biological research and have gained a reputation for themselves and the Organization.

In July 2003, researchers also witnessed the selection of scientists in grade B. Total 35 candidates were called for interview. Out of which, only three candidates were selected in the final rounds. Candidates from various parts of the country attended the interview. The time slot of 30 minutes was reserved by selection committee for interviewing each candidate.

Majority of the candidates who came to the interview had Ph. D degree in molecular biology. Those candidates, who did not have Ph. D, had several years of research experience. As informed by one candidate, only one third of the applicants were called for interview and selection committee may have tough time to select the right candidate since there were many competent fellows who attended the interview. The Organization provided travelling allowance to all the candidates.

For new scientists, induction is done at two levels. The fresh researchers are inducted at Grade B level. However, very senior scientists can enter laterally at Grade E or F level.

For selection of supporting staff under various sections and groups, the Organization Director, Group Heads of the section along with external experts, constitute a selection committee to conduct the exercise.

This committee does the job of identifying the capability and suitability of person for particular section or group. Generally, they look for experienced candidates with good track record. Like scientific staff, the supporting staff of the Scientific Organization is also expected to be competent enough to do their work with dedication. Most of them are hard-working and deliver what is expected from them. Their official timings are not restricted to specific working hours. Many of them work during unusual hours as well to complete the task on time.

It has become part of customs for Scientific Organization employees to distribute sweets among colleagues when someone joins newly or is promoted to a higher grade. A small get together is organized by newly joined persons and they are congratulated by other colleagues as well as wished good luck by them.

Induction is also important for grooming employees for a long and successful career. The basic purpose is to facilitate employees to understand the organization's culture and its challenges and acquire a sense of belongingness to it. In Scientific Organization, induction is done through participation in the research activities, attending meetings and seminars and open discussions with senior scientists. It is mostly informal because those who join the organization come from similar work environment i.e. either from academic institution or a research organization. There is no specific training programme designed for induction of scientists.

Hallmark of Scientific Organization

In this process, one learns to adjust/adapt to the Scientific Organization's work culture. Seniors provide orientation to the newly joined person, and to acquaint them with the work system. In this organization, any newly recruited person is treated as a part of organization's family. He is made more comfortable with people around and provided guidelines to familiarize with campus and its facilities. As per the feedback given by many Scientists, generally a new recruit does not take much time to adjust with the Scientific Organization's system, since it has open work culture, even though, training and socialization process varies from one group or section to other. Moreover, a senior scientist who joins the laboratory is given full-fledged facility to start the research work. This includes all facilities for experiments and manpower assistance to run the laboratory. This is the hallmark of this organization. The same has been followed since its inception; even though it is not so in many other CSIR labs. They further cited that getting all research assistance when someone joins is not possible elsewhere. In other places they are requested to write about the project and get funding from outside agencies to start the research work. This delays research work and denies speedy progress. In Scientific Organization, a newly joined senior scientist is provided full-fledged facilities, special finance package, to start the research work. This enables them to get acquainted with the system fast without facing any problems and obviously it helps in speedy progress of the research work. In fact, research scholars also do not take much time to get acquainted with the system. This system has been constantly admired by many of the scientists across the country.

In case of research scholars, six months course work is given to all the scholars. During this period, instrumentation group takes care of research scholars to get acquainted with instruments facilities available in the organization. Further, Laboratory technician provides necessary training required by the research scholar with regards to laboratory techniques, lab instruments and chemicals available. Group leaders guide the new scholar in thinking for an independent research subject and make him/her well conversant with all the processes and stand on their own. Scholars have the freedom to select their areas of interest as their research topic. However, majority of them work on areas, which broadly come under specialization area of the group, so that they do not face problems while continuing their research in future. Their seniors help in research problems and in acquiring wide range of research exposure to the field.

Within the organization, supporting groups have their own approach to training and socialization. For instance, in security group, senior security officers explain working environment and key tasks undertaken by the security group to new recruits. Responsibilities of a security staff are taught. Then only the security person is allowed to start work. Security officers observe the person for three months in order to identify his performance at work. If the work does not match with expected result, he is given time to improve. Security staff improves through this process and continues to maintain the standards of security service of Scientific Organization. As informed by security officer, most of the security personnel do not take much time to adjust with security system as they generally come from defense services background.

In case of Animal house, a newcomer has to go through all the stages of work pertaining to Animal house. The supervisors and technicians of the animal house are also sent for 3 months training programme at National Institute of Nutrition. Other aspects of dealing with animals are learnt on the job with the able guidance of senior scientists.

In case of engineering group, a new recruit works as an intern along with a senior staff member with whom he is directly associated. Then, 3 months training is given to them for familiarization with instruments and other repair works. Sometimes, they are sent outside institution as well for maintenance training so that they can acquire clear understanding of their role and responsibility.

Learning on the Job and Pursuing Further Education

Learning on the job is given prime importance at the Scientific Organization. Development opportunities are provided to scientists through participation in seminars and conferences related to his field of research. All scientists who have done significant work on a project and who need to sound on their findings with professional colleagues in other part of the world are encouraged to do so. Sometimes, scientists are sent to global labs on deputation. Reciprocally, it is quite common that this Scientific Organization receives senior scientists from abroad who spend several weeks with a particular research lab.

By and large, organizing seminar/lecture and presentation is given prime importance by the members of scientific community in this organization. It is also considered as an important opportunity for learning and sharing scientific knowledge among the scientists. It further helps scientist to take up new challenges and such exercise also enables people to look at scientific research more critically.

Within the organization, seminars and presentations are conducted every alternate day. It may be student's seminar, instrumentation experts' seminar or delegate scientists' presentation and so on. It goes on throughout the year and more or less it becomes part of the daily routine in the campus. The participation of scientists and research scholars in the seminar/presentation is quite encouraging.

Doctoral students' seminars are held every Saturday evening at 4.00 pm. They present paper on some areas of research findings. It is organized to improve the presentation skill of students and ability to face scholars in academic setting of Scientific Organization. It is designed to have more proximity among scientific community, provide common platform for sharing views and ideas on current research. Observations made on student seminar are as follows: Senior scientists also come along with their students to attend the seminar. The discussion is held in a light and informal atmosphere and both students and senior scientists share jokes with the audience in the seminar hall. Students begin their presentation with greeting people. The duration of presentation is 30 minutes and another 30 minutes is utilized for discussions.

In every presentation, there are lots of questions raised from fellow students and a few from scientists as well. Scholars try to answer most of the questions seriously while discussions are on so much so that it occasionally overlaps the time limit. It's compulsory for each and every scholar who is pursuing PhD in Scientific Organization, to present their findings/observations in research seminars. During presentation, students are expected to be confident. Most seminars are similar in terms of their pattern and way of interaction with audience during the presentation except difference in their topics.

Apart from this, there are other distinguished lectures delivered by various intellectuals and experts from outside the Scientific Organization.

The Research committee meeting is held once a year. It is confined to the team members in respective projects. These include Scientists, group leaders and project leaders. Experts, senior scientists from CSIR laboratory and other external members also participate in assessing and reviewing the research works in progress.

During field work, it was observed that research committee meeting was conducted for two days. On the first day of meeting, Director of organization delivered the introductory speech and briefly explained about the ongoing research works and also highlighted research findings of the Scientists in various fields.

Afterwards, group leaders and project leaders presented the progress of their ongoing research works and findings. After completion of each presentation, experts asked questions and clarifications. Sometimes scientists also questioned their colleagues. There were a lot of discussions and many suggestions came from experts' side to improve the quality of research work. They even suggested some scientists to keep in touch with distinguished scientists abroad for finding out issues related to their work. It was noticed that none of the research scholars' asked questions in the research committee meeting. Research scholars' generally listened to whatever discussions and interactions happening between scientists and experts. Group leaders and project leaders used the word '*WE*' while presenting their progress of research work. This clearly proved that most of the scientific research was done collectively.

Performance Management System

Overall performance of the organization is based on contribution made by every individual working in the organization. It is important to understand how individual performance is being assessed at different levels. There are various ways of assessing the performance of individual in various groups and sections of the Scientific Organization.

In Scientific Organization, scientists, supporting staff and general staff have to submit self-assessment report every year. Director verifies the accuracy of the self-assessment report submitted by the scientists and group heads based on day-to-day information and observation. Within a group, subordinate staff-members submit their report to the group leader. After verifying the report, it is transmitted to the Director who grades the staff performance as outstanding/excellent/very good/good/satisfactory/poor.

Assessment of Support Staff

As informed by many staff members, most of the employees usually get either very good or excellent ratings. For lower grade staff, organization selects best performing staff and group. The criteria of grading are mainly on their performance as per the work assigned by group leader, which includes punctuality, working beyond official call, cleanliness of building and so on.

For selecting best supporting group, group leaders and scientists meet every month. In this meeting, director asks scientists to express their difficulties in the Laboratory. Supporting group leaders are asked to explain complaints from scientists. Director attempts to find out the group which gets minimum number of complaints from scientists' community. This is the measure of quality of service rendered by supporting group. All these are cross-checked and duly appreciated. Most of the employees work with 100 per cent interest and sincerity because of encouragement from the institution. The Director presents awards in the form of cash/ certificate on 26 January every year.

Assessment of Scientists

As far as scientists' performance is concerned, they don't have any concrete and clear-cut parameters for assessment. However, there are few parameters which majority of the scientists consider as important. At first, they generally look for the number of publications and quality of journal where article is published. For example, there are few scientific journals like *Cell, Nature, and Science,* which have been highly rated by the scientific community across the world. The journal reflects the quality of article written by scientists. Last year one of our scientists got his article published in *Science Journal* and got appreciated by all.

While assessing the performance of the scientists, it is also important to find out number of projects taken up by him/her, particularly those that are externally funded. External agencies fund projects to those scientists who have the desired calibre and excellence in their area of research. A scientist's performance is partly determined by the number of projects he/she has handled. Afterwards, it is important to examine, whether project is getting funded by national or international funding agencies. Prima facie, getting a project from international agency is a big challenge. It is easier to get national funding though. Besides this, total amount of grant sanctioned for a particular project is also taken into consideration since it shows how big the project is. One of the scientists, who received rupees three crores grant for an international project, received highest level of appreciation by fellow scientists in the organization.

In few cases, Scientific Organization can not adhere to the above mentioned criteria as there are some areas of research which require considerable time to get results and being published in scientific journal. In such a case, they review the progress made by scientist in the last few years.

Promotion Criteria

Scientific Organization framed a common promotion policy where a scientist is promoted every five years. Actually, it is widely followed by many CSIR institutions in the country. However, this organization has added few more criteria to identify deserving staff/employees for promotion. For instance, fifty percent of the weightage is given to annual appraisal report and other fifty percent is based on the performance in the interview conducted by experts. The interview committee is formed according to the respective discipline. The Director is the chairman of all interview committees. As told by the head of supporting services, due to his outstanding performance in consecutive years in the organization, he got promotion within three years. However, some of the research scholars expressed that a few senior scientists have been given promotion on face value without much contribution made by them.

Research Scholars

Scientific Organization imparts research-oriented training to the doctoral students of Jawaharlal Nehru University, New Delhi. Besides this, post-doctoral research fellows sponsored by CSIR, or the Department of Biotechnology (DBT), or the Department of Science and Technology (DST), Govt. of India, New Delhi, are also given opportunity to do research here. On an average, at any given time, there are nearly 100 such researchers at the Scientific Organization. The Centre also provides training in specific areas of modern biology, besides conducting courses and workshops from time to time for these scholars.

During the course of PhD programme, every research scholar receives scholarship for five years from CSIR or UGC. Initial two years are considered as JRF in which a monthly grant of sixteen thousands rupees is provided and the remaining three years are considered as SRF with payment of eighteen thousands rupees per month as stipend.

There is a system of assessing the work done by a research scholar during the two years period. Before a scholarship is converted into senior research fellowship, every research scholar has to submit two years of work progress report to the scientific committee. The committee examines the quality of report and reviews the performance during the interview and presentation made by the research scholar.

On approval by the committee, the research scholar is given permission to convert into SRF. As informed by research scholars, so far nobody in the organization has been rejected from converting into SRF. Most of the people get SRF without much difficulty as they have been working constantly with dedication. Practice of celebration like distributing sweets is also followed when a person gets promotion in the organization. Sometimes it is extended to people working in other section whom he or she is familiar with.

Moment of Separation

The superannuation of an employee is an important event in Scientific Organization. For retiring scientists or other employees, farewell party is organized by the section or group members. As informed by employees, one or two staff members take responsibility of organizing the party and collect some contributions from each staff member working in group or unit. They present memento or gift to retiring person. This is done at the group level.

For the retiring person, a grand farewell party is organized the under the supervision of other administrative staff members. This is organized in the form of a formal function in the presence of Director. During this function, many of the colleagues speak about the person and his contribution towards the organization's success and growth. Director also speaks about the retiring person on this occasion. Farewell function is held at Santiniketan areas of the organization that is nearby main entrance. After finishing all formalities, other colleagues' go to see off the retired employee at his or her residence.

Third Section

Structure and Stratification of the Organization

Organization structure is stratified into different hierarchy. Within the scientific community, there are different grades i.e. Scientists-B; scientists-C; Scientists-D and E; Scientists-F; and Scientists-G which is almost equal to director rank.

Supporting staff is classified as Group I/II/III/IV employees respectively. Among scientific community, it is difficult to distinguish hierarchy of scientists because their behavior is not bound by Grades. Despite different status levels among scientists, their role seems to be similar in the entire laboratory. Scientists work very informally with other scientists irrespective of their grades. Their grades can be classified by referring to their official records; not by observing their work behavior. In fact, scientists are recognized or distinguished by their work, research results, publication, rewards and so on. It is not by the seniority or grade.

Leadership and Decision-making

Leadership has been the key in shaping the working culture and functioning of the Scientific Organization, as it sets the future trends of the organization. As informed by senior scientists and administrators, the organization has emerged as one of the best molecular biological research centres in the country, because of the leadership of its founder Director P.M. Bhargava. Several older employees mentioned that he had exceptional quality in judging candidates whether they were scientists or other supporting staff. He selected persons who have excellent skills in their respective fields and strong desire to work for betterment of the institution. He is the one, who inculcated congenial work culture and created a pleasant ambience in the organization. This continues even today.

Bhargava believed that scientific communities need, working environment which gives high esteem to the scientists who work with undivided attention on seeking research result. He has successfully set the culture of cooperation among the staff, transparency and concern for others, congenial environment for open sharing of feelings, thoughts, ideas and, as peers and equals based on job not on hierarchy. He treated all employees equally, be it a worker or a scientist.

Even today, employees of the organization give credit to the founder director for his long-term vision, which has become a major asset for ensuring good performance of the Lab. Today, the Scientific Organization is highly regarded by the scientific community, because of its member's commitment and dedication towards institution. The present leadership is strengthening the tradition set by the founder and taking it to reach the next level. Younger scientists appreciate the leadership of the present director; even founder director who lives in Hyderabad has high praise for the work carried out by his successor.

Since this organization is part of CSIR laboratory, its decision-making process is quite similar to other Labs. They follow CSIR rules and regulation for planning, budgeting and purchasing and so on. Within the institution, Director is the final authority to approve any proposal and recommendation made by individuals or the team leaders, committees, task forces and so on. However, in most of the cases the approvals are quick and hassle free. In fact, there are several committees of scientists and administrators involved in the decision-making process; however director gives the final approval.

As informed by an employee, in one of the cases, supporting service staff member had put up an indent for buying more smoke detector, which had to be placed in few of the rooms within the organization. It was approved by the purchasing committee and sent for director's approval. However, Director initially declined to approve it due to shortage of funds during the fag end of the financial year. Later, in his usual round, Director noticed that some of the rooms did not have smoke detector. Then, he immediately instructed supporting staff to install it soon. He immediately approved the proposal submitted by staff and asked the concerned staff to install it as soon as possible.

However, research related decisions are taken within the concerned Groups. In this regard, leaders or heads are given freedom to take their own decision to ensure quality of work. Within the group, decisions are generally made after consultation with other members of the group. The Scientific Organization ensured that the convenience and suitability of the group is always taken into account. In general, lots of freedom is provided to the scientists and research scholars in pursuing their work. Scientists often share, that pressure does not come from the top, it is from within; every scientists wants to do better quality of research. Healthy competitive environment is prevalent among the scientific community. They are quite keen on finding out the new emerging areas in biological research so that they can catch up with the trend. This is one of the reasons why this organization has emerged as a global research institution.

Work autonomy is observed among the scientists as well as research scholars. Flexibility of work schedule among Scientists and research scholars is common in most of the laboratories. They set their own work timings;. As expressed by scientists, scientific research requires freedom of thinking and freedom of work schedule in order to extract high quality of research from individuals. Imposing external ideas destructs greater thinking, blocks scientists to think on their own. In order to promote the quality of research, high level of autonomy is practiced by the scientific community.

In many of the Labs, scientists and research scholars work as per their own comfortable timings without getting any complain from group leaders or seniors. They set work schedule according to their convenience; however it is known to others in the group. It is an accepted practice that the scientists will take their own decisions on conducting research experiments. Some of the staff however, reported that working style of present Director is partly authoritarian in nature as compared to the style of the founder director. He is known for his short temper, go-and-get-it-done approach but sometime he is down to earth with people around him.

The Organization continues to excel in biological research under his leadership too. Recently, the All India Conference of Intellectuals (AICOI), New Delhi has conferred the prestigious Intellectuals' Award 'The great son of the soil' upon the director of the organization for his outstanding contributions to Science and Technology particularly for the development of a universal probe on DNA Fingerprinting technology.

Communication and Information Sharing

Communication system prevalent in the campus, a determinant of the standard of work culture. Communication facilities available in the campus is in highly advanced form. At the institutional level, CCTVs are installed in all the blocks/wings of buildings in order to circulate any related information within the organization staff.

CCTVs flash important information like daily food menu, seminar notice, lecturers, viva voice notice, loan notice, birthday wishes, informing about the instrumental problems, job advertisement and so on. In addition to these, they also put up notice board with detailed information especially for jobs and programmes. All the official information is flashed through CCTVs.

Employees and scholars keep watching CCTV whenever they step into building in order to get current campus news. Besides this, the Scientific Organization also offers Hindi-learning programme for non-Hindi speaking employees. It is compulsory for the employees to learn Hindi as national language. Every day CCTV flashes, 'Today's

Hindi word' as part of popularizing Hindi language among employ. It is noticed that people in the organization communicate either in English or Hindi most of the time and some sections of employees communicate in Telugu language as well. In the past, CCTV flashed information on lost money by displaying this message – *'Found some money; loser can contact security'* and greetings like, *'Congratulation to Director Lalji for getting extension as director till his superannuation'*. Clock timings of the country like Tokyo, London, New York are also displayed at the reception areas as to help scientists who frequently contact abroad via telephone services.

Through this well maintained system of communication, everyone in the organization is aware of what is happening around the campus. Every employee goes through CCTV everyday as a part of their daily routine in the organization.

At the intra group level, scientists and staff prefer oral mode of communication. It is commonly seen that the scientists come out of their office and talk to other subordinates on their desk itself. They generally practice face-to-face interaction. Telephone is also used for contacting other people working in other section or building. Telephonic conversation is noticed among group heads and section heads, seeking emergency requirement and other important matter. When telephonic conversation does not resolve the problem, they also talk face to face to discuss and resolve the issue. Such discussion and interaction helps to get employees of the organization more close to each other.

On the whole, such informal communication makes research work in this organization more friendly, alert and progressive. Frequent exchange of information is also important as it helps in improving the quality of relationship within organization.

There are various kinds of information exchanges within the organization such as exchange of information at institutional level, group level or across group/section. As mentioned earlier, at institutional level, information is shared and exchanged through various means like CCTV, telephone and notice board and so on. This information is very general kind of information, which can be shared by all the employees in the organization. By and large, this system is applicable to employees of all the sections in the campus.

Repair and Replacement Process

Sharing of information among staff is done as a part of their daily official duty in order to identify problems and plan the work assignment for the next day. For instance, supporting services group headed by Anand Rao looks after centrally located instruments like tube light, furniture, electronics installed in the building. Basically they offer coordinating service and solve any kind of problems arising in the building. It is compulsory that one person of this group goes around nook and corners of the building to identify casualty in any areas or instruments. This is noted down in daily complaint sheet and brought back to section head's room. The group head goes through the complaint sheet and informs appropriate staff to rectify the problems and if necessary, also informs other technical groups as well. In this group, as a part of their daily duty, every staff member knows about the status of availability of items like tube light, fan, or other electrical items and so on. and whether these items are working properly or not. Responsibility of rectifying the problems and identifying casualty lies with the staff of this group on rotation basis but their daily work report is shared among all staff members in order to rectify problems without any delay. As a result of this system, it is hard to find out any non-functioning tube light, bulb, fan, AC, electric switch and so on. These facilities are kept in order in the building all the time.

The same system is followed in other groups like instrumentation and engineering section as well. It is common to receive some complaints on non-functioning of instruments or machines from the scientific community. Everyday supporting group finds out and discusses their daily activity under the supervision of group head and allocates the work according to the needs of the scientific staff. Due to the frequent exchange of such information it is easy for them to carry out their duty more effectively. As pointed out by head of Photography, they (three staff members are there in photo laboratory) share all information and keep on updating their work schedule. It is necessary to mention here that scientists are able to do high quality research because of strong support provided by support staff like engineering, instrumentation, fine chemical, supporting services and so on. Their support service makes scientific research work smooth and fast.

Informal Relations

Exchange of information among scientific community within the organization is noticed quite often during tea or lunch breaks. There is a daily interaction among the laboratory people on all kind of topics. Something new that comes up in scientific research is always shared among group members. They discuss it with their group leader and senior scientist. On the other hand, group leader also keeps informing about new happenings in the scientific world especially on biological research to all his fellow scientists who are working under his supervision. Besides this, they also share their personal information as well with group members. In fact, there are two coffee rooms on the second floor of the main building where many scientists meet and exchange information, express their views and discuss on findings. While having coffee, a few scientists discuss about their research work. Most of them believe that coffee room is a good place for scientific discussions especially during breaks due to its ambience and scope for informal interaction. Scientists prefer to spend tea break in coffee room.

Each scientist in the organization knows about other fellow scientists' areas of research in which they are currently engaged in. In general, the kiosk centre of campus is also considered to be one of the important places for sharing information during tea break. Every morning, around 10.30 am., people gather at the kiosk centre for having tea and snacks. This kiosk centre provides a common platform to interact and share information among employees working in different units and groups. They discuss a lot about both their professional and personnel life.

A group of Laboratory Technicians (temporary staff) was found discussing about how to get permanent position in the organization. Their discussion was revolving around the fact that they have been working for the past fifteen years and have submitted many proposals to the director for making their job permanent. Despite all the efforts made by the staff, nothing has materialized so far. Technicians expressed their unhappiness towards the higher authority of the organization.

Usually, all kind of discussions takes place in kiosk centre among different groups and across different sections. Besides this, discussions and interactions take place across the people during lunch hours too. It was experienced during field work that one lady receptionist shared dining table with a lady scientist and discussed about their family related matters as well. Similarly, a group of scientists seriously discussed about their ongoing projects and shared views on their research findings. On the other hand, two technicians were talking about their children's education and future prospects. Further, they discussed about declining food quality in the canteen. Cross sectional interaction of scientists and other supporting staff are rarely seen during working hours. Lunch and tea breaks therefore provide a conducive environment to communicate and share information among the members irrespective of groups and grades.

Working hour is from 9.30 am to 6.00 pm. It can be seen that most of the staff members moves out of the campus after 6.00 pm. People exchange pleasantries like *'bye-bye; see you tomorrow'*, to each other while leaving the campus.

Life after 6.00 pm is limited only to the scientific community, especially research scholars in the organization. Laboratories are open round-the-clock and research scholars' work in the late night. As informed by research scholars, it is comfortable to work in the night time because of availability of common instruments for doing scientific experiment. Common instruments are not easily available during day time. They could concentrate more on their experiment without wasting time. There is a bus service in the night for dropping Scientific Staff and Scholars who do not stay in the campus. Scientific staff members are found appreciating transport service provided by the organization.

Life in the campus goes on 24×7, throughout the year because of its' constant engagement in scientific research on molecular biology. This flexible system provides great opportunity for scientific community to work for maximum hours. It also helps in speedy progress of research.

Open and Cohesive Work Group

This Scientific Organization is known for its open work culture which was initiated by its founder Director. It continues till date. All the facilities available in the organization are common to all members and it can be availed by any person. They have centralized instrumentation facility which is commonly used by all the scientists. All the rooms and laboratories are kept open throughout the day. It is observed that member of the organization get into any room or laboratory without taking prior permission from the concerned person. They feel free to meet any person either scientists or officers in the organization. Open culture is an accepted norm and value in this Scientific Organization. This is also one of the important factors that distinguish the Scientific Organization's work culture.

Scientists always look for high level of cooperation among staff. Unlike other research laboratories established in India, cooperation among the group and across groups is very well maintained in the organization. There are many scientific groups in the campus; each group has to work with full dedication coordinating with others to fulfill its own responsibility. As a result of this, scientific research flows smoothly without much obstacles.

It was experienced that a research scholar got disappointed to see the final results of the experiment. Later, he called up 3 of his seniors to discuss about the experiment. They had serious discussion for almost one hour. During their course of discussion, seniors enlightened him with lots of suggestions. One of the seniors told him that *it happens to everyone at the initial stage of research. So don't worry, 'lageerahoo' (joke).*

Another PDF lady commented, *'You didn't sleep properly yesterday night, that's why your experiment results are that way; so don't try to do things in a hurry and it's always better to do it at a slow pace with care.'* Other senior scholars advised him to go through the experiment once again. In the meantime, senior scientist invited the entire lab mates to come for tea and they discussed about the progress of their respective research work while having tea. Immediately after this they went to attend weekly lab meeting in the committee room. It is observed that scholars have a very tight schedule in the laboratory and they spend most of the day there busy in research work.

Unity and Cooperation

As informed by one staff member of animal house, their work is never affected because of the absence of one or the other members. Staff present in the office willingly takes care of extra workload. Sometimes even head of animal house assists his subordinates in cleaning and feeding animals. For instance, head of the animal house helped his staff in storing the medicines brought from the market. As a group, they also provide full cooperation to scientists and researchers in supplying animals for their experiment. They seldom receive complaint from scientific community. Their service has been well received and appreciated by scientific staff. While doing their duty, they also help each other.

Similar attitude is noticed in other groups like engineering services and instrumentation and support services, and so on. All these groups work in full coordination with each other. It was also noticed that group leader (senior scientist) came out from his room to taste the sweet distributed by one of the PDF scholar on occasion of becoming father of a newborn baby. Group leader enquired about health condition of PDF fellow's wife. Such incidences are common in most of the groups in the organization.

One informant quoted, Director of the organization is very dedicated to his work and provides full cooperation to all the members of the organization. He frequently takes round of all the buildings and sections to supervise overall functioning of the campus. He processes file very fast and never keeps any file in pending state and that is well appreciated by many of the employees. As a result of his strong cooperation, work in campus moves at a very fast pace.

Cooperation among the scientific community is also very strong, same as seen in the support groups. They seek each other's help while carrying out research projects. Scientists are always ready to help new comers. It is frequently noticed that senior scientists go to other colleagues for clarifying doubts on their experiment. There is always reciprocal response from other colleagues too. Sometimes, two-group leaders also work together on certain projects that may be difficult and time consuming for one scientist to perform alone. There are several joint projects taken up by scientists, which cannot be carried out without having proper cooperation among the scientists.

As a whole, cooperation among scientific staff is strong with regards to their research work. Director also provides full cooperation to his subordinates. Besides this, scientists conduct weekly meeting with lab mates to examine the problems and progress of the research. Apart from this, formal seminar and presentations are also organized in the group once in three months. It is mandatory for all the scholars to give presentation on their work progress and experiment done during the last three months. As informed by senior scientist, it is organized to improve presentation skill of the students.

During the field work, a group conducted weekly meeting in the laboratory. Senior Scientists, Research Scholars and Project Assistants attended the meeting. As narrated by a Research Scholar, group leader asked all his scholars to explain about the progress of their experiments done during the last week and cross check their findings. Later, he gave many suggestions for proceeding further with the experiments. This meeting helped in enhancing research skills of the young scientists and moreover, to understand what other colleagues were doing as they shared their experience.

Mutual Concern and Professional Interdependence

As far research scholars are concerned, they have very casual and informal relationship among themselves. Helping each other in research work is common but they also help each other's in their personal matters as well. For instance, once a lady scholar from a laboratory came to borrow 100 rupees from a fellow research scholar from another Lab. After borrowing money from another research scholar, she said, *'Remind me after five days, otherwise I will forget to return your money back'*. Another research scholar distributed sweets among her colleagues in the laboratory and wing mates for getting his first JRF scholarship money. Another Ph. D scholar also distributed sweets on the occasion of his thesis submission. Such type of small get-together is often noticed in this organization across groups and departments. Occasions like birthday, thesis submission, getting fellowship and so on are celebrated with personal touch.

Once a research scholar met with an accident and got injured seriously. He was admitted to hospital. Research scholars looked after him in the hospital. Every day, at least one or two research scholar would go to attend him in the hospital on rotation basis without affecting their research work. This incident reflects their concern about each other.

It is also observed that research scholars cooperate with laboratory technicians in getting the supply of laboratory requirements such as chemical, tubes, distilled water and so on. Helping each other is quite common among people of this organization.

As mentioned earlier, people in the Scientific Organization, work within their work groups and across other groups as well. It is difficult to carry out any assignment without seeking support from each other. Collective work pattern and mutual cooperation is more evident among members of the organization.

Quality of scientific work is mostly reflected in their publication of research findings. It is found that most of the research articles published in scientific journals are co-authored by at least 2 to 4 scientists. It was noted by research scholars that it was difficult to write any article without taking support from other friends or superiors. Most of the experiments are carried out by the scholars with proper guidance of senior scientists. Once the experiment is through, they plan to write an article with cooperation of their group leader. Moreover, getting the article published is group leader's responsibility. In this process, the involvement of minimum 2 to 3 scientists is quite evident.

Further, it was pointed out that while group leaders can publish article alone they prefer to author with others. This is because partly, it is time-consuming to do experiment alone, since they are involved in various administrative works, and primarily to demonstrate that research is a collective enterprise. Therefore, bench work is allocated among the scholars and writing part is done collectively with the group leader. Allocations of workload helps in accomplishing the experiment faster, which is very important for scientific works. Every week, new findings are coming up in biological research. If someone has carried out an experiment successfully; then there is no point in doing the same research elsewhere. They also strongly believe that team work would help in enhancing quality of research since it helps to pool in various thoughts. Hence, most of the scientists prefer to work in a group for achieving results. They include names of all the scientists, even technician whoever is involved in producing research results. Even in research committee meeting, while presenting the progress report of their research work, they use the word 'WE'.

It's clearly reflected that research works are done collectively in the organization. However, there are some laboratories, which do not have many scholars. In such a case, like other colleagues, group leaders are also engaged in bench work. The same work culture prevails in support groups as well. Whenever problems occur in any group or section, they solve it by consulting with all the members of the group. When problems can't be solved within group they approach the Director for intervention. In this organization, work culture, functioning and processing is very transparent. Everyone knows and shares it willingly.

Power Distance

Scientific Organization has good working atmosphere where it is hard to find hierarchy existing between superior and subordinates. Collective work culture is being one unique feature in the Campus. All the people in the organization work collectively and maintain cordial relationship with their members. It is also noticed that officers or scientists' do not write their designation on nameplate on their door. Only names are written on their respective doors. Everybody is treated equally.

It is very clear from the observations during tea time and lunch breaks, many of the scientists join their research scholars during lunch time almost every day. For instance, a scientist likes to have tea along with his research scholars and indulges in lengthy discussion about their ongoing project work. Afterwards, he does not allow his colleagues to pay money; he only pays the bill. Students also talk and interact freely with him; even exchange jokes with him.

A queue system is adopted during lunch time and even senior scientists and officers join the queue and serve themselves. There is no specific dining table for different grades of employees. All employees are free to sit and have food on any of the tables inside the canteen. This also reflects on non-existence of hierarchy system in the organization. However, despite of following a non-hierarchical system, it can also be seen that most of the groups which consists of four to five people come for tea or lunch, are either from same laboratory group or section or units. Therefore, interactions and discussions are largely seen among the similar grade of people who have been working in the same field or units.

On the occasion of festivals, the group members ensure to greet each other personally. The research scholar visits group leader's house to play 'holi' along with friends. They play 'holi' along with group leader's family members as well. After that, group leader offers sweets to all those who visit his house for playing 'holi'.

Scholars further stated that sometimes group leader invites all his research students and other staff members to his house for dinner. They feel very comfortable interacting with group leader. As a result, research scholars do not experience pressure and enjoy freedom to do research work. At the same time they are expected to conform to norms and follow the system, like attending weekly meetings, group meetings reviews, presentation and so on, which keep them fully occupied. Similar work culture prevails in other laboratories. There are, however, a few exceptions like some group leaders maintain formal relationship with their research scholars. For instance, a group leader who has been working for the past twenty years in this organization, maintains very formal relationship with scholars. Laboratory members are asked to come on time and they should inform him in advance if somebody wants to arrive late to office. He keeps visiting laboratory quite often. Scholars do not feel comfortable to work in his presence. This is often talked about in the organization as an example of deviance. However, as a whole Scientific Organization has a friendly work environment across the groups.

In a prize distribution ceremony of a 'Photography' competition, the director was invited as the chief guest. He spoke for about 15 minutes and while delivering his speech, he also cracked joke and also congratulated the vice president of the club for encouraging competitive spirit. He also suggested that there should not be a binding theme; it should be open to all kind of photography, encouraging various ideas/styles of diverse groups within the organization. Even though it would be a difficult task for the selection committee to select a winner with such talents around. He also thanked and congratulated all the participants and winners. While presenting the first prize, the director asked, *'Where did you click this photograph?' 'From Nehru Zoological Park'*, the participant replied. The director quipped jokingly, *'I thought it was clicked in our campus'*. Later on, tea and snacks were served. It was noticed that everyone stood in queue. He spent 30 minutes interacting with other staff members and scientists who had gathered there.

In engineering services, subordinates talk and move freely with their group head. They have tea together and share their thoughts and feelings. As informed by head of engineering services, there are 44 engineering staff members working under his supervision and nobody has registered a complaint against his work style. He maintains good relationship with his subordinates, which is appreciated by them. They freely walk into the head's room without knocking the door. Head's room is kept open when he moves out. According to his subordinates, strong support, encouragement and help from their superiors enhance their effectiveness at work. As a whole, such working relationship is prevalent in the whole campus whether it is a scientific group or any other supporting group.

Dealing with Uncertainty

In the Scientific Organization, people are aware of uncertainty in research. It is a part of their daily research work. There is no guarantee in getting proper result from all the experiment done by scientists. According to informants, failures of experiments are more than successful result; one has to face failures in research to get a successful result in scientific research. Every scientist has come across many difficulties in doing research. To avoid such problems, they frequently interact and consult within group as well as outside group. Most of the scientists have got genuine interests on their research work. They don't follow specific working hours and their work is based on result. Level of satisfaction is depending upon the kind of result that comes from experiment. Dealing with uncertainty is common in scientific research. As informed by scientists, to survive in scientific world; they need to explore new research topics and create new ideas that require lots of reading and energy. Only a person who has genuine interest in this field can be a scientist. As a whole, encountering uncertainty is a common phenomenon in scientific research.

Scientific Organization and Society

Scientific Organization is well connected with scientific societies around the world for various activities. It publishes Annual Report, containing the ongoing research activities, which are widely circulated nationally and internationally. Popularizing science is yet another mission that takes science to the doorstep of the common man. Towards fulfilling this objective, the scientists make contributions to newspapers; magazines and so on and participate in science programmes on television and radio. Further, to reach a larger national audience, a popular science magazine in Hindi (JIGYASA - meaning curiosity) was brought out. The magazine contains articles contributed by the Scientific Organization scientists and is well received by the public.

The Centre receives a large number of visitors throughout the year. They also organize an Open House on the 26 September every year to mark the occasion of the Foundation Day of its parent body CSIR and receives on an average 5,000 to 7,000 visitors for the programme. The laboratory also receives professional visitors from India and abroad as well as students from various universities in the country. The laboratory is also visited by various international delegations, from time to time, sponsored by the Government and other scientific agencies.

Several staff members of the organization have been associated with a voluntary group of scientists/engineers called 'Bhaskaracharya Mandal', which is named after the famous Indian astronomer and mathematician, Bhaskaracharya, to motivate and develop mathematical and intellectual skills among educationally deprived children, through fun games, puzzles and stories and so on.

A few years ago, few staff members from the organization formed a group to help children from economically weaker section of the society to pursue primary education. These children were selected from a local government primary school and were provided with books, uniforms and other materials in addition to direct financial assistance for extracurricular activities. Scientists have committed themselves to such beneficiary programmes for almost five years now, to help these children complete their primary education.

One of the most historic events in the Scientific Organization with vast social implications has been the development of DNA fingerprinting technology, as a fall out of present director's basic research on the mechanism of sex determination. This technology has transformed forensic science in the country and has helped solve a number of famous cases such as that of the assassination of Prime Minister Rajiv Gandhi and of Chief Minister of Punjab.

This technology has also been used extensively in settling parental disputes, in identification of missing children and of mutilated bodies, for identifying the culprit in cases of rape and murder, and settling disputes regarding exchange of babies in hospitals. At the request of various police bodies such as the National Police Academy, the Andhra Pradesh Police Academy, the Andhra Pradesh Judicial Academy, Administrative Staff College of India, Hyderabad, and the National Bureau of Crime Records, New Delhi. Presentations have been frequently organized on familiarizing the participants with the DNA fingerprinting technology. The participants include senior civil servants, police officials, Judges and also experts from forensic/criminal investigating agencies of India and abroad. Such half-day sessions are followed by visits to various laboratory facilities.

A Bioinformatics Centre (BIC) was also established in the Scientific Organization in 1986, under the sponsorship of Department of Biotechnology, Government of India. Its principal objective was to serve as a hub for national network, providing related information by accessing several scientific databases from India and abroad. It has an Internet facility provided by the National Informatics Centre (NIC), New Delhi. Since its inception, the BIC has been functioning round the clock contributing significantly to modern biological research. The staff also played an important role in writing national science textbooks under the umbrella of National Council of Educational Research and training, for students of class VI and above.

Besides this, employees also made generous contribution towards natural calamities like flood, epidemics, tsunami and so on.

5

Case Study of Seacom Pvt Ltd

First Section

Seacom Pvt. Ltd is one of the largest Indian IT companies providing software solutions worldwide. It offers a wide array of solutions customized for a range of key verticals and horizontals. Right from strategy consulting to implementing IT solutions for customers, Seacom straddles the entire IT space. It has excellent domain competencies in verticals such as automotive, banking and financial services, insurance and healthcare, manufacturing and telecom-infrastructure-media-entertainment-semiconductors (TIMES). As a diverse end-to-end IT solutions provider, Seacom offers a wide range of expertise aimed at helping customers re-engineer and re-invent their businesses to compete successfully in an ever-changing marketplace.

The company's unique right-sourcing delivery model facilitates it to leverage local competencies to offer global competitiveness to its customers. Right sourcing is a global delivery model which offers customers an optimal combination of onsite, offshore and offsite services in near-shore delivery facilities, providing crucial time–cost benefits.

Consulting and IT solutions have resulted in technology-intensive transformations that have met most of the stringent international quality standards. Seacom has developed a unique quality hallmark, called eSCM (e-Sourcing Capability Maturity) Model, for IT-enabled services (ITES), in collaboration with Carnegie Mellon University and Accenture. A business continuity model (BCM) which essentially comprises strategic plans for contingencies allows it to continue mission-critical operations of customers even in the most challenging times.

Historical Background

Seacom was established in the year 1989 by Ram. Today, it is recognized as a world-class IT company. He came from a family of farmers. His grandfather was an enterprising farmer who ventured out of traditional agriculture into agribusiness and bought a sugar mill. The venture backfired and the family lost a fortune. Ram's father moved to Hyderabad and became one of the first farmers to start commercial grape production around Hyderabad.

As the family's fortune improved, Ram the eldest son was sent to the USA in 1975 to get an MBA degree from Ohio after which he completed his B.Com from Loyola College. He returned to India filled with ambition and new ideas and tried his hand at different businesses, including cotton-spinning and construction. This earned him his bread and butter. He had brought back a small computer back from the USA. Recognizing the potential of information technology in the future, he took the plunge in this new business, even though he had limited knowledge of the field and incorporated Seacom in the year 1989. He very soon realized that there could be higher margins if one could convince companies abroad that Indian companies could develop the software in India and upload it to the US companies' mainframe computers through a satellite data link. Seacom was one of the first companies to get a dedicated 64 kbps data link for such 'offshore' development. Seacom was among the first Indian companies to make the unique paradigm shift from onsite-led operations to offshore-driven ones.

Philosophy

Company's stated philosophy is 'To leverage information, knowledge and technology to enhance human endeavour'.

Values

The values which the organization upholds and are its guiding parameters include:

- Pursuit of excellence
- Entrepreneurship
- Customer orientation

These values have led to the creation of a unique organizational structure, with every functional unit designated as an independent business enterprise, each responsible for managing its own resource management and its profits and losses. The company encourages an environment of openness and trust, where employees are free to share ideas and collaborate in finding solutions. Meeting customer expectation was uniformly accepted across the organization; in fact employees worked on projects dealing with a particular customer at a particular point of time. They remained focused on customer brief.

Goals of the Organization

In the last three years, Seacom has been given prime importance to be featured consistently in industry analyst ratings as one of the top global professional IT services providers. Company aims at achieving the following goals:

- A reputation of excellence in the global markets
- Benchmarking Seacom against the leading players in all its market segments
- Offering a complete range of services to customers, from consulting to BPO, in the professional IT services domain.

The imperatives arising from Seacom's strategic intent which were highlighted in the 'North Star' are:

- Global presence, with a strong revenue potential in each of the major geographies that are the declared domains of composition
- Investment in maturing the Global Delivery Model
- To scale up operations quickly in the declared geographies

- Increasing the proportion of consulting among the full spectrum of services for MITS and BPOs, including Application Development, Application Support and Maintenance.
- Significant enhancement of brand equity, focusing on the communication of company's strengths and overall image.

These strategic imperatives focus on enhancing revenue and profitability.

Location and Manpower

Seacom's network is spread in 45 countries and across six continents. Over 17,000 dedicated and highly skilled IT professionals are employed in its development centres in India, the USA, the UK, the UAE, Canada, Singapore, Malaysia, China, Japan, Australia and Hungary and serve over 325 global companies, including over 104 Fortune 500 corporations. The employees are drawn from across the country. The percentage of women employee working in the company is about 20%. The company has strategic technology and marketing alliances with over 50 top-notch companies that provide support for delivering end-to-end services to its customers.

Organization Structure

Seacom has built its organization around a 'network of circles', which is a non-hierarchical network based on a collaboratively driven mode of functioning. Each circle focuses on a specific set of business offerings based on its competency profile. The result is an internal culture where new ideas are nurtured and acted upon and new competencies are developed. This way Seacom continuously provides services right across the IT value chain.

At the centre of the Network of Circles is the customer, whose business requirements are the driving force. Accordingly, the circles are categorized as:

Verticals Business Units (VBUs; based on the customer's line of business): VBUs offer best-in-class business solutions, building domain expertise and leveraging HCU. This unit addresses customers in different industries or sectors. In the US market, VBUs assume end-to-end responsibility for business development, solution architecting, project management, relationship management, pre-sales, programme management, delivery and brand building.

In other geographies, the Regional Business Units (RBUs) handle both business development and relationship management for the VBUs. Select high-value customers (Platinum Customers) are globally serviced entirely by VBUs. The VBUs in Seacom have been classified into three groups:

1. Commercial and healthcare business includes the following verticals: banking and financial services, healthcare, life insurance and pharma, REINS, travel and transportation/government, insurance (P&C) and retails.
2. MEGA includes the following verticals: manufacturing, automotive, energy and utilities.
3. TIMES includes the following verticals: telecom/media and entertainment, infrastructure and semiconductor.

Horizontal competency units (HCUs; based on competency requirements): HCUs focus on building competencies in various technology platforms, packages and processes. They offer IT solutions across the whole range of industry verticals. The HCUs in Seacom currently include: consulting and enterprise solutions, engineering solution, enterprise applications, business intelligence solutions, embedded systems, managed IT services, quality consulting, SAP solutions, spatial services and GIS.

Regional Business Units (RBUs; based on the regions the unit operates in): RBUs focus on the earmarked geographies: Canada, Latin America, Europe, APAC, Middle East, Africa and India (USA being the only vertical market). In these markets, all the accounts are managed by the relevant RBUs in their territories. VBUs and HCUs have the responsibility for the alliances that they own and manage. In the case of alliance management, the VBUs and HCUs are expected to utilize RBUs in the respective territories for local contact and day-to-day management of the alliance partner. When an alliance partner becomes a customer, this will be owned and managed globally by the respective HCU and VBU.

The company has expertise in the following areas of business:

- Software development services
- Engineering services
- Systems integration
- ERP solutions
- Customer relationship management
- Supply chain management
- Product development
- Electronic commerce
- Consulting
- IT outsourcing

Seacom's subsidiary, Seacom Pvt. Ltd Infoway (SIFY), provides internet access and hosting services and network and network-enabled services.

Seacom's BPO subsidiary, Nipuna, provides a host of business process outsourcing services.

Seacom's wide range of business consulting and IT skills services have helped businesses to re-engineer and re-invent their products, services and processes to compete successfully in an ever-changing marketplace.

Seacom's state-of-the-art software development centres around the world work with a variety of business and technology partners to design and implement projects onsite, offshore and offsite.

The organization emphasizes on acquiring an in-depth knowledge of the customer's context and needs and designs solutions customized to these needs. Seacom's business ideas and products have resulted in technology-intensive transformations that have met the most stringent international quality standards.

Simultaneously, Seacom teams proactively work on turning new ideas into products designed to meet global market needs. One such product is Vision Compass, a web-enabled collaborative enterprise management software.

Seacom has developed strategic alliances with leaders in several technical areas. Through a web of over 50 technology and business partnerships, Seacom offers clients comprehensive, cutting-edge solutions.

Seacom is one of the high-performing organizations across the globe. It is also among the few companies around the world to attain the top rating of level 5 in the Capability Maturity Model (CMM) constituted by Carnegie-Mellon University's software engineering institute.

Seacom's foray into corporate data and internet services too was path-breaking. While several e-mail companies were languishing in the pre-internet days due to unreasonably high license fees and port charges by Dot, SIFY moved into this space in 1995. It invested heavily in TCP/IP networks when the only internet service provider was VSNL, due to monopoly of government in this sector. At that time companies could only be listed in India after three years of profitable business, while internet connectivity required large funding for infrastructure and acquisitions.

Seacom quickly moved to list SIFY on NASDAQ with great success. On 19 October 1999 it became the first internet company from India to be listed in the global markets. In June 1999, SIFY reached a milestone with its subscriber base crossing the 200,000 mark. SIFY posted a profit of Rs.67 crore for the year ended 31 March 2000 against Rs.10 crore in the previous year. While high-flying SIFY has caught people's imagination, the flagship Seacom Computer Services, a software services company, has grown from a turnover of less than Rs.4.7 crore in the year 1993 to Rs.679 crore in 2000 (146 times). Its net profit also increased 149 times from Rs.90 lakh to Rs.134 crore.

Today, Seacom has become a benchmark success story in Andhra Pradesh. Seacom now has six development centres in India, seven overseas centres and marketing offices in over 30 countries. The company provides services to over 140 multinational and Fortune 500 clients, many of them among the largest corporations in the world.

To increase technology competency continuously, the company has started a Tech Guru scheme. These are top-line tech professionals from the global IT industry, who come to the impressive Seacom Technology Centre (STC), Hyderabad, and conduct courses for about two weeks. Till now, about 30 such professionals have visited the centre.

It has tied up with Computer Associates International to provide online access to advanced e-business applications for small and medium enterprises.

Second Section

Enculturation and Rite-de-passage

This process is common in most of the organizations. It facilitates how one learns about the organization culture and grows within the organization.

Entry and Induction

As an initial step for entry to the organization, Seacom recruitment is done by conducting campus interviews in various engineering and management institutes across the country. In Seacom, the recruitment system is transparent and based on merit only.

Induction is a formal process in Seacom to help new entrants to understand Seacom's diversity and culture, a formal induction programme is periodically organized by Seacom's Learning Centre. This programme is designed to orient associates to the organizations design and direction in the Seacom way and the guiding principles of the company. The induction programme also provides the new entrants an opportunity to network and interact with each other and with senior leaders in the organization. Associates are encouraged to attend the induction programme in person. In view of time, schedule and cost implications, a web-based induction programme has been made available for associates outside India. Associates traveling to India on business can also plan and align their visit, where feasible, with the company's induction programme schedule.

In addition to this programme, specific circle-based induction programmes are also facilitated by the unit HRs to do the following:

- Enable associates meet other circle associates and understand the business model of the circle that they have joined.
- Orient associates on travel, logistics and statutory issues before traveling to countries outside India.

The various types of Induction programmes in Seacom are as follows:

- ELTP: Long-duration programme for fresh graduate trainees
- SIP: Enables transition of new associates into Seacom
- Asset: Soft skills training programme tailor made for associates of VBU
- Unit induction programme: These are unit-specific induction programmes initiated on request by the unit.

Learning on the Job and Continuing Education

Learning on the job is given importance in Seacom. Several programmes are organized in technical areas, management areas, software skills, domain training, project management, team effectiveness and change management.

Besides this, plenty of modules are available on the e-learning platform as well through Intranet which allows employees to learn at their pace and at their desk itself. Organization development and consulting efforts in the areas of visioning, building a cohesive culture, associate engagement and enabling change are a continuing feature.

The project leaders are trained on negotiation skills and senior managers on strategic management, business leadership and performance management systems. Every employee charts his career path which is vetted by the reviewing officer once before it is implemented by the human resource management group. For the top management, Seacom organizes a retreat, a learning workshop where all general managers, presidents and CEOs sit together and discuss the industry's future and the operating strategies for the company. Sometimes, leading global consultants are also invited to the retreat. The corporate division is then assigned the task of implementing the strategies.

Individual learning: Seacom has a stipulated training programme of minimum 40 hours per year for each employee. These personal training hours are over and above the regular project or need-based learning hours and organization-based learning hours.

Besides this, Seacom gives the following opportunities for continuing education to its associates:

- Facilitation for certification programmes
- Tie-up with BITS, Pilani, for MS programmes through distance education
- Limited sponsorship for MBA at ISB, Hyderabad
- Sponsorship for appropriate external seminars and knowledge-sharing forums
- Opportunities to present papers and attend internal annual conferences
- Acquiring a foreign language skill (spoken)
- Sabbatical for pursuing higher education.

Managing Knowledge and Recreating Competence

Based on Seacom's organizational and operational philosophy, it has commitment to staying on the cutting edge of the expertise. This is ensured by continually upgrading existing competencies and creating new ones, at the organization level as well as the individual level. Seacom has in place specific mechanisms to convert individual and group expertise into organizational knowledge and to draw business value from this knowledge by using it to upgrade and enhance organizational capabilities.

From a fledgling software company operating with a few service offerings in the year 1988, today Seacom has grown to an organization that operates across multiple domains and technologies. In the recent years, with domains and technologies becoming interdisciplinary, customers demand IT solutions that span across various domains and technologies. Business excellence comes from a strong knowledge base. Therefore, those who realize and act upon this will stay ahead in the new economy. This business need led to the conception of an organization-wide 'Knowledge Initiative' (KI) in Seacom.

Knowledge Management Initiative

Seacom's KI fosters a culture of creating and sharing a pool of knowledge across the organization that is in addition to managing existing knowledge resources. Associates have access to a query-based knowledge management system called the 'Knowledge Repository' that allows them to gain the advantage of collective experience, thus optimizing their own time on activities that are built upon them rather than repeating this experience.

The aim is to create a culture of effective communication and knowledge-sharing across the organization via exchange of information, ideas, thoughts, solutions, technologies and best practices and leveraging this 'Combined Intelligence' to offer winning solutions to global customers. A by-product of KI is the automation of certain routine query-based tasks, leading to a considerable saving of talent and time which is put for the search of more creative and efficient knowledge solutions.

While implementing change management, KI challenged several prevailing assumptions in the field of knowledge management implementation and introduced many innovative practices. Some of the innovative services include:

- *K-Radio*: Associates at all levels spend significant time reading and responding to mails. The knowledge team latched onto this practice and modelled the 'K-Radio' service around it. Through K-Radio queries posted by associates are channelled to the mail boxes of the right audience, and their email replies are tracked and logged in the repository. Thus, with 'K-Radio', the precious floating knowledge gets logged at one place.
- *K-Mobile*: K-Mobile is a simple off-the-shelf SMS (mobile messaging in GSM phones) technology to facilitate requesting of key documents by associates while on the move. This document-request-and-delivery service is entirely automated with very inexpensive technology and little programming effort.
- *Pathshala*: These are tacit knowledge-sharing sessions organized across the organization. These sessions serve two prime purposes: documenting tacit knowledge of the associates while they share their experiences and creating awareness about KI and its services.
- *Helpdesk Services*: A dedicated team attends to the queries and requests of the associates 24×7, thus making this initiative more customer-friendly and reachable.

Some of the prevailing assumptions which KI challenged in the field of KM implementation are as follows: *For it to be successful, the initiative has to be launched with a Big-Bang, and* unlike the typical KM implementations KI started with very little publicity. However, in just two years, it found what is probably the most effective vehicle of promotion: a loyal customer base, which gladly endorsed the services of KI.

The practical, solution-based shop-floor approach adopted by KI created positive customer perceptions and experiences, which spread quickly across the organization through strong word-of-mouth. Thus, in spite of being released without a big-bang premiere, the 'show' became a super hit.

One needs on-the-wall campaign to communicate effectively to create a unique identity for self. KI shunned the prevailing practices and adopted more customer-friendly approaches such as follows:

Introducing tacit knowledge-sharing sessions in the organization, like Pathshala or publishing a book based on the experiential knowledge shared by associates, generated a lot of interest due to highly relevant content. The messages of KI success stories were embedded within the knowledge transcripts. A subtle and positive communication through a book brought in the required awareness among more than 4000 associates. Also carried out was a novel experiment of a 'friendly hard-to-throw-away brochure'. Every internal conference or event was viewed by KI as a unique opportunity for communication. KI showcased success stories to the target associates by putting up stalls and display booths in several of these events across various locations.

People should change their behaviour to align themselves with the new processes of the organization. People do not shift their 'habits' easily. Therefore, many process implementations are treated as a burden by employees, as it requires them to spend extra time and effort to adopt them. To avoid this, KI made the smart choice of designing processes and services around associate's behaviour. 'K-Radio' and 'K-Mobile' services are perfect examples of this.

Brand-building by associates is an explicit activity that requires additional time and effort. In KI, communication, internal as well as external, is an integral part of every team member's role. Team members are encouraged to make an effort on writing papers and articles for the work they do, whether it's a small feature development or roll-out of a new service. Writing about their own work makes them feel proud of their contribution and efforts and builds strong ownership in the unit.

Till date, KI, with a team size of five associates (core team), has submitted nine papers in internal and external conferences. This effort (on thought leadership) not only made the KI core team members proud of themselves – leading to high morale and visibility across the company – but also contributed to building trust with customers and associates.

Performance Management System and Intra-organization Mobility

Seacom has an elaborate performance management system. The complete process is automated by using a web-based tool 'PCMS'. The main features of the PCMS include:

- A 360 degree approach
- Division of competencies into technical and leadership competencies

- Normalization process to remove any discrepancies in the ratings
- Appraisals on the basis of goals set at the start of the appraisal cycle
- Project closure appraisals at the completion of the project are done only for the people in that team. The parameters are set by the group and the client/manager.
- The following flow is observed for goal setting for performance: An executive is expected to set his annual goals and objectives and his project manager is required to confirm. Towards the end of the year the executive measures his achievements against the objectives set, which is reviewed by his superiors. There is also a feedback mechanism. It is interesting to note that in Seacom almost all objectives set are measurable. They have systematic annual performance review countersigned by the reviewing officer. This record constitutes an important input towards the development and promotion decisions related to the employees. Since there are not many levels of hierarchy and avenues for promotion, they have an elaborate system of review, reward and recognition on the job. Every employee or group achieving excellent performance is generously recognized and sometimes financially rewarded. Graduating from team leader to project leader is an important event in Seacom and these calls for wide celebration.

In Seacom there aren't many cases of superannuation till date. But separation calls for elaborate exit interview the inputs of which are then shared with the leadership.

Third Section

Organization Stratification

Employees are categorized into the following grades: vice president, project line leaders, project managers and associates. Seacom's organizational structure and processes are designed and aligned around customer requirements. The organizational design is geared to increase customer confidence and customer delight and to enhance customer competitiveness and success. Organizational design has evolved dynamically over the years to meet market and customer requirements. At the same time, the design nurtures the core practices of entrepreneurship, non-hierarchical operating structure and end-to-end responsibilities. Seacom acknowledges the importance of customers by placing them at the centre of its universe. The circles (units), the building blocks of the enterprises, are organized in a non-hierarchical networked fashion as depicted, to enable collaboration and end-to-end responsibilities and promote entrepreneurship and real-time distributed leadership.

Along with the responsibility of achieving well-defined goals, the circles also have considerable freedom to make business decision related to market strategy alongside investment in competency building and infrastructure. Circles are a distinguished feature of Seacom; each circle is an aggregation of processes and/or service offering and is responsible and accountable for its domain area with a defined scope of operation. Each circle makes its own business justification and contributes to the broader organizational goals by providing services to internal and external customers.

Seacom's organizational structure reflects commitment to making the customer the driving force of all initiatives.

Seacom's processes are oriented to give the organization a sharp insight into customer needs. Seacom acts on these inputs and translates them into solutions for the customer.

Seacom's believes in the 5C approach.

- Communication
- Collaboration
- Competency enhancement
- Customer intimacy
- Competitive edge

Leadership and Decision-making

Seacom was established under the dynamic leadership of Ram. He had the courage, the will power and the vision to face all the odds to shape up 'Seacom' His entrepreneurship is indeed an example for generations to come. He has always believed that to really succeed one must have a vision and must be ready to take risks. That's the reason Secom's management style is unique. It does not function as a normal pyramidal hierarchy. Every department or division is formed as a circle where the head operates as a CEO of an enterprise, with all the responsibility of running an independent company, including making profits. The company's attrition rate is half of the industry's turnover rate of 15% per annum. The leadership has in essence adopted the Japanese way of doing things.

With the theme 'Growth through Leadership', the 2004 Asia Business Leader Award sought to recognize leaders who had looked beyond cost-cutting and restructuring to achieve growth. The underlying belief was that such achievements in leadership would be possible only with a high degree of customer orientation supported by a strong corporate culture.

The top leaders work in consultation with the team leaders. Seacom is committed to provide each associate with the appropriate workforce, based on the level and responsibility being discharged. A standard work kit is provided based on the associate's nature of work, which could include a cell phone, business cards and a laptop. Workplace design and equipment are chosen with care to meet the highest ergonomic standards. Each associate is an ambassador of the company.

When an associate is deputed to a client site, he or she is representing the organization. In every interaction, associate needs to maintain high standards of professional integrity. Seacom provides freedom of expression and an air of informality. The company encourages associates to voice a counter viewpoint without the fear of retribution. Feedback is taken in the context of the process and not the person involved and hence is perceived as positive criticism. Innovative skills are the main instrument for enhancing potential of the company associates. In order to improve, Seacom permits lots of autonomy so that people can think independently and develop new concepts and ideas which can bring laurels to the company. It has been observed that the autonomy is more when the company is performing well, while things are a bit tight during crisis. On the whole, work autonomy is given to all the associates.

Communication and Information Sharing

The communication system is quite open in nature. Employees are courteous and demonstrate sensitivity and respect for those involved in the exchange. Advanced technologies are used to enhance effectiveness of communication. The market and corporate communications circle is the single point of contact for all external (media, vendors, agencies-related) communication. Any contact with the external media is linked through this circle. Common information is frequently updated and communicated through administrator e-mails to associates (e.g., Administrator_ HST or Administrator_NJP for associates based at STC, Hyderabad, India, and New Jersey, USA, respectively).

Mails that communicate information which is of interest to all associates or for those associates in a given location shall be sent through these mail IDs (e.g., audit schedules at a given location, information about awards won by the company etc.). To prevent information overload, company-wide information by any circle should be routed through corporate HR. Besides these formal routes, employees also communicate through direct face-to-face interaction, telephonic conversation and group e-mails. As a whole, the communication system is very effective and every employee is aware of the day-to-day happenings in the company business and other related issues.

The company has about 17,000 employees working at different locations. An average team consists of 6–10 members. The company encourages sharing of knowledge and work experience among group members. Daily market news and company-related information is disseminated through Seacom intranet, and company newsletters, queries pertaining to HR issues like leaves, contributions and are put up online.

Employees share new developments in the company and its future challenges during knowledge-sharing sessions. Similarly, when projects end, company selects the best case study for sharing their successful experiences. The company also conducts various meets like best practices and Seacom conference, which provides opportunities to share successful work experience of projects done by other associates across the groups. This kind of information and experience sharing helps in improving the work competency of other groups. Such a work culture has helped Seacom emerge as a major player in the market.

Open and Cohesive Work Group

The vision and the goals of the organization are clearly communicated through the intranet and employee handbook. Similarly, all information and circulars pertaining to company's performance, projects, accomplishments and so on are posted on the intranet in an effort to ensure transparency.

Company encourages transparency and openness in its work culture, which helps people to focus more on work rather than on trivial issues of rules, regulations and policies. The transparent administration makes people feel free to do work. This helps in improving the overall efficiency of people and work quality.

Team work is key for bringing success in any company. In a company like Seacom, there are several projects taken up by groups or teams. As mentioned earlier, each team or group consists of 6–10 associates who work with high level of cooperation and collaboration. As a close unit, work group members share a great deal of support and freely communicate with each other, which helps them in improving their performance. While this sometimes leads to the formation of subgroups within the organization the performance within these groups is very high. People not only discuss about better ways of doing things and finding solutions to their problems but also help each other. This increases the overall work efficiency and also affects the performance of the organization in a positive sense by decreasing the time wasted in communication. People share their joys together and come closer and thus enjoy a close rapport. This in turn positively affects the performance of the individual and the organization as a whole.

Events like birthdays are celebrated with much involvement within the unit (with songs, cakes, gifts and all), which helps in developing attachment among employees. During data collection, the birthday celebration of the group head was witnessed. While he was cutting the cake, the fellow employees sang birthday songs and gave him a gift as well. His seat was especially decorated for the purpose. In the GE group, people receive gifts like baseball bats or balls and so on as a token of appreciation.

While doing project, every group or team is free to seek technical or knowledge assistance from other group. These groups are also known for their dedication towards customers' satisfaction. This is possible because of their strong cooperation across the groups. For instance, independent groups are given freedom to handle each client as they want and according to their needs. The client can manage them independently with assistance from Seacom. The policies followed are of the client's own company. All the verticals and horizontal groups focus towards the satisfaction of the client who is their customer. The client can give direct feedback to the associates with whom they are concerned.

Commitment towards customers can be seen in the way the business model has changed from being Seacom-centred to business-centred. The documents, policies and the literature on the intranet also reflect this. Client delight is one of the parameters in performance appraisals.

This means that Seacom is a highly customer-focused organization. The result is in terms of better deliverable quality, less cycle time and enhanced customer delight. All these can be attributed to their team work.

Power Distance

The company discourages hierarchical barriers and associates are free to reach one another. In Seacom, project leaders, team leaders or divisional leaders are accountable for performance, but they work with their team as peers. The whole work group celebrates success together, sometimes go for picnic along with their family members and meet socially on birthdays. There are occasions when all the project leaders across the divisions sit together to deal with common problems. Since project leadership rotates, such meeting broadens their horizon and enables the project leader to take charge and improve performance.

In Seacom, people greet each other informally. Even the seniors have to wait for their turn in the cafeterias, in the buses and at various counters. It is not like that seniors enter and juniors get up to offer them seat. They have to wait for their turn. Sometimes, employees play music on their work stations in the evening, but it is very slow so as not to disturb others.

In this organization, if the boss needs to speak to his team members he himself goes to the subordinates' seat and tells him the work to be done, the deadlines and so on. If anything has to be discussed with the seniors, the subordinates simply go and speak to them. They skip levels to meet their seniors. Here, people do not have to wait long for the sake of meeting their seniors so as to get a nod to a simple decision which could otherwise delay the work for long. This informality speeds up things, which in turn has a positive effect on the cycle time of completion of the project. Thus, informality results in lesser loopholes, effective completion of tasks, clearer ideas and so on, which have an overall effect on the performance of the individual and the company.

Chores like bringing tea and coffee and fetching papers are done by employees themselves. There is only one helper for the whole group. Everybody is being treated equally and there is no one especially assigned for the so-called menial jobs.

This kind of an attitude really helps the organization as people do not wait for someone to come and do a job for them. They know they have to do it. They move around themselves, which brings them closer to each other and in direct contact. There is less waiting time for each task to get accomplished.

The employees address each other informally. Even the subordinates address their seniors with nicknames or abbreviations. For example, they used to call 'Thiagrajan' as 'Thiagu'. Employees address each other by their first names. An employee is accountable for himself, to his work and to his responsibilities. However, despite this informal cultural pattern, there are occasions when care is taken to give due respect to seniors and bosses by offering them front and prominent seats during functions and parties.

This shows that there is still a senior–junior factor in Seacom. Similarly, all major decision-making is done by seniors themselves. This also ensures that the experience of their services is being used appropriately. On the whole, the informality like skipping level to meet seniors and going and discussing with juniors at their workplace has a very positive effect on the performance of the individual as well as the company. The informal relationships and freedom are encouraged and practiced within the framework of company's policies and practices.

Dealing with Uncertainty

Dealing with uncertainty is quite common in Seacom since every project is different and every assignment calls for different rules to be set. Every customer is also different and has to be dealt in a different manner. Everyone has to deal with uncertainty. The customer orientation, collaborative team effort and models like the BCM help the company in dealing with uncertainties.

Fourth Section

Seacom and Society

Seacom believes that wealth creation is incomplete unless it contributes to the betterment of society as a whole. Every society is judged by the opportunities that it provides its citizens to create wealth and obtain a continuously improved quality of life. Creators of business or market value must constantly look for ways in which this value can be used to fulfill the larger social responsibility. This is one way in which an organization reaffirms its role as a contributing member of the social and economic milieu it occupies. When all levels of a society gain from economic growth, the engines of that growth are further energized.

As a larger expression of its mission and core values, Seacom is actively involved in a variety of public service projects serving underprivileged groups in urban, semi-urban and rural areas. Working through *Alambana*, an umbrella organization that brings together committed Seacom associates and their spouses, the company contributes to social causes and organizes initiatives for social change, primarily in the areas of education, environment and healthcare, areas which are inextricably tied to overall development and quality of life.

About Alambana

In Sanskrit, Alambana means 'support'. Formed in October 2000, Seacom Alambana is a volunteer-based charitable trust that identifies, plans, implements and supports projects that attempt to narrow the digital and economic divide. Each of Alambana's activities makes use of Seacom's intellectual capital to create social equity and add value to society. The volunteers who run Alambana include committed Seacom associates and their family members. Associates see Alambana as an opportunity to go beyond the cheque book charity, so they spend a considerable amount of time and effort on planning and supervising projects.

Alambana also draws upon Seacom's project management experience to turn each of its projects into economically sound business ventures that provide employment opportunities for the underprivileged and grow into self-sustaining entities. For this reason, all Alambana projects depend on the active and long-term participation of a committed group of people. And for the same reason, Alambana does not fund third-party projects or one-time charitable activities.

Alambana's first project was inaugurated by Ram on 4 October 2000 in Secunderabad. A dedicated team of Seacom IT professionals and their spouses have put in more than 2000 hours of their time to help in this venture. A full-time computer teacher has also been appointed.

The students are trained in English, personality development, typing and basic IT skills like MS-Office in the initial phase of a three-month training module designed by Seacom Learning Centre (SLC). At the end of this period the students are proficient in handling data entry, scanning services and creation of HTML pages. There are plans to train the students in elementary programming languages like C, C+ + and so on.

Additional skills would be imparted to the students based on project requirements. Alambana does not charge its beneficiaries for any of the costs associated with training.

Three batches of about 20 students each have already completed the course and the fourth batch is undergoing training. A batch of students are undergoing training on software design as part of the training for building a website for a customer in Singapore.

Alambana also coordinates the individual contributions of Seacom associates for relief purposes during disasters. For instance, during natural calamities like earthquake in Gujarat, tsunami and so on Alambana collected clothes and medicines from associates which were donated to the Chief Minister's Relief Fund.

The Saregudam Project

The children of Saregudam, a village near STC, had no access to primary education as the only school in the village was closed for many years and was in ruins. Every day, children had to walk miles and cross the dangerous Medchal highway on their way to school. The village had a literacy level of less than 5%, and the village school had fallen into disrepair, lacking a teacher and a proper building.

Moved by the plight of the children, a few GE IDC employees of Seacom revived the village school by appointing a teacher, distributing uniforms to children and monitoring the progress of these kids on a continuous basis.

Alambana intends to take IT to rural areas in order to increase their productivity. The vision is to evolve an integrated village development programme for a quantum increase of entrepreneurship in the village, leveraging the existing resources. Plans are underway to replicate similar initiatives in more villages. Besides this, the social initiatives of Seacom also include activities involving the family members of the employees. Seacom Utsav is an annual event celebrated globally, in which the families of Seacom associates participate. It is marked by the spirit of fun and joy and usually conducted in December or January every year. As part of the celebrations, various cultural, literary and sports competitions are held.

Another initiative is *Samanvay* which functions as Seacom's family learning centre. It is basically an initiative of SLC for the parents, spouse and children of associates. It seeks to foster an environment of learning among Seacom employees and their families, through a variety of learning activities designed to stimulate the mind and enhance learning. This has been rolled out in Hyderabad, India, and is being extended to other cities within and outside India, in a phased manner.

6

Case Study of Telcom Company Pvt Ltd

First Section

Telcom Products Company (TPC) is a US$2 billion company with a global vision of providing comfort, health and convenience to millions of people worldwide. It gives an impetus for the company's steady diversification into new frontiers. And today, this cooling giant's products are available in over a 100 countries across the globe. Telcom is an independent global manufacturer of hermetic compressors for air conditioning and refrigeration products, gasoline engines and power train components for lawn and garden applications, submersible pumps and small electric motors. In addition to this, Telcom has many other subsidiaries that not only sell products within Telcom but to other countries as well. Their products are sold in about 120 countries around the world.

TPC entered India through a dual acquisition of Shriram India Electrical Limited (SIEL) Compressors Limited, Hyderabad, and the Compressor Division of Whirlpool India Limited at Ballabgarh in July 1997. The company's investments in India, which currently stand at US$80 million, are likely to go up to US$100 million in near future. Telcom Products India Limited (TPIL) is a fully owned subsidiary of TPC. TPIL is the largest independent manufacturer of compressors in the country. TPIL are the manufacturers and exporters of reciprocating, air and fluid gas compressors for air-conditioning, refrigeration and coolers. Telcom's range of compressors is widely used in air conditioners, refrigerators and commercial refrigeration applications. Today TPIL is the largest independent manufacturer of both air conditioner and refrigerator compressors in India.

Computer-Aided Design and Computer-Aided Engineering Services (CADEM)

CADEM is located in Hyderabad with a well-qualified and highly motivated team of about 40 individuals. These professionals who have strong hands-on experience in various CAD, CAE and CAM packages are from engineering background. Thus, the company has created an exceptional talent pool to cater to all design, analysis and manufacturing needs. A unique combination of domain knowledge and best usage of cutting-edge technologies enhances the ability to understand clients' needs better and to plan and execute efficiently thereby delivering the products faster. It offers the advantages of 24×7 operation, leveraging time zone differentials, moving from concept to product in the shortest possible time.

Company information security is a combination of leading industry standards (firewall, intrusion detection system, virtual private network etc.) and functional/conceptual policies. Recovery of information is possible because of the disaster recovery management system.

As part of system security, company offers its clients secure and dedicated FTP services. They use RF connectivity with backup to ensure quick and uninterrupted data transmission. Data integrity is maintained through virus detection and removal systems. Physical security of your data is ensured through different means such as fire detection and extinguishing systems, burglar alarm systems, and access right to control systems given to authorized personnel only.

With a commitment to provide its customers with the best of services, Telcom has a wide, integrated network that provides prompt, accessible after-sales services and technological assistance. The network includes four regional sales offices in Delhi, Mumbai, Kolkata and Chennai; two branch sales offices in Secunderabad and Ahmedabad; six depots in Faridabad, Indore, Chandigarh, Bhubaneswar, Silvassa and Pune; 194 registered dealers and 600 registered assemblers in different regions of the country.

Historical Background

From its humble beginning in 1934, when Ray Herrick founded the Company, Telcom Products Company has earned a respected position in the manufacturing and sale of products for the refrigeration and lawn and garden industry. Through its dedicated workforce committed to quality, it has grown to become a world-class company producing mechanical products for health, comfort and convenience.

Today, Telcom products are sold in over 100 countries around the world. Headquartered in Telcom, Michigan USA, nearly 20,000 people are working around the world to develop and manufacture state-of-the-art products for hundreds of applications. The workforce is excited about leading Telcom into the twenty-first century and Telcom is continually seeking support from dynamic, talented people with similar visions to work in the factories, design, testing and research facilities, sales, customer service, administrative offices and so on. People can make a real difference in the way company operates.

Lala Shriram established Shriram Refrigeration Industries Limited in 1961. SRI as it is popularly known is one of the units of Shriram Group of Industries with its headquarters located at Delhi. This is located in the vast industrial area of Balanagar Township. Soon after its inception, SRI started manufacturing hermetically sealed compressors. The factory had only 100 employees working in a small workshop setup covering an area of 1 acre and a paid-up capital of Rs.50 lakh.

Later, the company diversified its activities and started the production of water coolers and diesel engines in the financial year 1967–1968. The company also started manufacturing electric motors. In a drive to further diversify its activities in the refrigeration field, the company started with the production of split air conditioners also. The products of the company were popularly known with the brand name of SHRIRAM and USHA.

Shriram Refrigeration was taken over by TPC during the year 1997 with the acquisition of SIEL and also the compressor division of Whirlpool of India Limited. Telcom India has become the leader in the manufacture of hermetically sealed compressors catering to all the segments of AC&R industry in India.

TPC is a full-line, independent, global manufacturer of hermetic compressors for air conditioning and refrigeration products, gasoline engines, power train components for lawn and garden applications, and pumps.

Expansion of Telcom

In 1930, TPC started when Ray W. Herrick opened the Hillsdale Machine and Tool Company of Hillsdale, Michigan. A former employee of Ford Motor Company, Ray Herrick initially produced parts for automobiles as well as electrical refrigerator components, small tools and toys. Then the company moved to Telcom, Michigan, a small town 60 miles southwest of Detroit, and Ray Herrick renamed his company after its new hometown. After a gap of three years, the company went public with an offering of 25,000 shares. It wasn't long before the company realized the future of TPC was not in automobile industry but in the burgeoning new refrigeration industry.

By 1939, Telcom was able to produce 160,000 compressors per year for mechanical refrigerators. The compressor production halted during World War II as the company's output switched to shell casings. After the World War was over, Telcom resumed manufacturing compressors and expanded its product base to include compressors for window air conditioners.

In 1950s, the company acquired two Wisconsin-based small engine manufacturers, Lauson Engine and Power Products. The addition of these two companies made Telcom's presence an important factor in the expanding outdoor power equipment industry. Today Telcom has over 30 principal locations producing compressors, engines and pumps with operating facilities in Brazil, Canada, France, India, Italy and the United States.

Vision: We are not going to simply provide compressors. We are going to provide customer solutions.

Value: Telcom works for customers to meet their expectations. Telcom is in business not merely to sell a product but to sell service, because here people are committed to total customer satisfaction by delivering quality products and focusing on customer delight. The company has realized the value of customers. Earlier, it used to be a seller's market. Now, with the liberalization of economy, customer rules the show. The company provides the best-in-class after-sales services. They have several service centres and customers' needs are duly taken care of. The suppliers and dealers are particularly happy with the speed of functioning and how their concerns are taken seriously. Even the finance department people know that dealers are satisfied with the company as they proudly flaunt it in front of outsiders.

Mission: Be recognized as the world leader in the supply of refrigeration and air-conditioning compressor.

Location and Manpower

This is the first compressor-manufacturing facility in India. Built on 55 acres of land, the manufacturing facility at Hyderabad, Andhra Pradesh, caters to air-conditioning and commercial refrigeration applications. The facility is both ISO 9001 and 14001 certified. One of the four global technology development centres (TDC) of TPC is located in this facility. The in-house application engineering testing facility is well-equipped to optimize and ensure performance improvement of the appliance. Employees working in the company are drawn from across the country. Since it is located in Hyderabad, majority of the lower-level employees belong to Andhra Pradesh. Female employees are not even 1 percent of the total workforce.

High-performing Organization

Telcom is a prominent player in the refrigeration and air-conditioning compressors industry. Telcom is also one of the high-performing branches across the globe. It has a market share of 56% in air-conditioner compressors, and over 30% in refrigerator compressors. Out of the Rs.300 crore turnover in the financial year 2002, a revenue of Rs.40 crore was generated from exports and TPIL's targeted 25% sales growth. Company had registered an 84% leap in export earnings with a turnover of Rs.110 crore from sale of compressors and pump kits for air-conditioning applications during the period January–June 2004. Telcom India, with its two units – one near Hyderabad and the other at Ballabhgarh – recorded turnover of Rs.480 crore in 2004 and had projected revenues of Rs.600 crore in 2005.

Company exports were mainly to Saudi Arabia, the UAE, Bahrain, Iran, Korea, Nepal, China, Bangladesh and a few other countries. It has commenced its quiet engagement in China by shipping a small quantity of reciprocating compressors to Gree, perhaps the largest maker of air-conditioners in the world. The Indian subsidiary of the US$2 billion Nasdaq-listed Telcom Products Company of the United States is projected to ship about 40,000–50,000 compressors to China in 2004. It geared up this number to 150,000 in 2005. Telcom makes about 600,000 reciprocating compressors (in the range of 1–2.5 tones) for air-conditioners at its Hyderabad facility. Out of this, about 400,000 compressors are exported.

Telcom was the first company in India to manufacture high-precision rotary compressors for the air-conditioning industry. As informed by the employees, the Hyderabad unit has a capacity to manufacture 750,000 units annually, and it supplies these compressors to air conditioner companies in India. Telcom India has commissioned a state-of-the-art rotary compressor manufacturing facility at its Balanagar plant in Hyderabad.

Telcom is a leading supplier of compressors to LG, Voltas, Hitachi and Blue Star in India and to Gree and Midea of China, Alessa of Saudi Arabia and Vestel of Turkey.

The rotary manufacturing facility, spread over 48,000 sq. ft. and the only rotary compressor plant, is of Telcom in the entire Asia-Pacific region, including China, apart from those in the United States and Brazil.

Telcom compressors provide the dual advantage of cooling and heating options and can take temperatures of up to 54°C under ambient conditions. This was not possible earlier.

Awards

Besides, on the occasion of May Day (1 May 2001) celebrations, Government of Andhra Pradesh has conferred the Best Management Award to the Hyderabad plant for outstanding performance in the maintenance of industrial relations, labour welfare and productivity. For the future, Telcom sees an opportunity in motor manufacturing in India, which is the second largest constituent in its global sales after compressors.

Second Section

Enculturation: Rite-de-passage

Entry and Induction

In Telcom, recruitment of employees is done through different sources based on category. Company gives advertisement in newspapers for recruiting diploma engineering staff of the company, and graduate engineering staff are recruited through campus interview. However, experienced staff member joining at the executive level are recruited with the help of consultants. As informed by Assistant Manager, HRD, there is no recruitment for staff and workmen for the past ten years in the company.

The company looks for very strong technical skills and an outgoing and active personality. Orientation is given to newly recruited staff. The period of orientation is decided upon on the cadre in which they join. In case of management trainees, fresher who is recruited from campus is on orientation for one month. This gives them the opportunity to know the culture, work systems, people and get accustomed to the environment. Everyone has a caring attitude towards a newly recruited staff member. During this period, the recruited staff member visits different departments for few days so that he gets acquainted with the whole process of the company. One person from every department is allotted to guide the new member.

Experienced people who join company in the executive grade are given orientation for 7–10 days to get acquainted with the system. During these days, they will have interactive sessions with unit heads of the company. Managing director sends circulation to unit heads in advance to fix schedules for interaction. During these interactions, respective heads share their work experience with the company and explain each and every part and process of the system followed by the company to the new member.

Holder of diploma engineering is also provided an orientation training of 10 days duration at the Hyderabad centre.

Learning on the Job and Continuing Education

The company also provides the opportunities to learn through challenging assignments, realistic appraisals, structured counselling and on-the-job and class-room training. Company tries to move employees from one responsibility to another and try to do this as often as possible.

At Telcom, the focus is on continuous up-gradation of skills, enabling managers to focus on their work. Training tends to be concentrated in specific discipline requirements, and in view of this Telcom uses identification and analysis technique, which formalizes the process in the company. Employees participate in training programmes, and the emphasis is on developing their talent from within. They are encouraged to work on cutting-edge projects.

The employees have freedom to try out new things all the time, and this helps them to learn every moment in and out making forays to touch new heights of performance and achieving individual goals by transforming ideas into actions.

Telcom doesn't only prefer to excel but strives to be perfect in all areas. The company's HR model focuses on performance as a core in all its aspects. In establishing a performance-driven culture, the company has initiated certain HR processes to nurture and sustain it. The company believes in recruiting the best talent from the industry and in retaining and developing them through innovative compensation and reward system. This has necessitated that the company relook its approach to compensation as well as its practice to motivate employees towards top-class performance. The company realizes that each individual must be motivated and developed to handle the future challenges of the business. A number of employees are sent to the United States for a visit to the Michigan plant, so as to learn the way of working there and learn new technology for business development as well.

Performance Management System

The system emphasizes on assessing the potential of individual for their development and growth. It objectively assesses performance vis-à-vis plan so as to link it to compensation and reward. The system leverages the process of business and planning and extends the same up to the individual level for objective goal setting. It defines targets in the beginning of the year so as to reduce ambiguities at the year-end appraisal.

Company follows a specific performance management system (PMS), in which executives have to fix their goals or targets in the beginning of the year itself. It is divided into four quarters – April, June, October and December – for assessing their overall performance.

In April: review and study of the goals and making work strategies to accomplish them. Based on this, employees start working in a direction to meet the target or goals set for the year. In June: review of the progress of the work done during the last months to determine what are the requirements for achieving these goals. The personality development and other work behaviour in the company are assessed in October, and in December it is assessed whether or not yearly goal or target set by the executives have been achieved. As a whole, annual appraisal concludes with a presentation of the goals achieved during the year, in front of the senior, internal customer and HR. HR acts as a moderator.

Employees are given promotion based on this appraisal format. As informed by HRD staff, there is no fixed period for promotion in Telcom; it wholly depends on the performance of the individual. There are cases where employees get promotion or incentives every year based on their performance. Promotion system is applicable only for executive grades like diploma engineers, graduate engineers and other senior executives.

Workmen's performance is assessed by the unit heads and reports are sent to the managing director. Their performance appraisal is based on daily assignment done in the unit. This category of staff do not have any promotion system but are provided salary increments based on their performance. If production targets are reached, then workers get gold coins. In an interview, a worker flaunted his gold ring and proudly said 'yeh mujhe meri company ne dee hai' (This is given to me by my company.)

Special Projects (SPs). The objective of the scheme is to promote new ideas which would result in quality improvement or wastage/cost reduction. This scheme is applicable to the entire officers up to grade 10. An SP can be qualified for a reward if it falls outside the functional/routine responsibility of the employee. SPs can either be individual or team and in case of team SPs it is very essential to ensure that all the members involved in the process of effective implementation are included. All team SPs should have cross-functional team members. Each SP identified should be sent to HRD for evaluation along with a list of team member's detailed activities. This includes time frame required for completing each activity as well as the entire SP and the role played by each member of the team.

Suggestion Reward Scheme

The objective of this scheme is to promote new ideas in design, processes and commercial areas of the company's business, which would result in improvement in quality and reduction in waste and cost. Suggestions qualified for reward should be outside the scope of the expected duties that go normally with the function/job responsibility of the employee.

The scheme is applicable to all the employees of TPIL below the level of managers. The suggestion committee consists of seven members and will evaluate and monitor the implementation of each suggestion. A chairman heads the committee.

Retirement

Retirement is considered as one of the important events among the Telcom employees. It is marked with a grand celebration. It is important to mention that the company encourages staff to work for company post-retirement as well. It is especially done for people who made a valuable contribution towards company's growth.

As observed during data collection, a senior staff member was working in the company's chemical department post his retirement as well. Many a times, Telcom has called back retired employees to extend their work term with them, and the employees are also willing to work with Telcom even after retirement. Most of the people don't want to leave Telecom for any reason, and when asked why they don't want to leave, they simply reply that the company has given them so much, which they never expected for them. The company has taken good care of them and their family and they want to stay here and keep growing with the company.

Usually, based on the performance of an employee, the outstanding amount to be paid by him to the company like loans under housing finance scheme are written off. Even cell phones are also given to them at the time of retirement.

Spandan: The Heartbeat of Telcom

Spandan is quarterly in-house magazine being released from Hyderabad covering the entire Telcom India. The magazine is helping them to bring all the employees and their family members together.

Telcom collaborates with employees as well as their families for celebration. Some regular celebrations happen on the annual day, including officers' get-together, picnics and so on. Celebrations associated with different festivals are also part of their joyous moments. Family is important for the company; it is given special attention and the company ensures that employees are stress free at the family level. Annual day is celebrated in the presence of family members of the employees present there. The officer's get-together also calls for the family members of all the officers to be present at a pre-decided venue for the party. This gives the employees an opportunity to gel with each other at the family level as well.

Telcom recognizes and rewards its employees. It honours individuals and teams for specific outstanding achievements that have had major impact on company's operations. In 1999, one of the motor shops was named as 'tiger' after it produced a massive number of compressors. This boosted the morale of the employees immensely; they got the sense of achievement as they were being noticed by the management. They received cash rewards as well. The name still prevails and that motor shop is still referred to as 'Tiger'. The employee suggestions scheme was also started to recognize the efforts and value them in an appropriate way.

Telcom acknowledges their people not only for the work done but also for their achievements in other areas as well. Telcom encourages its people to participate in sports conducted by different associations. The newsletter celebrates the achievements in other fields as well. Employees get a letter of appreciation from the company to complement them on their achievements. Their certificates are published in the newsletter.

Company follows the culture of wearing the same uniform for all employees. Two pairs of uniform, one pair of shoes and two pairs of socks are supplied to all employees except to the officers of commercial departments. All employees who are issued the uniform are expected to come to factory strictly in uniform.

Why Monday off? The industrial area from Balanagar to Jedimeethla remains closed on Mondays, so employees wanted to spend time with their families. Moreover, on Sundays, banks, markets and so on remain closed. So Monday gives them time to finish pending work. The decision was taken on employees' request. Staff and officers can go out on personal work for 1.5 hours, thrice a month, at the discretion of superiors/HOD. If an employee gets transferred in the middle of the academic year of his or her children, he or she can maintain two residences till academic year gets over so as to facilitate the admission of children to new place. HRA will be paid at both locations by the company. Company wants to give employees the feel that it is working for their betterment. Company tries to instil a sense of belonging into the employees. A benevolent fund of Rs.1 deducted from the salary of all the employees towards this fund. On death of any employee, Rs.5,000 is given to the family as funeral expenses. On the death of child/spouse of employees, Rs.500 given from the fund.

The birthdays of employees are remembered, and a letter of best wishes is put on the notice board. Sweet packet is also given. The caring attitude of company is visible even towards construction workers; Rs.10,000 is sanctioned for new clothes for their children if workers finish their work within the given time frame. Employees are provided with monetary support to maintain the position or status of a particular job post. Usually, based on the performance of an employee the remaining amount to be paid by him back to the company like HFS is written off. Even cell phones are gifted to them at the time of retirement. Workers are also given gold coins, when they meet the target set for them in production. Employees are given gifts once every year. This is to make them feel a part of team Telcom. The gift could be a rice cooker, OTG and so on.

An employee is happy, if he feels that the company cares for him. The sense of belonging is very apparent in the Telcomsians. They all care for the company as 'their company', and this sense of belonging is very apparent in the way they speak about Telcom.

Third Section

Structure and Stratification of the Organization

Like any other manufacturing company, Telcom also has an organizational structure which is categorized into various grades: managing director, vice president, senior general manager, senior deputy general manager, senior manager, manager, senior engineering, production engineering, supervisors and workers. As a whole, company assignments are carried out by various divisions like air conditioners, refrigeration, commercial air conditioning, commercial refrigeration, condensing units, CADEM Centre, quality management, management services, executive director office, finance and accounting, HR, planning and development, and hospital administration. These units are headed by senior manager or SDGM and assisted by other subordinates.

Telcom functions in two shifts; first shift starts at 6.45 am and ends at 3.15 pm, and the second shift starts at 3.45 am and ends at 11.30 pm. The employees who are working in the factory follow the above schedule. However, administrative staff member have a different work timing, from 8.30 am to 4.30 pm, and this timing pertains only to the administrative building staff.

Security personnel are posted in various entry points of the company so as to look after safety of the company as well as the staff. There is close scrutiny of the visitors by the security personnel at the main entry point. Nobody is permitted to go inside the company unless they get prior permission from the concerned official. Visitors are issued temporary entry pass for meeting company officials.

Leadership and Decision-Making

The leadership of an organization is one feature which greatly influences its culture. The leader determines the terms by which the employees will behave. It is usually seen in organizations that employees usually behave in the way their leader does. The working of the organization and the beliefs and values get modified as per the directives from their leader.

The employees boast of having a capable leader. Vipin Sondhi is the Managing Director of the organization; he is working in this post for the last three years. Before him, the company was headed by Madhavan. In fact the workers and staff give the credit of turning Telcom around to Madhavan. According to workmen, it was under him that Telcom underwent the turbulent times of getting everything together and starting afresh. Workers themselves admit that before him, under the leadership of Shriram's, they were not interested in the company and its growth at all. It was Madhavan who proved a catalyst to the change reaction. He gave them a vision to excel and take Telcom to this new heights. Workmen admit that there never was any orientation among them regarding the vision of the company and what they can contribute for its fulfilment. They just worked for the sake of it and never thought much about it. It was due to the reason that even the company never bothered or oriented them to do their bit for the company.

In fact, the workers' relations were strained with the management and workmen didn't have any focus as to what they are doing and why they are doing it. They admit that the company meant nothing to them, then just a way to earn livelihood. But after Telcom's take over in 1996, Madhavan made them realize what is their worth. They got a new focus and the zeal to do something extraordinary. They were made responsible and answerable to produce results. Their views and suggestions were taken seriously, and they were encouraged to do so as well. This kind of importance given to them helped the company in many ways. Moreover, the workmen believed in what the company was doing because the leader himself was involved. He led them to this belief that they are the best.

His enthusiasm and energy were contagious and spread to the workmen level as well. The perspective of the employees got clearer when they came to know what was expected of them and why was it expected from them.

The present leader Sondhi is also considered as a dynamic leader by a lot of employees. He is a hard worker and has a particular vision for the company and the employees. The employees show the same commitment; they are also hard-working and believe that they can help Telcom reach the level they want it to.

Sondhi is said to be a capable leader but is not as experienced as Madhavan was. Madhavan used to hold a monthly meeting with all the employees and used to address the workers as well. But Sondhi has changed to them quarterly meetings with the officers only. In fact the workmen have this query that why they haven't seen their MD talking to them as the previous one used to.

But the answer comes from them; they know that the present MD is handling both the units (Ballabhgarh and Hyderabad) and he is very busy. Moreover, at the time of Madhavan, the workers needed more motivation and information. The team spirit had to be aroused and the mammoth task of turning the company around had to be accomplished. Now, even the workmen believe that they don't need to be addressed as frequently by the MD, as their superiors provide them with all the information at the shop floor itself. And they understand the busy schedule of their MD. Still they do want to meet him personally sometimes, other than giving personal letters to them quarterly, informing them about the progress of the company. The attitude of Sondhi has channelled down to the lowest-rung cadre; they all believe in working hard, they think about the company as their own and they want to witness it reaching new heights. Telcom always takes a long-term view of any situation, for it is company's intention to stay in business as long as it can generate the resources each year to grow from one level to another.

The core member committee takes the strategic decisions for the company. Telcom has adopted two levels of decision-making: (a) unit-level team, which consists of all unit heads, looks after micro-level planning and decision-making of unit-level works. It is conducted once in a month or so based on requirement; (b) executive-level team, which consists of managing director, vice president, senior managers and heads of HRD, looks after the overall functioning of the company. It is conducted quarterly. The quarterly meeting involves decisions about where the company is headed to and what are the current market requirements. In an effort to grow further, the company is planning to focus more on exports and R&D.

Telcom believes in freedom of expression. Hence, employees have the freedom to try out new things, and this helps them to learn every moment and strive towards touch new heights in performance. The workers agree that they are given freedom to try out new methods of doing their work, and mistakes are treated as lessons learnt but experimentation goes on. A worker talked about how he tried to experiment with the way compressors are assembled and said he was encouraged to do that.

As informed by employees, a major shift in the culture of the company from Shriram to Telcom is the decentralization of power. Every unit can take its own decision for their own benefit. This is because the company has come of ages and is gearing for a new drive towards excellence. And in this drive, company is looking for the support of employees. Creativity is one thing which is always welcomed by Telcom. They want their employees to experiment so that they can find ways to excel. Hence, there is more freedom in decision-making after Telcom took over. The core committee team, that is, ELT takes major decisions but does so based on feedback from lower levels.

Problems are also discussed at the department level, and, if problems go out of hand they are forwarded to a higher level. A senior staff member expressed that even Shriram culture's was also good but it was a bit strict and employees didn't have this much freedom at that time. As a whole, there is autonomy at the section/departmental level, but strategic decisions are taken by ELT.

Telcom believes in quality of work–life balance, which enhances employee productivity. It takes care of all the needs of employee; for example, when a manager is transferred to a new place or unit in a different location, the company ensures that relocation is taken care of, enabling the managers to focus only on their work. The company actually pays all the relocation expenses and has in fact handled the admissions of the employees' children in schools as well. Executives are given furnishing allowances to maintain their standard of living.

Recognition and rewards are an integral part of the culture at Telcom. This is not only for the employees but is extended to their family as well. Employees' kids, who excel in academics, are awarded scholarships. The company even gives award to its employees for their suggestions which are useful for the company. A worker in Hyderabad unit got a monetary reward of 5% of the amount he saved for the company. These strategies are properly designed and executed by the core committee to earn more loyalty from the employer towards the company.

Communication and Information Sharing

Communication plays an important role in any organization. The channels of communication decide as to what kind of culture does the company has. It is the communication technique and the ways which lead to the development of trust in any employee and strengthening his or her loyalty towards the organization.

Communication is an important medium which disseminates relevant information to the employees. In Telcom noticeboards are one of the main platforms for disseminating company news. Noticeboards are located in all the nooks and corners of the company. For instance, some health safety measures are also placed on the notice board. The most amazing thing is that people don't hide anything from anyone, and information flows freely. These days, the noticeboards are boasting about lean manufacturing. Every year, 4th March is celebrated as safety day in the company, and on this day noticeboards are full of safety issues on this day. During data collection, we noticed that the noticeboard at gate no. 2 very strongly instructed that staff should come in uniform and otherwise half-day wage-cut will be levied as penalty. Company policy also considers the following as seven deadly sins not to be committed by Telcom family: *inconsistent product quality, slow response to market place, lack of competition and competitive products, uncompetitive cost structure, inadequate employee involvement, unresponsive customer service and inefficient resource allocation*. This notice is put up in most of the work places inside the company.

Telcom has this culture of open communication; nobody hides anything from anyone. The information is out and open, and anyone can clarify doubts from anybody. Employees are well-informed about what their goals are and in what direction the company is headed; thus, they know how much is the demand and how much they need to produce.

Canteen is not a very noisy place even during lunch time, with about 200 people occupying the place. Employees don't roam around in canteen for chit-chat as they move to their respective departments as soon as the lunch is over. On 11 March 2004, increment letters were distributed but it was not like the previous year. Though it was low compared to the previous year, employees haven't shown their unhappiness overtly.

A quarterly meeting is held at Telcom where the managing director interacts with the officers of the company. Here, the future plans and problems are discussed. There is a tradition of the quarterly letter which is sent from MD to the workers informing them about the performance of the company and motivating them to work harder to achieve the pinnacle of success. Important announcements are circulated through noticeboard and e-mails.

The informal channel of communication, grapevine, is always open. No organization can escape from it. The information does flow faster through this channel, but this is not the only channel for the employees to rely upon. A lot of things are shared through noticeboard; it could be about a virus on the loose or medical tips about preventing heart diseases. The company also takes special care to keep its employees health-conscious. They want their people to be fit mentally and physically. The employees do prefer to have open feedback and are not hesitant about walking up to their colleagues or superiors to give them a feedback on the job done. Company provides telephone for all officers at home as well.

The wellbeing of the communication channels is proved through the amount of trust and relationship it develops. And the employees seem to trust their company for what it says. After all, which company's accounts and costing department would give a presentation on how much scrap they sold and how much waste they have got. The way sharing of information takes place in Telcom has led to an environment where even the workers know what the market is looking for and where the market is headed. With this kind of information being circulated, even the workers are capable of understanding what the customer is looking for and can give his or her suggestion to improve the product and work towards customers satisfaction. As informed by employees, the suggestion scheme from workers has led to a saving of Rs.2.9 lakh in the year 2002 to Rs.4.1 lakh in the year 2003.

Open and Cohesive Work Group

Openness, respect for individuals, teamwork, integrity, trust and flexibility are the much-spoken about topics in Telcom. Talking of respect, during one of the interviews with a manager, we *were asked to interview his senior (in years of service to the company, not designation) first who was just sitting next to him (this senior was not on the list of people we had chosen to interview).* The problems are solved by mutual discussion. If the problem is big, then everyone comes together and solves it with the help of concerned departmental heads and the top executives.

In another instance, *a fire broke out in the IT department. The teamwork and concern for each other was seen there. How everyone had come together to take control of the situation was remarkable. People were running back and forth with sand buckets and fire extinguishers to put down the fire. Nobody settled down till everyone was out of the building and situation was in control.* Similarly, in 2001, a *company-owned land was occupied by some political group. Everyone got together to fight for it and got the land back. Company representations were made to Prime Minister and so on.*

Discipline is one thing which unifies the vagrants in any organization. Openness and cohesiveness may be common nowadays, but when it comes to binding them all and keeping them under control discipline is required. It is not about being a dictator but being able to keep things under control. The timings of coming to factory have to be followed strictly; there is a half-day wage-cut if a worker punches in late. It shows that Telcom does follow certain rules and regulations. The officers have got the internet facility, but they can't use the messenger service for reasons best understood without mentioning.

As mentioned earlier, employee's suggestions are valuable for the company and they are encouraged to make suggestions. That is why the company has a Suggestion Reward Scheme, to reward the best suggestions given by employees which helped the company to perform better. The healthy competition that prevails in Telcom ensures that the company stands to gain.

As expressed by a few employees, Telcom does care about the difficulties of employees and gives due regards to their problems. The company gives extra support to the employees because it values them. The employees are never left to handle their chores themselves; if there is something the company can do, it always does it. It could be anything, transferring an employee because his son is undergoing treatment at a different place or reimbursement of relocation expenses. If feasible, even transfers are given to employees on the basis of their family problems. One employee was transferred from Mumbai to Chennai because his son needed treatment for a disease in Chennai after every three months. This kind of caring attitude is appreciated by the employees, and they show their gratitude in turn by performing beyond the expected levels.

As the company was taken over by the American group, everyone on board has taken up the mammoth task of bringing Telcom back to business. This action was taken in a very positive manner by everyone at Telcom. Workers are still reminiscent of the days when Telcom was going through the turning-around phase. This growing together has cemented the bond between the employees and the company.

Moreover, with the many welfare programmes being run for the employees, Telcom has really won their hearts. The salary has also increased manifold after Telcom took over. As informed by employees, employees are more happy and satisfied now. In Telcom a worker can earn up to Rs.25,000/month.

Telcom has this family feeling prominent everywhere; a new person is welcomed so openly and warmly that he or she immediately feels as a part of the family. The employees children are called 'young Telcomsians', and they are given scholarships if they perform well in studies. The food is served in the canteen at subsidized rates of Rs.8.50/meal. The company has provided the employees with a sports room and even a gym.

The kind of considerations given to the employees and their families do generate a sense of belonging among the employees. The company gets a special place in the heart of employees. People believe they are needed by the company and the company values them; this does wonders for the employees' loyalty to the company. This is what makes Telcom stand apart.

Power Distance

It is also noticed that subordinates can call their superiors by their first name. Workers feel free to talk to superiors and their problems do get solved. Any employee who is curious can ask anyone about anything. Employees maintain cordial relations with each other irrespective of the department they work in. They generally converse in Telugu language. The people are very open. One can easily walk into anyone's cabin. The superiors don't mind doing their own work rather than calling subordinates for simple work.

Employees feel free to talk to their superiors, and they usually call each other by their first names; this may not be very prevalent on the shop floor. Cracking jokes is also a part of conversation. Employees agree that they can speak to their superiors anytime. The transparency gives rise to trust, which is very essential in building rapport with employees.

There is a hierarchical setup; everything is permission bound but that is not required in every situation. Employees do agree that they have requisite autonomy but they are more used to getting permissions from their superiors before doing anything that is not a routine task.

It is noticed that employees walk over to do small things and superiors' even walk up to their subordinates to tell them any work they want them to do. This really shows that this company which was a family-run business is breaking free from the shackles of hierarchy.

Even a worker admits that now there is no gap between superiors and subordinates; they all work for their company and that is what they have in mind while working. The workers even assure their superiors of delivering higher amount of production and that they need not worry about it. The superiors discuss their problems with the subordinates and vice versa. If problems come up in the organization then everyone sits together and solve it after discussions. The workers are expected and encouraged to give suggestions.

Since the information flows freely, almost everyone knows what is going on and even if anyone asks them they are pretty open about disclosing what they know. Hiding is not a part of the Telcom culture; they gather up everything so that it becomes visible. Despite all these we noticed that canteen has few tables which are supposed to be for officials at the top level. Other employees are not supposed to sit there. Workmen have their lunch 30 minutes before the management cadre.

It is also observed that employees (middle level) refer to each other as 'colleague'. The safety and training in charge, Srinivas, is lovingly called as 'safety Srinivas'. While entering into the factory, workers usually give way to officers to enter first if they also arrive with them. Respect is one attribute which is common for Telcom and its employees. By mutual respect it is meant that the company gives respect to its employees and vice versa and the employees give respect to each other as well.

As stated earlier, the atmosphere is like a family; employees are polite with each other and nobody is harsh or extra polite with anyone. People maintain their individuality and distance while performing their part of job in the big family of Telcom. The growth of employees is appreciated and is shown in the form of letter of appreciation by the MD, if any employee gets promoted. This not only motivates the employees but also helps them to focus on their goals. They are insinuated to achieve more and makes them loyal towards the company.

Dealing with Uncertainty

Since Telcom is a manufacturing company, amount of uncertainty is not that high due to the nature of work being more static. Most of the groups and sections are engaged constantly into same kind of work round the clock. However, the employees are well prepared to deal with all eventualities or unforeseen troubles. Sometimes, they do face uncertainty in meeting the deadline. Such cases were dealt with effectively. In the past, employees from the top most level to the junior level have witnessed Telcom going through the worst period but in those turbulent times as well, they stood firmly against all odds. The company was taken over by its American counterpart and this led to the sense of insecurity amongst all the employees at that moment but Telcom retained and reassured them all. Nobody was sacked and almost no one lost his or her job.

Fourth Section

Telcom and Society

Telcom has been constantly engaging itself in the upliftment of the society. For instance, Telcom Products India Private Limited and Confederation of Indian Industry, Lodhi Road, New Delhi, have jointly taken up a modest primary education project as part of corporate social responsibility. In all rural areas in the vicinity of Ballabgarh district, this facility was explored and finally a village called Samaypur situated on Ballabgarh Sohna Road was identified.

Leaders sat together with village Panchayat and elders to make them partners in the project, which ultimately was their own to sustain and nourish. This established basic trust between the villagers and Telcom representatives along with CII experts on education and social development. Second priority was Mahila Kendra as young girls were prone to leave primary or secondary school because of commuting issues and other social problems and could not even attend any vocational courses outside the village. A half-finished centre existed, which was renovated and made functional by Telcom and basic tailoring classes were started. Seven sewing machines were installed at this centre on 9 April 2004.

Progress of This Project

Cutting and tailoring led to vocational revenue generation – Telcom is already getting all shoe covers made by this centre.

From October 2004, candle making and handicrafts training were started at Mahila Kendra. Exhibition-cum-sale of these products was inaugurated by Managing Director Vipin Sondhi on 10 November 2004 at the lawns of Ballabgarh plant. This was a very modest but encouraging step towards creating a cooperative for women of Samaypur village.

- Health and welfare clinic started functioning at the newly built Anganwadi centre
- Interventions at primary school Samaypur
- Newly renovated school building was inaugurated by Shaila Sondhi in the presence of S. Sen, Deputy Director, CII, New Delhi, who has been a constant source of guidance and encouragement along this arduous path of social responsibility
- School bags and stationary were provided for all students
- A small library was provided for children. Most of the books were from National Book Trust.
- On Van-Mahotsva, a tree plantation drive was initiated, and all primary school children were encouraged to plant trees and be custodians of this tree plantation

- Government initiative on mid-day meal programme was strengthened by providing cooking and serving utensils to all
- Linda Herrick, wife of Chairman Todd Herrick, visited the school. The children at primary school presented a colourful cultural programme
- A school health programme was started in December 2004. Construction of kitchenette and two more class-rooms are being planned.

A programme called for 'Literacy for All' was launched as a part of corporate social responsibility and bringing a qualitative and productive change in the lifestyle of illiterate workmen both at home and at work; Telcom initiated an 'Adult Literacy drive' on 21 May 2001. First batch of 25 out of a total of 55 identified workmen successfully completed basic 'Hindi Yatan Programme' in February 2002 and second batch of 18 passed out in December 2003. Company designated them as 'Siksha Sainiks', that is, torch bearers, of adult literacy in the society.

Apart from this, company employees have also made monitory contribution towards the welfare of the victims of earthquake in Gujarat and the tsunami victims.

7

Case Study of Heavy Electrical Company

First Section

Heavy Electrical Company (HEC) is the largest engineering and manufacturing enterprise in India in the energy-related/infrastructure sectors. HEC ranks amongst the top 10 power generation equipment manufacturers in the world. It was established more than 40 years ago when its first plant was set up in Bhopal ushering in the indigenous heavy electrical equipment industry in India, a dream that has been more than realized with a well-recognized track record performance.

It manufactures over 180 products under 30 major product groups. The origin of HEC can be traced back to 1956, when the Government of India set up Heavy Electricals of India Ltd (HEIL) in technical collaboration with AEI, UK (now GEC Alsthom). HEIL started manufacturing electric equipment at its plant in Bhopal. Later in 1959, the government set up a new venture with the name HEC with the objective of creating indigenous manufacturing base for power plant equipment. During the third five-year-plan period (1961–1966), HEC set up three plants in Hardwar, Hyderabad and Trichy, respectively. In 1974, on the recommendations of Action Committee on Public Enterprises, HEIL was merged with HEC. Over the years, HEC entered into several technical collaborations with international players and set up its plants all over the country. It has set up a number of new plants in various parts of the country. Currently, the company has 14 manufacturing units, 4 power sector regional centres, over 100 project sites, 8 service centres and 18 regional offices across India.

HEC's business is divided into three segments: power, industry and exports. Industry segment includes various sub-segments such as transmission, transportation, telecommunication and renewable energy.

- Vision: A world-class engineering enterprise committed to enhancing stakeholders' value
- Values: The zeal to excel and pursuit for change
- Integrity and fairness in all matters and respect for dignity and potential of individuals
- Strict adherence to committed deadlines
- Ensuring speedy response
- Foster learning, creativity and teamwork
- Loyalty and pride in the company.

Time is given a value in the organization; everyone trooped on time. The value of time was best noticed when the employees worked overtime to meet the deadline and their commitment to the customer. Likewise, working in a team, cooperation and collaboration were desired behaviours practiced widely.

Mission: To be an Indian multinational engineering enterprise providing total business solutions through quality products, systems and services in the fields of energy, industry, transportation, infrastructure and other potential areas.

Technology Upgradation

To remain competitive and meet customers' expectations, this organization lays great emphasis on the continuous upgradation of products and related technologies and development of new products. The company has upgraded its products to contemporary levels through continuous in-house efforts as well as through acquisition of new technologies from leading engineering organizations of the world. The corporate R&D Division at Hyderabad, spread over a 140-acre complex, leads HEC's research efforts in a number of important areas. Research and product development centres at other manufacturing divisions play a complementary role in its growth and development.

HEC investment in R&D is amongst the largest in the Indian corporate sector. In the recent past, it has introduced several state-of-the-art products: low-Nox oil/gas burners, large-capacity atmospheric fluidized bed combustion boilers, high-efficiency pelton hydro turbines, petroleum depot automation systems, 36kV gas-insulated sub stations, controlled shunt reactors (CSR), performance analysis, diagnostics and optimization (PADO) package for power plants and so on. The company has also transferred a few technologies developed in-house to other Indian companies for commercialization. The company is also engaged in research in futuristic areas, such as utility of super-conducting materials in power generation and industry and fuel cells for distributed, environment-friendly power generation.

Among overall earnings of the organization, power is the focal area of HEC. Power segment accounts for around 70% of the company's revenues. The company makes equipment for all types of power plants i.e. thermal (coal/gas), hydro and nuclear. It has installed equipment for over 90,000 MW of power generation for utilities, captive and industrial users. It accounts for nearly 65% of the total installed capacity in the country.

In industry segment, HEC manufactures major capital equipment and systems like captive power plants, industrial boilers, gas turbines, pumps, heat exchangers, electric machines, valves and forgings to a number of industries other than power utilities like metallurgical, mining, cement, paper, fertilizers, refineries and petrochemicals. It also manufactures a wide range of transmission products and systems, transportation and telecom equipment. It has developed and commercialized technologies for exploiting nonconventional and renewable sources of energy. HEC has emerged as a major manufacturer of wind electric generators up to 250 KW unit size.

HEC has exported its products and services to more than 60 countries. Its export ranges from individual products to complete power stations on turnkey basis and specialized after-sales services like Residual Life Assessment (RLA) studies/retrofitting/refurbishing/overhauling. They also include supply of HV/EHV substations.

Over the years, HEC has absorbed technology from several international players. It has several successful adaptations of global technology to its credit suiting Indian conditions such as modification of boiler design to function optimally with Indian coal which has higher ash content. They have indigenized most components and raw materials for power plants.

In its quest to become world class, HEC focuses on continual improvement in the quality of its products, services and performance leading to total customer satisfaction and business growth through dedication, commitment and teamwork.

HEC caters to core sectors of the Indian economy via power generation and transmission, industry, transportation, telecommunication, renewable energy, defence and so on. It has already attained ISO 9000 certification, and all the major units/divisions of HEC have been upgraded to the latest ISO 9001:2000 version of quality standard certification. They have secured ISO 14001 certification for environmental management systems and OHSAS-18001 certification for occupational health and safety management systems for all its major units/divisions.

Looking at continuous improvement in the financial performance and other allied activities of the company during the last few years, HEC has been selected as a high-performing organization.

Location, Manpower and Product Profile of the Hyderabad Unit

The Ramachandrapuram Unit of HEC, situated about 30 km from the historic city of Hyderabad, stands out as the perfect example of technological and industrial excellence. Its product range covers steam and gas turbines, electrical machines, compressors, pumps, heat exchangers, pulverizers, oil field equipment, switchgears and so on.

HEC unit based in Hyderabad has earned a reputation as one of its most important manufacturing units, contributing the lion's share in HEC corporation's overall business operations. The Hyderabad unit was set up in 1963 and started its operations with manufacturing of turbo-generator sets and auxiliaries for 60 and 110 MW thermal utility sets.

Over the years it has increased its capacity and diversified its operations to many other areas. Today, a wide range of products are manufactured in this unit, catering to the needs of variety of industries like fertilizers and chemicals, petrochemicals and refineries, paper, sugar, steel and so on.

This unit has collaborations with world-renowned MNCs like General Electric, USA; Siemens, Germany; NuovoPignone and so on.

Major products of the unit include the following.

Gas turbines: It is the largest gas turbine manufacturer in India, with the state-of-art facilities in all areas of gas turbine manufacture. It offers complete engineering solution in-house to meet specific customer requirement. With over 100 machines and cumulative fired hours of over 4 million hours, HEC has supplied gas turbines for a variety of applications in India and abroad.

Steam turbines: These have been playing an active role for almost four decades in its promise of 'bringing power to the people'. The art of steam turbine building has been perfected over a quarter of a century by the absorption of leading technologies and building up of experience for catering to every possible application in the product range.

Compressors: In the year 1970, HEC made its foray into centrifugal compressors with technical collaboration from NuovoPignone, Italy, and since then has been catering to the fertilizer, refinery, petrochemical and other process industries. It has built up a cumulative experience of more than 30 million hours of operations for various applications.

Turbo generators: HEC has manufactured turbo generators of ratings up to 560 MW and is in the process of going up to 660 MW. It has also the capability to take up the manufacture of rating up to 100 MW, suitable for thermal power generation, gas-based and combined cycle power generation as well as for driver's industrial applications like paper, sugar, cement, petrochemical, fertilizers and rayon industries.

Heat exchangers: HEC Hyderabad has supplied a variety of heat exchangers in large numbers for diversified applications. Among them are steam surface condensers, air evacuation system, feed water heaters, deaerators inter-stage gas coolers, process heat exchangers and steel and other industrial plants.

Pumps: HEC started manufacture of pumps during the mid-1960s under technical collaboration with M/s Sigma Lutin, Czechoslovakia, to meet the requirements of 60 MW, 110 MW and 210 MW thermal power stations.

Pulverizes: HEC also manufactures mills for pulverized coal-fired thermal and industrial boilers. Operating in different coal-fired thermal power stations in India, HEC has manufactured over 1,200 bowl mills and over 100 tube mills till date.

Switch gears: HEC is also involved in the design, commissioning and service of a wide range of switchgears catering to various applications like power station auxiliaries, power distribution, process industries, rural electrification, open cast mines and other applications.

- Oil rigs: HEC started manufacturing oil field equipment in collaboration with US Steel Engineers and Consultants (National Oil Well), Skytel Brewster USA and so on. After successful absorption of technology, HEC now has the capability to manufacture conventional deep-drilling rigs up to a depth of 9,000 meters, mobile rigs to a depth of 3,000 meters and well-servicing rigs to a well-depth of 6,100 meters. In addition, HEC has upgraded three rigs by installing an independent rotary drive system.

The campus looks very clean, and there is greenery all over. There are many transport facilities available for the employees. Auto rickshaw services are available to move around in the campus. The company provides housing facilities for the staff, and majority of the staff live inside the company premises. It's informed that turbine compressor/gas turbine unit, which is selected for the fieldwork in HEC, has the maximum number of employees. This division is one of the high-performing divisions in the organization. Employees are from various parts of the country. However, about 90% of the lower-grade employees are from Andhra Pradesh and Telangana. There are hardly any women working in the factory except a few in the administrative sections.

Performance of HEC Hyderabad (Ramachandrapuram)

HEC Hyderabad is one of the high-performing units, and it contributes the lion share to the overall performance of the whole company. During the year 2004–2005, HEC Hyderabad achieved a turnover of Rs.1,755 crore. The unit recorded the highest-ever PBT of Rs.308 crore. Its productivity improvement activities have resulted in a saving of Rs.82 crore. The year 2004–2005 opened with an order book of Rs.2,518 crore. During the year fresh orders were booked for Rs.2,683 crore. For the year 2005–2006, orders in hand are worth Rs.3,666 crore, which is the highest ever. This is a reflection of continued customer confidence as well as the success of competitive pricing and delivery strategies adopted by the unit.

Performance guarantee lists conducted on FR6 FA combined cycle plant at TNEB, Kuttalam, TNEB, Perungulam, GSEL, and Dhuvaram have achieved higher thermal efficiencies than the guarantee values.

The Hyderabad unit received an order for Rs.270 crore from RVUNL Dholpur, which consists of two sets of Fr.9E gas turbines and generators; export orders received from PDO, Oman, for compressors train for supply to Lekhwair and Yibal worth Rs.153 crore; order worth Rs.164 crore has been received from Reliance Industries for supply of gas TG sets. Repeat orders have been received from customers like Reliance Industries, ACC, Gujarat Ambuja Cements, HPCL, Jindal Steels, and PDO, Oman, amply demonstrating the confidence of customers in HEC equipment.

Awards and Recognitions

In the year 2004, HEC Hyderabad in its movements towards business excellence under the CII Model (TQM) has been recognized and awarded 'Commonwealth Certificate for Strong Commitment to Excel'. They continue to be certified for ISO 9001 for quality systems, ISO 14001 for Environment Management, and ISO 18001 for Occupational Health and Safety. Besides, Hyderabad unit has received various appreciations and awards during recent times.

INSAAN award for 'Excellence in Suggestion Scheme' among manufacturing companies was awarded to HEC Hyderabad for the year 2004.

Hyderabad unit was adjudged by QCFI, Hyderabad Chapter as 'Best Organization in Promoting Quality Circles' for the second consecutive year, that is, 2004 and 2005.

Prime Minister's Shram Vir Award was bagged by M. Sudhakar Reddy of TC/GT, for incorporating changes in manufacturing process, thus saving up to Rs.225 lakh.

Second Section

Enculturation: Rite-de-passage

As we noticed in societal culture where a community follows the rite-de-passage, it indicates ceremonies and rituals staring from birth, adolescence (sacred thread, ghotul, circumcision), adulthood including marriage, and of course death where a person's membership ceases for good. Similarly HEC also follows the *rite de passage,* which indicates admission or transition of membership of the employees from one level to another, leading to superannuation.

Entry and Induction

The company follows meticulous recruitment process primarily emphasizing advanced planning for manpower requirements. Recruitment to various posts is normally made at the induction level. The company's internal employees are considered for recruitment at posts, other than those at the entry level. In exceptional circumstances, however, and if candidates with suitable skill and experience are not available internally, recruitment to posts other than induction levels may be resorted to, with the prior approval of the corporate office. Recruitment to induction and other levels, approved by the competent authority, is normally made from the sources mentioned below:

- From employment exchanges as per the provisions of the Employment Exchanges (compulsory notification of vacancies) Act, 1959
- From open market through advertisement in the press
- By considering departmental candidates possessing the specified requirements
- From reputed engineering/management institutes through campus interviews.

Process of Recruitment

Unskilled, semiskilled, skilled and supervisory groups required to be filled by outside recruitment are notified to the appropriate employment exchange in the manner as provided in the relevant act from time to time. Simultaneously, an internal communication is also issued for the information of employees who may wish to be considered in the selection. Recruitment to the induction levels in the skilled and supervisory groups is from among the apprentices and trainee under the Apprentices Act.

Executives/Sr. Executives' cadre may be decided by the competent authority depending on the requirements of the post. Normally, an advertisement is issued in leading daily newspapers on pan India basis to tap the potential available in the open market. Simultaneously, a notification is sent to Directorate General of Employment and Training, Ministry of Labour, New Delhi, with a request to sponsor suitable candidates, if any registered on their roster. However, where the job is of a special nature which can be performed only by certain types of specialized personnel, the competent authority may decide to fill up the posts by persons on deputation from the central/state government and other public sector undertakings.

It is the endeavour of the company to help the government in achieving its objectives with respect to the upliftment of socioeconomic status of those belonging to weaker sections of the society. For this objective to be realized, the company does not spare any efforts to adhere to and follow the directives of the government concerning reservation of vacancies and concessions allowed to candidates belonging to scheduled caste/scheduled tribe, ex-servicemen, differently abled individuals, outstanding sportsmen and minority communities. All units/divisions are required to ensure fulfilment of requirements in this regard and send periodical returns to the corporate office as required.

Selection boards are constituted by the appointing authority/personnel heads to conduct tests/interviews and to select candidates for appointment to any posts in the company from among those called for such tests and interviews. For selection to posts falling within the purview of the unit management, unit selection boards are constituted as required, provided that in case of recruitment to executive post, a member of the central selection board is associated.

As explained by informants, company receives a huge number of applications for any post. From these applicants, the company selects the candidates with required skill and expertise. Thus, the company assembles quality-driven high-performing employees who are capable of bringing company into limelight.

Induction is a formal process and a structured programme. It inculcates knowledge about the company in totality, its structure and function, its technology and R&D system, and its strategy for growth. HEC organizes induction training programme for new recruits. The inauguration programme is conducted under the guidance of executive director and general managers. Duration of the training programme is one year, in which the new recruits are provided various trainings that help them to cope up with the company assignments. After one year of training, they are given permanent positions in the company.

Learning on the Job and Continuing Education

Continuous learning is given prime importance in the company. Company provides various training programmes for its employees to improve overall productivity level of the company. Important trainings programmes like advanced management programmes/strategic management programmes/ functional management programmes are provided for senior executives at all India level at the Human Research Development Institute (HRDI), Noida. With the help of Human Research Development Centre (HRDC), representatives of senior executives are also sent from Hyderabad unit to participate in the training programmes. It is useful for the company in enhancing the quality of work. Besides, various other programmes are also conducted at the unit level. Some of the important programme areas are as follows: (a) general manager programme; (b) moving ahead of performance (MAP)-based programmes for executives; (c) behavioural science; (d) health safety, environment and quality; (e) computers; (f) customer programmes; (g) other programmes like Hindi workshop/ Hindi Pragya/Hindi translation/HRD day/training coordinators meet/ special lectures and seminars on MAP programmes.

The above training programmes are scheduled in advance on an annual basis. The schedule thus formulated is circulated to all the concerned staff. This is aimed at providing good service to the company.

HEC's HRDI was set up in 1976 with the objective of developing HRD policies, integrating and co-coordinating HRD activities of various divisions and units, improving managerial effectiveness, nourishing a value system and establishing linkages for knowledge sharing. HRDI has so far conducted nearly 700 programmes covering nearly 16,000 senior executives. Notably, development of senior-level managers still remain the core activity of this institute. These programmes have contributed immensely in improving the effectiveness of the managerial cadre in HEC. This premier training institute has also played an important role in developing performance appraisal systems for board-level and below board-level senior positions for Navratna Public Sector Enterprises. With this assignment awarded by Indian Institute of foreign Trade, HEC's

HRDI is helping in providing a common platform for industries and academicians to share with each other their concern and improve their contribution in the area of management education.

Human Resource Development Institute (HRDI), the corporate training institute of the company in association with the Advanced Technical Education Centre (ATEC) in Hyderabad and the Human Resource Development Centre at the Units, is responsible for the total human resource development of the company. Furthermore, competency development assessment centre for senior executives is taken up by HRDI.

Health Safety and Environment Management

In its endeavour to become a world-class organization, HEC has committed itself to environmental causes giving due importance to growing global concern on issues related to environment, occupational health and safety. For fulfilling these obligations, various corporate policies have been formulated:

Environmental Policy

- The policy focuses on compliance with applicable environmental legislation/regulation.
- Continual improvement in environment management system to protect our natural environment and control pollution.
- Promotion of activities for conservation of resources by environmental management.
- Enhancement of environmental awareness among employees, customers and suppliers.
- HEC also assists and cooperates with concerned government agencies and regulatory bodies engaged in environmental activities, offering the company's capabilities in this field.
- Occupational health and safety policy: this policy emphasizes on:
  - Compliance with applicable legislation and regulation;
  - Setting objectives and targets to eliminate/control/minimize risks due to occupational and safety hazards;
  - Appropriate structured training of employees on occupational health and safety (OH&S) aspects;

- Formulation and maintenance of OH&S management programmes for continual improvement;
- Periodic review of OH&S management system to ensure its continuing suitably, adequacy and effectiveness;
- Communication of OH&S policy to all employees and interested parties;
- The major units of HEC have already earned international recognition by implementation of ISO 14001 Environmental Management System and OHSAS 18001 Occupational Health, Safety and Environmental Science.

Participation in the 'Global Compact' of the United Nations

The 'Global Compact' is a partnership between the United Nations, the business community, international labour and NGOs. It provides a forum for them to work together and improve corporate practices through co-operation rather than confrontation.

Organization has joined the 'Global Compact' of United Nations and has committed to support it and the share of core values enshrined in its nine principles:

1. Business should support and respect the protection of internationally proclaimed human rights and make sure they are not complicit in human rights abuses.
2. Business should uphold the freedom of association and the effective recognition of the right to collective bargaining.
3. The elimination of all forms of forced and compulsory labour.
4. The effective abolition of child labour.
5. Elimination of environment of discrimination.
6. Business should support a precautionary approach to environmental challenges.
7. Undertake initiatives to promote greater environmental responsibility and
8. Encourage the development and diffusion of environment-friendly technologies.

By joining the 'Global Compact', HEC is getting a unique opportunity of networking with corporate and sharing experience relating to social responsibility on global basis.

Performance Management System and Intra-organization Mobility

The company has an elaborate performance management system. Promotion of staff is applicable to all grades. Company follows yearly moving ahead to performance (MAP) system of performance appraisal for executive level staff since 2002. A performance cycle refers to the year for which individual performance is being evaluated. The performance cycle of MAP is one year coinciding with HEC's financial year. MAP follows an April–March cycle and consists of three key phases:

1. Performance and development planning: Development planning in MAP focuses on building individual capability using competencies. Competencies relevant to a role are predefined in its URR (Unique Role Responsibility) along with the desired proficiency level.

   Obtain appraiser's and reviewer's sign-off on performance development plan: At this stage, the appraisee discusses and finalizes the performance and development plan with the appraiser. Upon finalization, the appraiser would forward the performance and development plan to the reviewer for final sign-off.

   Editing the performance and development plan: Extraneous circumstances that significantly impact the performance and development plan of an appraisee may arise during the performance cycle. In such situation, the appraiser requires the reviewer's approval to edit the plan.
2. Midyear review: It is an interactive feedback session between the appraiser and appraisee, conducted during the month of October for the half-year ended September. It is a mid-cycle process for reviewing and tracking achievements thus reducing the scope for year-end surprises.
3. Final review: During the final phase, the appraiser will assess the appraisee's level of achievement on key result areas (KRAs), routine responsibilities and the demonstration of competencies. The final review is conducted in April. Performances of each KRA are given a rating as per the rating scale (1–5).

As informed by executives, this system provides transparency in the performance appraisal procedure. It helps in developing mutual understanding between these two persons. This system also aids in developing clarity regarding the roles and responsibilities of employees.

For other non-executives cadre, unit heads write assessment reports of subordinates to examine performance of the employees. Their performance assessment is done once a year. Assessment criteria are categorized into different parameters. The whole procedure of performance assessment is based on the parameters that reflect efficiency of the staff. This record is taken into consideration for giving promotion. A small tea party is organized at the unit level whenever an individual gets a promotion.

Retirement is the final stage, where the employment comes to an end. HEC provides several schemes and benefits for the retiring person. Apart from this, unit/department people give farewell party to the retired person. For organizing this function, they collect money from all the employees working in the same department. After the function, unit people send off the retiring person to his residence as a closing part of the function. This system is commonly practiced in all the groups.

Third Section

Structure and Stratification of the Organization

HEC organization structure is categorized into various grades, that is, SDGM, SM, M, senior engineer, production engineer, supervisors and workers. This classification is made on the basis of seniority, qualification, area of specialization and so on. Overall company assignments are carried out by various divisions like TC/GT, electrical, switchgear, HE/FAB, pumps, oil and pulverisers, spares management, central management, quality management, management services, executive director office, finance and accounting, HR, planning and development, hospital administration and so on. These divisions are headed by senior manager or DGM and assisted by other subordinates. There is clear hierarchy in grades of the employees, but hierarchy is not seen in their working behaviour. It is seen that employees perform their respected role in the company according to their position.

The organization functions according to the following timing; first shift starts at 6.45 am and ends at 3.15 pm; second starts at 3.45 pm and ends at 11.30 pm and third shift starts at 11.45 pm and ends at 7.00 am (this is only in the peak time; known as overtime through extra payment).

The employees who are working in the factory follow the above schedule. However, administrative staff have a different work timing, which starts from 8.30 am and ends at 4.30 pm in the evening, and it pertains only to administrative building staff. Generally, majority of the staff strictly follow the official timing set by the company, and they use automatic entry and exit system which is called 'Excess Control System', to determine the entry of unauthorized people inside the company. Security service of the company is taken care by CISF (Central Industrial Security Force). CISF personnel are posted in various entry points of the company so as to look after the safety of the company as well as staff. There is close scrutiny of the visitors by the security personnel at the main entry point. Nobody is permitted to go inside the company without prior permission from the concerned official. Visitors are issued temporary entry pass for meeting HEC officials. For the permanent and temporary employees, the company has issued 'Carmas system magnetic card' for entry and exit. Recording daily attendance of employees is made easier with this system. Moreover, it helps in controlling of staff who report late and move out from the company during unofficial hours. The main purpose of deploying CISF is to protect any kind of hazards in the HEC plant. This security force is known for its expert services provided to the Indian companies, and they are deputed to look after the government-undertaking buildings, companies, historical monuments and so on. As informed by the commandant officer, nowhere in the world is available this type of security organization except in India, and this is also owned by the Government of India. They are well-trained in various security activities.

Leadership and Decision-making

Decision-making is an important factor and has a strong impact on company's performance. Since it is a government-owned organization, HEC follows a centralized system of decision-making in terms of planning, budgeting, procurement and so on. All the planning is done at the top level and is then disseminated to the unit level. Executive director shoulders the responsibility of executing the company plan and implementing the same among the workforce. Besides, there are various committees to execute the overall functioning of the company. These committees take major responsibility in formulation and planning of the company. This is basically in tune with centralized system of functioning.

The company also gives freedom to individuals to take decisions pertaining to their day-to-day assignment. Head of every section or department or supervisor takes certain decisions on the work progress according to the needs of the company. Such decision-making process is quite common in the company, and nobody interferes in these matters. Every employee has the liberty to take certain decisions, provided it has a good impact on the company. The staff members in respective bays or sections formulate their regular work plans. Executive staff members look after the work progress of the bays and give direction to get positive results in stipulated time.

Customers are very happy about HEC products, especially the quality of service rendered by employees. Organization has enough potential to diversify into other products. As informed by managers, company is adopting advanced technologies of manufacturing. It continues to maintain its quality and aims at improving quality continuously. People are dedicated, ambitious and sincere towards their duties and responsibilities. Staff members are committed to overall development of the company.

After giving instructions related to company goals and targets for a year, work autonomy is provided to all the grades. To achieve targets, company keeps encouraging employees to create innovative ideas on carrying out certain assignments and provide more space to do experiments. As informed by majority of the employees, none of the employees has to work under stress. They work at their own will and interest. But nobody takes advantage of the freedom provided by the company. Majority of the employees have a strong sense of belonging towards the company. There was a case where a senior manager was reluctant to avail his leave for a long time in spite of his ill-health and even after availing it, he was duly concerned about the company assignment during his absence.

Employees have strong commitment towards their work, and especially senior employees carry out company-related assignment with dedication. It was also observed that the supervisors never asked staff to work who were sitting idle inside the bay. They automatically felt shy to sit alone for a long and immediately returned back to work. Such incidences were noticed more after the lunch break. It was noticed that people took small nap inside the bay and it so happened that a few people continued to sleep for long hours. In such cases, supervisors woke them up to engage in their respective assignments. Workers do not seek specific instructions from their superior while doing their day-to-day assignments. However, they do consult superior whenever they face problems in their work. Such work culture enhanced the commitment of the employees.

Communication and Information Sharing

Communication plays an important role in high-performing organizations like HEC. Formal mode of communication system followed in the HEC are noticeboards, which are put up in every section and building to disseminate formal information like holiday declaration, election notice, tender notice, slogan-writing competition, distribution of ID cards for employees, sports events, cultural programmes and so on. The company news is displayed regularly on the noticeboards. On the whole, communication system within HEC is very open. Employees learn what is happening in the company before receiving any formal communication.

This is because most of the employees prefer to have an informal mode of communication. Intercom facility is available to aid communication across far-placed units in the company. On the other hand, face-to-face interaction is more prevalent among the worker-level cadre. This system of interaction helps in creating a congenial environment and developing close relationships between employees. As informed by employees, all company or work-related information are shared and discussed openly. Work-related problems are discussed in groups, and sometimes additional help from higher authority is also sought if problem is not resolved at the lower level. Concerned authority gives serious thought to any problems related to company work as targets and goals are planned hand in hand. Problems are given immediate attention to avoid any hindrance to the assignment. The executive-level employees regularly inspect daily work done by other subordinates. They keep a constant check on their problems and work progress. Communication among workers and superiors are very open in nature.

Besides this, formal information is shared through noticeboard or e-mail. It provides common platform for information flow within the company, which can be shared by all the employees. Executive-level employees generally use e-mail as a formal and informal mode of communication within or outside the company, but it is not so in the case of shop-floor workers. Company regularly displays notices announcing important meetings and a welcome message on automatic electronics noticeboard is put up at the main entrance of the administration building.

In the case of TC/GT block, face-to-face interaction is commonly practiced among different grades of employees. One could notice the closeness and openness in relationships existing among employees irrespective of their positions and grades. They also communicate freely with employees from other bays whenever situation demands. It was noticed that there were lots of gossiping among the employees during community centre election. Employees gave great importance to the general secretary post because it gives them better status among the employees and provides some scope to make their own money as well. It can be considered as one of the main reasons for the high number of contestants in this election. At the same time, it was not the case with the International Club, for which the election was held simultaneously with community centre. All the committee members of the International Club were nominated through mutual consent without contesting election. It was quite interesting to see lobbying among the staff for community centre election.

As a whole, communication system prevalent in the organization is not well-equipped with high technology. In spite of this, information flow is very fast because of the close and informal relationships among employees across functions. Nobody is left out from knowing important information. Informal interaction among staff is quite common which instils a sense of unity and encourages group work.

The work groups are properly coordinated. There are several modes of sharing information in the HEC, such as sharing of policy/planning information through written information and sharing information through meetings and verbal interaction in and outside the company. A good amount of information sharing can be observed among the shop-floor workers regarding their regular procedure. As informed by staff, it is easy for any staff to take up the same assignment in the absence of another person. Exchange of shift is also part of sharing information on their work progress, and it is done on regular basis. It enables the second-shift staff to understand the whole progress made by the first-shift staff.

Group leaders also keep sharing their experience with other groups and help each other to handle their routine jobs better. Executives are responsible for goal-setting and allocation of resources required to meet targets. However, regular monitoring of work is done by subordinates and superiors. Supervisory staff members play mediators between artisans and executives and provide full-fledged supervision to artisans. There is regular exchange of information among these three groups. As a result, staff members are very clear about their targets and timings for taking up any assignment. Such incidents are seen in all the bays of TC/GT. They exchange their work plans and ideas on a regular basis.

Openness and Cohesive Work Group

One special feature of the company is its open work culture in the plant. Company information is put up on the website. It provides company profile and other related information which are regularly updated. Besides, there is always free interaction among the employees irrespective of grades. Lower-level staff members find it very comfortable to interact or share their ideas with superiors.

More open discussion is witnessed in canteen during lunch break. The shop-floor staff members are more open than other staff, and everyone has a caring attitude towards the new person who enters into the factory. It is common to see staff seeking clarification from notice or letter put up in the notice board. It is noticed that whenever executive staff goes around the bay for monitoring their work, they casually come forward and interact with executives and discuss their problems openly. Their interaction is more informal, but some issues they do discuss very seriously.

In some cases, subordinates call executives by nickname. All the company-related documents are put up on the company website to give a clear picture of the company profile to the outsiders. This reflects an open culture that prevails in the company. Through this, people are able to understand various manufacturing works carried out by the company. Cracking jokes is common among the employees. Though organization chart reflects a hierarchical system, regular work is not hindered by this hierarchy as there are high levels of interaction among different levels. For work-related issues, executives personally go to shop floor for in-depth discussion with their subordinates. Lower-level staff members are also involved in problem-solving. As informed by many employees, they have been working in the company for more than 10 years. Their long association with the company has resulted in developing close relationships between employees irrespective of their position in the hierarchy.

High-performing companies like HEC exhibit cooperation among employees at all levels. As informed by employees, work progress of the company is never affected by the absence of an individual. It is common to see staff coming in groups to help other colleagues whenever any problems occur in the machine or in company-related work. There was a case where one employee who suffered from paralysis was fully supported by colleagues in carrying out his assignment. They always worked hard to reach early to meet the target put up by the company without compromising on the quality of product. According to informants, there are four quarters of work phase in a year in which one quarter consists of three months. They set well-defined targets for each quarter. The workers exhibited remarkable commitment towards organizational goals. Workers are also offered incentives for any overtime work they put in for the achievement of targets.

It can be seen from the annual reports of the company that it has been consistently performing well in terms of productivity. Overall work environment in the company is well organized and employees are very friendly. Generally, employees are jovial while interacting with other colleagues. This is the specialty one can notice in the HEC organization. The employees balanced their professional and personnel relationships well. Whenever there were differences between two team members, other team members and supervisors intervened to sort it out. Employees are overzealous in showing their loyalty and pride towards the company. At the end of the shift, workers board the company bus to go back home and during their travel one can often hear them talking about what they achieved during the day and how well HEC is regarded in the country. They all introduced themselves as belonging to HEC; working in HEC enhanced their self-esteem. Apart from company work, they do discuss other family-related matters as well during leisure hours.

Team work is an asset to this company. A strong culture of team work inculcated in the company has helped them exhibit excellent performance and thus come into limelight. The constant growth of the company can be attributed to its team work culture. The company requires mutual support and coordination among various sections/departments for proper functioning. Without proper cooperation from all sections, it is difficult to manufacture or produce any instruments. For instance, for making a gas turbine, it requires service from different departments like engineering, management, finance and artisans. It is desirable to have proper coordination of work among these groups to get the required result. Company is performing well since inception because of the strong team work culture that prevails in the organization.

Organization gives prime importance to team or group work rather than individual since it is not possible to see successful result by one individual. As a result, congenial work culture is inculcated in the company which can motivate employees to produce quality output. In order to strengthen team work, there are regular interactions between different grades of employees and they discuss on various company assignments. For instance, executive staff concentrates more on setting the target and framing goals, monitoring work and utilization of resources. Whereas supervisors take care of reaching the goals and target set by the company with the help of artisans. They do take care of supervisory work as well as mediating between artisans and executive people. On the other hand, artisans also put in a lot of hard work in the process of manufacturing.

From the above description, it is clear that employees of all grades have to perform certain roles to achieve the target. Finally, it is the contribution of groups and teams rather than individuals alone that helps in enhancing overall company performance.

Power Distance

This is one of the focal areas of study and research into an organization. Superior and subordinate relationships reflect a lot about work environment prevailing in the organization. In HEC, the relationship between superiors and subordinates looks very informal and casual. During field work, it is quite common to see these two categories of employees moving closely inside the *bay* of the company. Sometimes, they also crack jokes with each other. Moreover, subordinates can walk into superior's room without giving any prior notice. It is frequently seen that subordinates often have the freedom of working inside the superior's room in his absence. Generally, executives do not stay in their respective rooms all the time since they move from one place to another. In their absence, rooms are kept open and other subordinates are allowed to access it when required. Subordinates used computer facilities available in executives' room.

It is also noticed that there is no formal respect shown by subordinate whenever they pass by or enter into the work place. In one incident, *SGM asked his subordinate to organize meeting for executives; subordinate replied, 'Sir, you take initiative since you are the right person to do the job according to the grade'; then SGM replied, 'this chair is just like musical chair because any person can come and occupy. Perhaps, you may be the one. It should keep changing from time to time so that I can move ahead for better position.'* Their interaction was very casual and cordial. This is more applicable in the factory areas, whereas such relationships are not so in the other departments or sections. It varies from one individual to another.

On the whole, they maintain a very cordial relationship, and mutual understanding among staff is also visible at the work place. *For example, one staff in TC/GT was drinking water from the same bottle that was used by DGM.* Such activities are noticed quite often inside the bay. Besides, they maintain close informal relationships outside the company as well. As informed by an insider, there is always regular exchange of invitation among superiors and subordinates for social gathering like marriage/ birthday and other occasions. Meeting in such gatherings brings them more closer to each other and it also expands their family bond relations with other off springs. As mentioned in the HEC report, there is monthly forum, which gives an opportunity for the executives and subordinates to interact on various issues. This helps in creating a congenial work atmosphere for employees.

Dealing with Uncertainty

Degree of uncertainty is not that high since the nature of work in company looks more static. Most of the groups and sections are set to follow similar kind of work throughout the year. But the employees are well prepared to deal with all eventualities. Sometimes they faced uncertainty in meeting deadlines. Such cases were dealt effectively.

Fourth Section

HEC and Society

HEC's contributions towards corporate social responsibility till date includes adoption of villages, free medical camps/charitable dispensaries, schools for the underprivileged and differently abled children, campaigning and promoting ban on child labour, disaster/natural calamity aid, employment for differently abled, widow resettlement, employment for ex-servicemen, irrigation using treated sewage, pollution-checking camps, plantation of millions of trees, energy conservation and conservation of natural resources through environmental management.

To express their solidarity with the flood victims and for rendering relief, employees of HEC have contributed one-day's salary amounting to a total of Rs.22.5 million to the Prime Minister's National Relief Fund. A cheque to this effect was handed over to the Prime Minister, Dr Manmohan Singh, by the Union Minister for Heavy Industries and Public Enterprises, Mr. Santosh Mohan Dev. HEC has also contributed a sum of Rs.60 lakh to the Chief Minister's Relief Fund as its contribution towards mitigating the suffering of flood victims in the state of Assam. HEC and its employees have always risen to the occasion and contributed generously for rendering relief to victims affected by natural calamities like the earthquake in Gujarat, the super cyclone in Orissa and the drought in Gujarat and Rajasthan, besides the Kargil war.

Reaching out to the distressed victims in the tsunami-affected states of Tamil Nadu, Andhra Pradesh, Kerala, Andaman and Nicobar Islands, employees of HEC have made a humble contribution of Rs.1 crore to the Prime Minister's National Relief Fund. HEC's manufacturing plant at Trichy, which is closest to the affected areas, swung into action by the morning of 27 December 2004 and handed over relief material including clothing and medicines to the district authorities by the afternoon of the same day.

Trucks went around HEC townships to collect relief materials from HEC employees and their families. The contributions included medicines, more than 20,000 packets of hygienically prepared food, 70,000 pieces of clothing, 1,500 kilograms of rice which were distributed among the victims. Similarly, HEC from other stations, for example, Chennai, also swung into action and have organized relief measures in coordination with local authorities.

Over the years, HEC has proved its capability as a leading supplier of gas turbines, steam turbine generators and boilers for captive thermal co-generation and combined cycle power projects for mining, metallurgical and various other industries like refineries, chemicals, fertilizers, petrochemicals, besides establishing itself as a supplier of gas turbine generators to utilities in India and the overseas market. As on date, HEC has executed contracts for over 500 steam turbines/gas turbine-based power plants in India and in abroad.

They share their growing concerns on issues related to Environment and Occupational Health and Safety (OHS) and is committed to protecting environment in and around their establishment and to providing safe and healthy environment to all their employees. For fulfilling these obligations, a Health, Safety and Environmental Policy has been formulated and implemented through management systems.

Under UNDP programme for specialized services in the area of Environment, HEC has set up a Pollution Control Research Institute (PCRI). They also have a Model Centre for Occupational Health Services at Trichy, which is a pioneer in this field in India. Today, it offers a wide range of occupational healthcare as well as expertise in work environment monitoring, toxicology, ergonomics and in organization of OHS to a multitude of industries for different sectors in India. Few ILO-sponsored candidates from African countries have undergone training at this model centre.

HEC is a member of CoRE (Corporate Roundtable on Development of Strategies for Environment) launched by The Energy Research Institute (TERI). CoRE is envisaged as a means to facilitate a proactive and catalytic role for industry in addressing the environmental problems plaguing India and helping the industry towards sustainability paradigm. CoRE is now a partner organization to the WBCSD (World Business Council for Sustainable Development). It has signed a memorandum of understanding with WBCSD, now called as CoRE-BCSD, India. Interfaces between companies such as HEC, TERI and the WBCSD provide an important link to address issues of sustainable development at the global level and to learn and exchange experience of the participating companies.

HEC's commitment to environmental issues can be seen as an integral part of its core business. In the field of nonconventional and renewable energy, HEC has successfully launched products like wind electric generators, solar heating systems, solar photovoltaic systems, solar lanterns and battery-powered road vehicles. Technology upgradation has been done to minimize environmental impact of fossil energy products, by way of low-NOx oil/gas burners, circulating fluidized bed combustion boilers and so on.

Occupational safety and health are basically associated with management functions like quality and production. It focuses on active participation from all employees and their families, with the aim of minimizing deterioration and eliminating loss of precious resources of men, machines and materials while ensuring process and product safety too.

HEC takes initiatives in pollution control, storage of hazardous chemicals, proper waste disposals and so on.

Celebrations

HEC celebrates National Safety Day on 4th March every year and distributes safety gifts and manuals to all the employees. As reported by safety staff, more contract workers are prone to accidents, as they are not well-acquainted with the regular working style of the company. Hence, company facilitates safety training programme for contract workers in order to avoid accidents.

International Club: This club is meant for providing recreation to executive-level employees in the company. There are a total 800 executives in this club. The club organizes various kinds of activities like cultural programmes and sports events as well as literary meets. This club provides library facility for its members who can borrow books for personal development and enrichment of knowledge. This club also organizes movie shows every weekend. Every member of the centre contributes Rs.50 per month as membership fee which is utilized for organizing a variety of programmes. Besides this, company sanctions an annual special grant of Rs.1 or 2 lakh for the functioning of this club.

Community Centre: This centre is set up for nonexecutive-level staff within the company and it has a total of 3,992 members. Each member pays Rs.5 per month as membership fee which comes to around Rs.20000 in total. The centre also gets sanction of the equivalent amount from management as grant. It is collected and sanctioned on a monthly basis. Centre is run by an elected body. The body consists of one general secretary and a secretary each for sports, cultural events, literary events and five executive members.

The whole team is headed by a general manager who acts as the president of the community centre. Committee appoints one treasurer and accountant to look after the centre's financial activities. They are appointed as a permanent cadre staff especially to look after the centre's activities. Tenure of the elected body is for two years. During field work we witnessed that election was held and many employees contested in the election. Community centre is considered to be one of the largest groups, which organizes several programmes and activities. Main activities organized by the club are national programmes like Republic Day, Independence Day, Gandhi Jayanti and so on. During these occasions, they organize marches by school children, CISF staff and so on. The centre also conducts drawing competition, essay competition for children and games like throw ball for lady employees on that occasion.

Executive director is the chief guest at the function. After the march past, ED distributes cash prizes to the meritorious sports men and workers. Many games are organized for children and spectators. In the evening, various cultural programmes are also organized. There is a huge crowd comprising from employees from all sections and their family members participates attend the events.

Apart from this, community centre conducts religious functions or programmes like Ugadi, Krishna Janmashtami, Ramadan and Christmas in a grand manner. Moreover, members also conduct state-wise drama competition. It is a 10-day programme and generally held between May 2 and May 10 every year. Participants are drawn from all over the country and competition is confined only to Telugu-speaking people. Company provides major portion of the fund for organizing drama competition. As noted by members, almost 20 teams take part in the competition every year, and each participant is given Rs.3,000 as preparation expenditure along with memento.

On every Saturday evening, small programmes like orchestra, dance programme and movies are arranged. In the month of October and November, interdepartmental drama competition is organized among the employees. All the activities are organized with lots of enthusiasm.

Apart from other cultural programmes, an inter-unit sports meet is also organized between August and November every year. Around 12 games are played between different units. Company also participated in state-level league tournaments in sports events like cricket, football and hockey. While the community centre committee is headed by the general secretary, supporting staff takes care of organizing these activities.

8

Summary and Conclusions

Preceding chapters have clearly described the trends of management culture in the four organizations discussed in detail. There appears to be enough similarities between the four organizations, but at the same time dissimilarities do exist over certain aspects which give separate identity to each organization apart from their good performance and track record. The present chapter summarizes the various findings made about the four organizations and conclusions that are drawn for further research.

To begin with, Scientific Organization is India's foremost research lab and has championed biotechnology revolution in the country and demonstrated application of biology in various fields such as pharmaceuticals, agriculture and security. Its research contribution is globally recognized.

Seacom Pvt. Ltd is one of the largest Indian companies in the IT sector providing software solutions worldwide. It has operations in nearly 45 countries across 6 continents and provides customized solutions to some of the largest corporations in the world.

HEC is again the largest electrical engineering and manufacturing enterprise in India. Besides registering consistent growth during the last decade, it is known for its innovations in energy and infrastructure sector. It is a multi-location corporation competing effectively with majors such as ABB and Siemens.

Telcom, originally an Indian company in the field of refrigerators and allied products, was taken over by the global industry leader, the Telcom Product Limited 10 years ago. It operates from 30 different locations and has presence in all major countries like United States, Brazil, Canada, France, Italy and India among others. It has consistently improved upon its own performance.

Since these high-performing organizations are engaged in different works like manufacturing, software and scientific research, it is obvious to notice differences in working hours and nature of work. For instance, Seacom starts in the morning and closes past midnight, scientific organization researcher's work based on work demands and aren't following any specific work hours. HEC is a two-shift company; work commences at 8 am and closes around midnight; it sometimes operates right through the night when deadlines have to be met. Telcom, unlike the other three organizations, operates between 8 am and 12 midnight covering only two shifts.

Cultural Contours: Analysis

The study first attempted to understand how these organizations enculturate new members. Enculturation is the process by which one acquires membership and psychological ownership of the organization, one becomes part of. It's mostly informal where members learn the culturally accepted behaviour through observation, imitation and mentoring. In all the four companies studied, it was discovered that all the new entrants learnt the cultural ropes by observing the behaviour of those who were already in the organization. While the organization manual had given broad indications about what they expected from an employee, they soon discovered that desirable and acceptable behaviour in the organization was best understood by observing the successful predecessor. In HEC and Telcom, reaching office on time was valued. In Scientific Organization and Seacom it was not so. The scientists and software engineers operated on a flexi schedule; however, most came before time and left after the office hours. There were very few truants in any of the four companies. All the members accepted the norms, if not excelled in it.

Likewise, most of the newcomers discover early in the career that in Seacom everyone was addressed by the first name, and the same was followed in Telcom. But in HEC and Scientific Organization, everyone was addressed by his first name only by peers and superiors. Superiors were addressed differently. Keeping their desk clean, spic and span, was expected by all employees of Telcom, HEC and Seacom. However, this was not so in Scientific Organization. Some scientists' desks were clean and well organized; others were not so and that was also accepted. Scientific Organization recognized individual differences and idiosyncrasies of some scientists.

Nevertheless, all these organizations had published documents on their corporate values, that is, ideal and desired behaviour expected by the employees of the company. Only some of these were observable in behaviour. Time was valued in HEC, and everyone trooped on time. The value of time was best noticed when the employees worked overtime to meet the deadline and their commitment to the customer. Likewise, working in a team, cooperation and collaboration were a desired behaviour practiced widely. Whenever there were differences between two team members, other members of the team and supervisors intervened to sort it out. The HEC employees were overenthusiastic in showing their loyalty and pride for the company. While employees travel in company bus after their shift, one often heard employees talking about what they achieved during the day and how well HEC was regarded in the country. They all introduced themselves as belonging to HEC; working in HEC enhanced their self-esteem.

In Telcom one could observe employees, right from the shop floor to the administrative offices, exhibiting high concern for customers. The only thing they knew from their superiors through announcements on the boards and newsletters and so on that they existed because of the customers. Their salary was actually paid by the customers. This was drilled in day in and day out, nonverbally, as well as verbally. And they all worked towards meeting their customers' expectations.

In its brochure, Seacom stated that its employees must uphold the values such as belief in people, pursuit for excellence, entrepreneurship and customer orientation.

Even though, Seacom employees work for clients who insist on strict secrecy, one can see that those working on a project were always willing and open to share ideas and assist in finding solutions. Trust was the mutual parameter on basis of which they operated together to achieve milestones in the project and also in the verticals to which they belonged. Meeting customer expectation was uniformly accepted across the organization; in fact, employees worked on projects dealing with a particular customer at a particular point of time. They remained focused on meeting customer expectation.

In Scientific Organization also one could see that scientists valued understanding among the scientific community as well as valued achievement, new discovery or innovation which made valuable contribution to the field they were researching in. Colleagueship was also valued, and members of every lab operated as members of an egalitarian family extending help whenever required. They were also generous in sharing knowledge and were equally open to sharing results particularly about instruments and ingredients for running experiments.

While there was no formal coaching of values in either of these organizations, employees acquired them through their observation of behaviour of elders and colleagues, superiors and subordinates in the organization. There was one value that was shared across these organizations, that is, value of entrepreneurship and excellence. They must achieve something more than what they have done in the past or what others have done elsewhere. This they believed kept them going.

Rite de passage

Organization culture also follows the *rite de passage* which indicates admission or transition of membership of the employees from one level to another, leading to superannuation. In societal culture *rite de passage* is concentrated with birth, adolescence (sacred thread, ghotul, and circumcision), and adulthood, including marriage, and of course death, where individual's membership ceases for good.

Likewise, in a corporate culture a member passes through various stages of work-life such as entry and induction, training and development, performance evaluation and promotions from one level to the other, and separation or retirement. While the rites and rituals vary from one organization to another, there is one shared custom of celebration, which marks transition from one level of membership to another in the organization. While in Scientific Organization and Seacom celebration is often marked by distribution of sweets to colleagues in the work group or division and shower of good will and greetings by all of them, in HEC and Telcom there is a formal assembly of colleagues to celebrate the occasion.

Entry and Induction

In all the four organizations, the members (with few exceptions) are recruited at the entry level; software engineer in Seacom, graduate engineer in HEC and Telcom, and junior scientist in Scientific Organization.

Recruitment is a rigorous process. Both HEC and Scientific Organization are public sector organizations and announce job openings through ads in Employment News and national newspapers; Seacom and Telcom also advertise but they prefer campus recruitment.

Recruitment is done in several stages. Vetting the vitae, group interview, personal interview and sometimes meeting with the heads of divisions where they would be placed. At every stage, there is filtering and only those who meet the profile are presented to the heads. The emphasis towards the final round is to ensure the cultural fit, interpersonal adaptability and attitude towards team work. There were several examples where candidates were rejected in the final stage because their fitness to the organization culture or inconsistency in their behaviour and attitude came into question and made them unsuitable for the organization.

All the four organizations consider induction phase important for grooming of employees for a long and successful career. While there are variations in the process of induction, its basic purpose is to facilitate employees to understand the organization and its challenges and acquire a sense of belongingness to it.

In Scientific Organization induction is through participation in research activities, attendance in meetings and seminars, and discussions with the senior scientists. It is informal. Those who enter the organization come from similar work environment, from academic institution to research organization.

However, in Seacom, HEC and Telcom, induction is a formal process though the durations vary. In Seacom, induction programmes are organized by Seacom's Learning Centre followed by a shorter programme organized by the unit to which new employees are posted. While the former enables the young associates to understand the characteristics of the company, the latter inducts them into the business model of the vertical and horizontal they get attached to.

The Seacom's Learning Centre whose ELTP programme runs into several weeks not only enable associates learn about Seacom's vision and values, work systems, performance management and development plans but also the nitty-gritties of the organization. It enables smooth co-option of new associates into the Seacom's system; ASSET, a soft skill programme is tailor-made for associates of a particular vertical. There are also unit induction programmes where associates learn about a particular unit.

Telcom organizes induction programme only when it inducts a large number of graduate trainees. It relies on brief training and long mentoring, which equips a fresher to become a part of the organization. HEC has a very structured induction programme. It inculcates knowledge about the company in totality, its structure and function, its technology and R&D system, and its strategy for growth. In all the four companies there is a system by which every executive is evaluated; towards the end of induction programme, a prognosis of his future in the company is recorded on his personal dossier.

Learning on the Job and Continuing Education

While learning on the job is emphasized in all the four organizations, be it research or IT or manufacturing, it is supplemented by ongoing education programmes for its employees. The nature of ongoing education is dependent on the desired outcome of the performance appraisal where an employee's strength, weaknesses and improvement areas are highlighted.

In HEC, the executive who moves from one level to another has to undergo training programmes on supervisory, middle management, general management, advanced management, strategic management and even functional area programmes, designed to equip him or her to accomplish higher responsibilities. Likewise, some are nominated for behavioural programmes and others on health and safety, environment, quality, computers and customer-oriented programmes.

Seacom organizes programmes in technical areas, management areas, software skills, domain training, project management, team effectiveness and change management. The project leaders are trained on negotiation skills; senior managers are trained on strategic management, business leadership and performance management systems. Every employee charts his or her own career path; once vetted by the reviewing officer, it is implemented by the human resource management group. For the top management, Seacom organizes a retreat, a learning workshop where all general managers, presidents and CEOs sit together and discuss industry's future and operating strategies for the company. Sometimes a leading global consultant is also invited to the retreat. The corporate division is then charged with the task of implementation.

In Scientific Organization, development opportunities are provided to scientists through participation in seminars and conferences related to their field of research. All scientists who have done significant work on a project and need to sound their findings with professional colleagues in other parts of the world are encouraged to do so. Sometimes scientists are sent on deputation to the labs abroad. Scientific Organization also has visiting senior scientists from abroad who spend several weeks with a particular research lab.

Telcom does not have its own learning centre, but it nominates their executives to external training programmes which may enhance their skills and competency. The senior executives are often sent to plants in other countries, to learn new work practices to be implemented in-house on their return.

Performance Management System and Intra-organization Mobility

All the four companies in the study have elaborate performance management systems. An executive is expected to set his or her own annual goals and objectives and his project manager is required to approve it. Towards the end of the year, the executive measures his or her achievements against the set objectives, which is then reviewed by his or her superiors and feedback is shared with the executive.

It is interesting to note that in Seacom almost all objectives set are measurable; in Telcom and HEC nearly 75% of objectives are measurable and in Scientific Organization the process milestones achieved are the only indicators of performance. Perhaps in scientific labs, it has not been possible to establish measurable parameters of performance. Yet in all these companies there is an annual performance review countersigned by the Reviewing Officer. This record constitutes as an important input towards development and promotion decisions related to the employee.

Scientific Organization, Seacom and Telcom are structurally flat organizations. There aren't many levels of hierarchy and avenues for promotion; therefore, they have an elaborate system of review, reward and recognition on the job. Every employee or group achieving excellent performance is generously recognized, sometime financially also rewarded.

But, financial reward is a rare event in all the four organizations. HEC has several layers of hierarchy and high performers do get promoted at least once in five years. While graduating from team leader to project leader is an important event in Seacom, in Scientific Organization a scientist is up for promotion review every five years; promotion to higher level is a big event in Telcom and HEC. All these call for a big celebration which is a must, howsoever big or small scale it may be.

The superannuation of an employee in the organization is an important event in all the four organizations. Here, the members of the group or division pool their contributions and organize a function. Scientific Organization arranges a grand farewell party for retiring scientists where the director is always present, so is the case of Telcom. However, in HEC it is a divisional and departmental affair. In Seacom, there aren't many examples of superannuation till date. In Telcom, retired employees are engaged to work in the company as long as they are physically fit.

Communication and Information Sharing

Communication is the life line of an organization, so is the availability of relevant information. In all the four organizations studied, there is open communication and information sharing. Withholding information and communication is seen as sacrilege. Although each company has its own mode of communication and information exchange, Seacom operates on intranet for internal mail. This is an organization-wide platform across all locations in six continents. In Telcom, noticeboards disseminate information. These are located in all the nooks and corners of the company premises. Employees are free to respond; HR coordinates the exchange. In Scientific Organization, CCTVs are located across the campus. In HEC too there are noticeboards, but they often use fail-safe informal channels of communication. The employees learn what is happening in the company much faster than it takes for formal communication to disseminate information. In the other three organizations, communication is instantaneous with little room for informal grapewine.

CCTVs at Scientific Organization flash throughout the day information regarding research projects, seminars, canteen administrative facilities and birthday greetings; news related to important research projects are also flashed. Appreciations for publication achievements, promotion and superannuation are also conveyed through CCTV. In Seacom, intranet is a state-of-art technology where information is not only shared but also sourced. It is the platform for knowledge management; in order to avoid information overload there are points of contact and dissemination in every circle or verticals. Information relevant to the employees are frequently updated and communicated on the intranet.

Information of interest to all associates in a given location is routed differently. Information about awards won by the company is shared on the intranet platform. Depending on the nature of information, dissemination and the recipient audience, group mail IDs have been created by Seacom. In Telcom, quarterly newsletter from CEO is sent to all the employees which keeps them informed about the progress of the company and the future plans. In addition, there are monthly and quarterly meetings which act as forum for sharing information, discussion and decision.

Besides formal channels of communication, there are also informal channels in all the four organizations. During tea/lunch breaks, small groups meet and exchange information; they make fun and enjoy discussions about achievements as well as faux pas. Informal communication is functional in the company. It releases tension and creates bonhomie and belongingness. It is also true that the people with shared interests converge; birds of the same feather flock together.

Informal exchange at group and project level strengthens belongingness to the organization. In scientific organization, any new scientific research is always shared and every scientist knows the area of research that colleagues are engaged in. In HEC sharing of information during the change of shift is critical. It is structured; it enables the new shift employees to understand the work completed by the first shift and the tasks ahead in the next.

Open and Cohesive Work Group

Information sharing, knowledge sharing and open culture are accepted norms and valued in all the four organizations, so are employees' cooperation and collaboration in their work groups; Telcom and HEC has shop-floor work groups engaged in special tasks. These groups are cohesive where members support each other. Cooperation to achieve their group goals is assured; also there is assurance for support to other groups which need their assistance from time to time.

In Scientific Organization, this is clearly visible when one research group needs assistance from another. This is also seen in Telcom and HEC where operation and maintenance groups have to work hand in hand. It has been observed that a group's work is never affected because of the absence of one of its members; other colleagues willingly carry extra work load. Employees openly seek help from each other while performing their job and seniors or superiors often help juniors and subordinates.

This is reciprocal in nature. One example is from HEC where a member suffered partial paralysis. In order that he does not lose his pay, the colleagues helped in carrying out his assignment in rotation. This was also observed in Telcom where colleagues came to each other's help in solving technical problems experienced on a shop floor. In Scientific Organization there are examples of group leaders working on joint research projects, where two groups are required to collaborate for speedy results. Scientific Organization's record shows that most of these joint projects deliver successful results. One can observe cooperative culture outside the lab too. A colleague who was injured in an accident was looked after by colleagues in rotation in the hospital, until he recovered fully.

Cooperation does not mean absence of differences. There are examples where differences were openly argued and sorted out. In Telcom and HEC differences on shop floor is a regular phenomenon but they are always resolved with mutual discussion to the satisfaction of both parties. If differences could not be resolved at the peer level, the superior intervened and sorted it out. Institutional mechanism is in place to promote cooperative behaviour.

Power Distance

Hofstede (1991) pointed out that the national culture of India reflects high power distance. There is unequal relationship between superiors and subordinates and this inequality is an accepted behaviour. However, in these four organizations this is not true; each of them has low power distance.

Participant observation has shown that all the four organizations nurture good working relationships between superiors and subordinates. The superior, a formal head, may be the boss but behaviourally he operates as a colleague. In HEC, superior–subordinate relationship is informal. They mingle freely. Subordinates do not require special permission for reaching and speaking to their superiors. All executives are accessible at all time. They share common dining table, use boss's office for discussion and have the freedom to reallocate work to achieve timely results. This contributes to the quality of work-life and reinforces trustworthy relationship.

Telcom is a multinational company with an Indian origin, and the interaction between superiors and subordinates is informal in nature. They call each other by first name. Bosses do not mind walking up to the subordinates in case they need to discuss something. The performance appraisal system is not confidential; everybody knows where they stand. They can seek information from their superiors about their group, about themselves and the organization with ease. In Telcom, feedback on individual's work progress and his or her future plans is regularly given. This actually leads to enhanced understanding and cooperation. It has also brought in an atmosphere of openness among the staff and enabled employees to converge their energies on meeting the business goals. In Telecom, the employee's involvement and commitment to work are equally high. The culture of mutual discussion among employees and superiors, vendors and customers has also empowered people to deliver high performance.

In Seacom, project leader, team leader or divisional leader are accountable for performance, but they work with their team as peers. The whole work group celebrates success together. Sometimes they go for picnic along with their family members and meet socially on birthdays. However, there are occasions when all the project leaders across the division sit together to deal with common problems. Since project leadership keeps on rotating and such meetings broaden their horizon and enables project leader to take charge and improve performance. Seacom bosses also walk up to subordinates when they need inputs. Every employee collects his tea from a common pot and buses their trays in the canteen cup, and even superiors do not allow someone else to do his errand. Nobody is subordinate. This attitude has created a peer culture in Seacom. An employee is accountable to him or herself, to his or her work, to his or her responsibilities; however, there is a collective work culture over which power distance has no bearing at all.

In Scientific Organization it goes a little further; nobody displays his or her designation on the door or status with how they behave; there is a strong value for expertise and knowledge and this can come from any scientist, senior or junior. Sometimes senior scientists do not allow juniors to pay for tea in the cafeteria but it does not reflect hierarchical attitude. It shows concern and care for young colleagues. A great example of team work in Scientific Organization is the authorship of publications. All the Scientific Organization publications carry joint names, sometimes of all the members of the team who have worked on the project. The project leader does not take the credit but shares it with everyone. This is part of the Scientific Organization culture.

Likewise in Telcom and HEC, one notices team culture even beyond work groups. For producing gas turbine or compressor it requires support from different groups, like engineering, maintenance and finance. And the support is always available both in Telcom and HEC. Sharing of work is the credo in these companies, and cooperative work culture promotes high performance.

Regular interface and interaction between interdependent work groups ensure cooperation. In HEC and Telcom executives concentrate on setting targets and goals, monitoring work, providing resources and supporting the employees on the shop floor to accomplish goals. They mediate between the workers and the supervisors when required. And the employees carry out the tasks as per manufacturing plans. Each employee has a role which is interdependent on other roles. It's the contribution from one person to the other that ensures performance. In Seacom external support is seldom required; every work group is self-sufficient in completing the task assigned, but in Scientific Organization support from the staff in and outside the lab is very critical for success. The support is always available; it does not require any intervention from superiors.

Leadership and Decision-making

All the four companies operate with assigned leaders who are the official role-holders in the team or in the project. All these leaders work in consultation with the leadership team. More often than not, they use consultative style of decision-making. Every team is autonomous but it operates in different forms. In HEC, members of the team, once they agree on the goals, have all the freedom to achieve results. This autonomy enhances the commitment of the employees. They work more sincerely for achievement of results. There are no examples where a team misused the freedom earned by them.

The leadership style in Telcom is also consultative. Every member has the freedom to express his or her opinion; once discussed openly they arrive at a consensus; if not, the leader can convey the decision based on points and counterpoints raised in consultation. This approach gives freedom to the employees to try out new approaches and help them to learn different ways of improving performance. They greatly appreciate the freedom to try out new methods of doing work. Here mistakes are treated as lessons to be learnt and not to be repeated. Thus, performance keeps improving.

In Scientific Organization, though the team leaders have more expertise and experience than others they always consult the young scientists. They report that these consultations have improved their judgment. All scientists enjoy autonomy; everybody works based on his or her work priorities and timelines and follow a flexible work schedule. Working hours are set by themselves, which are known to others also. As indicated by the Scientific Organization scientists, research requires freedom of thought and experimental work culture in order to generate high-quality performance. Since creativity is a must for research lab, autonomy is must for a research scientist. Scientific organization provides autonomy to the scientific community but makes them accountable. In several laboratories, scientists decide on their own timings, without any constraint from group leaders. They work during day or night and take decisions as to how to conduct their experiments. This culture of empowerment, they believe, has contributed towards high performance of scientific organization.

Dealing with Uncertainty

Our earlier survey had shown that Indian organizations are characterized by high uncertainty avoidance. This however was not true for the four organizations studied. In Scientific Organization work is full of uncertainties. In Seacom, every project is a different project; every assignment calls for different rules of the game; every customer is a different customer and has to be dealt with differently.

Everyone has to deal with uncertainty. For Telcom and HEC, the degree of uncertainty is not that high, yet the employees are prepared to deal with all eventualities. There were several occasions when they faced uncertainty in their projects. One related to the deadline in HEC and the other related to employee welfare in Telcom. Both these issues were dealt with effectively. It was obvious that employees in all the four organizations had high achievement orientation. Ambiguity and uncertainty did not matter. There was no case where an employee wanted to achieve his objectives at the cost of other colleagues. There were no examples of undercutting. They all followed win-win strategy.

Conclusion of the Study

The study brings out three cultural characteristics which distinguish high-performing organizations.

- Competence-based membership, the hallmark of Scientific Organization, Seacom, HEC and Telcom.
- Commitment to time, task, objectives and goals; this is what drives their high performance.
- Contribution to the organization and its environment; this makes high-performing organization a valued corporate citizen.

Unlike in the Indian culture where family and kinship define the pattern of relationship, in these high-performing organizations it's the competency and merit which earn one's membership in the organization. Cooperation, trust, win-win behaviour and quality of relationship are key cultural characteristics. What is right gets valued and preferred. The organizational goals are well defined and adherence to organizational values is their anchor.

In all the four organizations, employees are well aware of their individual identity but primarily within the organization they act as an integral part of the working group, division and organization to which they belong. It is their collective orientation and the culture of team work which contributes to their high performance. In all these organizations, it is also interesting to note that the employees differentiate between work relationship and personal friendship. To them, achievement of work objectives is important; nurturing personal friendship is also valued. High performance is the function of task competence as well as competence in interpersonal relationship.

Commitment to deadlines, organizational goals, commitment to exceed their own best past performance is the essence of high-performing organizations. Most societies and organizations have varying time orientation, in terms of the past, the present and the future. However, in these four organizations the past is not considered important. Creating preferred future is the key. And present accomplishment is certainly of importance. While current achievement is important, future promise, plans and goals are of greater relevance to these enterprises. It was widely observed that in all the four organizations, including Scientific Organization, employees believed that time once lost was lost forever; meeting deadline was sacred, and optimizing use of time as a resource was of utmost concern.

Another distinctive cultural characteristic is related to employees' concern and contribution to the organization and society at large. Not that individual members were not concerned about their personal growth but most of them believed that their growth will come only when the organization grow, when organization has a brand equity and respect in the society. Being a part of the larger society, employees highlighted the contribution their organization had made to the society; HEC, in energy; Scientific Organization, in biotechnology and new economy; Telcom, quality of life; and Seacom, in driving the growth of national economy. Being a high-performing organization is not enough for the employees; they are equally concerned about the role the organization plays in the development of the larger society to which they belong.

It must however be noted that except for Scientific Organization, all these high-performing organizations are overwhelmingly male dominated. Telcom has just a handful of female employees; in Seacom and HEC, you could see them in only administrative functions. The usual explanation that it is the reflection of the gender divide in Indian society has not cut the ice yet. This needs to be explored.

There is another aspect which needs to be flagged – Indian national culture; it is believed to be deeply embedded in promoting family, kinship, relationship and concern for people. This study does not endorse the same. In high-performing organizations, membership is based on competence, not relationship or kinship. Commitment to achieve organizational excellence, assertiveness in behaviour (not aggressiveness) and personal dignity are also important for those who are part of high-performing organizations. And what sets these organizations apart is their culture of appreciation; appreciating others for whatever they are worth, whether it is Scientific Organization, Seacom, Telcom or HEC.

On the basis of this study it can be concluded that organizational culture has a positive impact on the performance. It further shows that a strong organizational culture is very helpful for the new employees to adopt the organizational values and gain competitive advantage under specific set of conditions unique to their organization. Earlier, scholars viewed that employee's commitment and group efficiency play a crucial role in adopting the value and beliefs of the organization and enhancing the performance of the organization. It also shows that culture is good only if it fits the industry or the firm's strategy. Finally, an organizational culture that encourages confidence and risk taking among employees have leadership that produces change and focuses on the changing needs of customers' for successful socialization; it also helps in enhancing performance, job satisfaction and intention to stay with the organization and reduces levels of distress symptoms and boosts employees' commitment towards organizational goals and welfare.

The impact of societal culture (Indian Culture) on the management of corporate organization in India. It is highlighted (Sinha, 1991) that Indian management, ownership and management are not differentiated; almost invariably, these overlap. It is centred around the chief; for example, family head, religious head, the king, and the chief executive of an organization or the head of the institution in contemporary sense. It is rooted in its traditional style of decision-making. Hierarchy is the key to management coordination. Horizontal peer-level coordination, so typical of Japanese society, is almost absent in the Indian scene. Presumably, members of an Indian organization look for top-down guidance. It emphasizes on the lifelong employment and job security. There is a societal assumption that membership in a family, caste and corporate group has to be permanent. Although security and lifelong employment have been traditionally valued in India, in contemporary management there is much debate about its efficacy.

Indian management has is its own concerns with the job identity. An Indian derives his or her identity from the social group to which he or she belongs, his or her occupation and the job he or she performs. These are so interlinked that in his or her work organization, his or her first attempt is invariably to establish a reference group and job identity. It is the centralization of power and authority and the decentralization of activities. This has emerged from the powerful belief that the chief has a *Mana* and is the storehouse of energy, authority and power. Even in organizations which have decentralized authority, one finds that people do not exercise their delegated authority and power. There is strong conviction in Indian society that power and authority flow from the fountainhead – the chief executive, the centre of the organization (Kakkar, 1974).

Indian management values loyalty, sometimes unquestioned loyalty – to the king, chief, head of the family and chief executive. There is often confusion between loyalty to the king or the country and loyalty to the chief and or the organization. The assumption is that the king and the country and the chief executive and the organization are synonymous. This is a matter of great debate. Some researchers have commented that Indian society fosters dependency thus calling for loyalty and fellowship and playing to the tune of the supervisors or authority figure (Sinha, 1986).

There is a preference for an open-door policy. The king must be accessible, the head of the joint family must listen, and the chief executive must be approachable not only to those who are close to him but also to anyone in his organization. It also has two parallel information systems – the formal, which is structured either top-down or bottom-up, and the informal, which is unstructured and criss-crosses the organization hierarchy like a grapevine. The former is slow; the latter is faster. The skills of shifting information from one system to another and using them effectively are considered important assets for successful managers. Performance in the context of Indian management requires pressure and persuasion. Deadlines, targets and crises are great motivators and challenges in the Indian society. The pressure to meet deadlines works so well in Indian management.

Indian management values individual excellence. It recognizes individuals who make distinguished contributions in whatever field of endeavour they are. In Indian society, one does not look for the same qualities in every man. Rather one recognizes individual differences and respects excellence in whatever field one distinguishes him or herself. It is believed that in a team not all members are alike. In fact, they should not be alike but be as five fingers with different lengths and shapes and bound together in one hand. Collective wisdom is valued in Indian society. Teamwork always commands attention. The Blind Man and the Lame Man joining hands together to compensate for each other's deficiencies is a household story. An effective team consists of people with different views, values, perceptions, professions, skills and wisdom working for a common goal so that together they convert energy into synergy and the competence of individual is translated into excellence through teamwork.

Many of the features highlighted by Sinha are found in the present study with few modifications and little variations. It also largely depends on nature of the organizations like small or large scale, public or private, and traditional or modern organizations. It is noticed that not all these characteristics are desirable for Indian managers to practice and pursue. In fact, there is an unrelenting debate in the country about the desirability of these characteristics, that is, whether ownership and management should be differentiated; whether chief executives should have so much authority; whether hierarchy should be the major method of management coordination; whether paternalistic, directed, nurturing leadership is most appropriate for an Indian organization; whether one should accept Indian managers are best solo players and that do not care about team work; whether organizational behaviour needs modification, and if so, which new aspects of behaviour should be implemented and promoted. These are burning issues for Indian management professionals, which can be proven further by conducting intensive studies on the topic.

References

Adler, N.J. (1983). A typology of management studies involving culture. *Journal of International Business Studies*, 14(2), 29–47.

Adler, N.J. (1983). Cross-cultural management: Issues to be faced. *International Studies of Man and Organization*, 13(1–2), 1–45.

Altekar, A.S. (1978). *State and government in English India*. New Delhi: Motilal Lala Banarsi Das.

Amba-Rao, S.C., Petrick, J.A., Gupta, J.N.D. & Von der Embse, T.J. (2000). Comparative performance appraisal practices and management values among foreign and domestic firms India. *International Journal of Human Resource Management*, 11(1), 60–89.

Arora, D. (2005). *Foreign multinationals in India: Adapting to India's work culture and management practices*. http://people.f3.htw berlin.de/Professoren/Arora/discussion_paper/Foreign_Multinationals_in_India-Dayanand_Arora.pdf (Retrieved 30 January 2013)

Awasthi, V.N., Chow, C.W. & Wu, A. (1998) Performance measure and resource expenditure choices in a teamwork environment: The effects of national culture. *Management Accounting Research*, 9(2), 119–38.

Axel, M. (1995). Toward an analysis of Japanese-style management: A psycho-cultural and socio-historical approach. *Management International Review*, 35(2), 57–73.

Bala, M., Chalil, G.R.B. & Gupta, A. (2012). Emic and etic: Different lenses for research in culture: Unique features of culture in Indian context. *Management and Labour Studies*, 37(1), 45–60.

Barbara, M., Harzing, A.W.K. & Mirza, H. (2004). Host country specific factors and the transfer of human resource management practices in multinational companies. *International Journal of Manpower*, 25(6), 518–534.

Barney, J.B. (1986). Organizational culture: Can it be a source of sustained competitive advantage? *Academy of Management Review*, 11(3), 656–665.

Barry, G. (2008). Cross-cultural management research: Assumptions, evidence, and suggested directions. *International Journal of Cross-Cultural Management*, 8(3), 259–274.

Bercovitch, J. & Foulkes, J. (2012). Cross-cultural effects in conflict management: Examining the nature and relationship between culture and international mediation. *International Journal of Cross-Cultural Management*, 12(1), 25–47.

Bhal, K.T. & Debnath, N. (2006). Conceptualizing and measuring Gunas predictors of workplace ethics of Indian professionals. *International Journal of Cross-Cultural Management*, 6(2), 169–188.

Bhaskaran, S. & Sukumaran, N. (2007) National culture, business culture and management practices: Consequential relationships? *Cross-Cultural Management: An International Journal*, 14(1), 54–67.

Bidney, D. (1953). The concept of culture and some cultural fallacies. In *Theoretical Anthropology*, ed. D. Bidney (pp. 23–53). New York: Columbia University Press.

Black, B. (1999). National culture and high commitment management. *Employee Relations*, 21(4), 389–404.

Bloom, B., Chesney-Lind, M. & Owen, B. (1994). *Women in California prisons: Hidden victims of the war on drugs.* San Francisco, CA: Center on Juvenile and Criminal Justice.

Bruce, K. & Singh, H. (1988). The effect of national culture on the choice of entry mode. *Journal of International Business Studies*, 19(3), 411–432.

Chang, L. (2002). Cross-cultural differences in international management using Kluckhohn–Strodtbek Framework. *Journal of American Academy of Business*, 2(1), 20–27.

Chee, T.S. (1992). Culture and management teaching: The case of Malay culture. *Journal of Management Education*, 16(4), 61–71.

Chen, M. (1995). *Asian management systems: Chinese, Japanese, and Korean styles of business*. London: International Thomson Press.

Chevrier, S. (2009). Is national culture still relevant to management in a global context? The case of Switzerland. *International Journal of Cross-Cultural Management*, 9(2), 169–183.

Child, J. (1981). Culture, contingency and capitalism in the cross-national study of organizations. In *Research in Organizational Behavior Middlesex* (pp. 303–356), ed. L.L. Cummings & B.M. Staw. London: JAI Press.

Chow, C.W., Shields, M.D. & Wu, A. (1999). The importance of national culture in the design of and preference for management control multinational operations. *Accounting, Organizations and Society*, 24(5/6), 441–461.

Chow, C.W., Shields, M.D. & Chan, Y.K. (1991). The effects of management controls and national culture on manufacturing performance: An empirical investigation. *Accounting, Organizations and Society*, 16(3), 209–226.

Christophe Lejeune, A.V. (2009). Organizational culture and effectiveness in business schools: A test of the accreditation impact. *Journal of Management Development*, 28(8), 728–741.

Chui, A.C.W., Lloyd, A.E. & Kwok, C.C.Y. (2002). The determination of capital structure: Is national culture a missing piece to the puzzle? *Journal of International Business Studies*, 33(1), 99–127.

Coen, H. (2011). Cross-cultural perception and power dynamics across changing organizational and national contexts: Curaçao and the Netherlands. *Human Relations*, 64(5), 653.

Costas, J. (2012). We are all friends here: Reinforcing paradoxes of normative control in a culture of friendship. *Journal of Management Inquiry*, 21(4), 377–395.

Cragg, C. (1995). *The new Taipans*. London: Century Business.

Cummings, L.L. & Schmidt, S.M. (1972). Managerial attitudes of Greeks: The roles of culture and industrialization. *Administrative Science Quarterly*, 17(2), 265–272.

Currie, G. & Kerrin, M. (2004). The limits of a technological fix to knowledge management epistemological, political and cultural issues in the case of intranet implementation. *Management Learning*, 35(1), 9–29.

d'Iribarne, P. (2009). National cultures and organizations in search of a theory: An interpretative approach. *International Journal of Cross-Cultural Management*, 9(3), 309–321.

Daulatram, B.L. (2003) Organizational culture and job satisfaction. *Journal of Business and Industrial Marketing*, 18(3), 219–236.

Daun, A. (1998). Describing a national culture: Is it at all possible? *Ethnologia Scandinavica*, 28, 5–19.

Dayal, I. & Daya, A.K. (1978). *Organization for management in developing countries*. New Delhi: Concept Publishing.

De Hilal, A.V.G. (2006). Brazilian national culture, organizational culture and cultural agreement: Findings from a multinational company. *International Journal of Cross-Cultural Management*, 6(2), 139–167.

Deltamont, S. (2012). *Handbook of qualitative research in education*. London: Edward Elgar.

Denison, D.R. & Mishra, A.K. (1995). Toward a theory of organizational culture and effectiveness. *Organization Science*, 6(2), 204–223.

Denison, D.R. (1984). Bringing corporate culture to the bottom line. *Organizational Dynamics*, 13(2), 5–22.

Denison, D.R. (1990). *Corporate culture and organizational effectiveness*. New York: John Wiley.

Dominic, B. (2012). Cultural theory and conflict management in organizations: How does theory shape our understanding of culture in practice? *International Journal of Cross-Cultural Management*, 12(1), 9–24.

du Plessis, Y. (2011). Exploring teamwork paradoxes challenging 21st-century cross-cultural conflict management in a multicultural organizational context. *International Journal of Cross-Cultural Management*, 12(1), 49–71.

Eccles, R.G., Ioannou, I. & Serafeim, G. (2012). *The impact of a corporate culture of sustainability on corporate behavior and performance* (Working Paper 12–035). http://www.hbs.edu/faculty/Publication%20Files/12-035.pdf (Retrieved 30 January 2012)

Edwinah, A. (2012). Corporate culture and organizational effectiveness: A study of the Nigerian banking industry. *European Journal of Business and Management*, 4(8), 212–228.

Barinaga, E. (2007). 'Cultural diversity' at work: 'National culture' as a discourse organizing an international project group. *Human Relations*, 60(2), 315–340.

Fetterman, D.M. (1998). *Ethnography: Step by step*. Thousand Oaks, CA: Sage.

Ford, J.B. & Honeycutt, Jr., E.D. (1992). Japanese national culture as a basis for understanding Japanese business practices. *Business Horizons*, 35(6), 27–34.

Fukuyama, F. (1995). *Trust: Social Virtues and the creation of prosperity*. New York: Free Press.

Gertsen, M.C. & Zolner, M. (2012). Recontextualization of the corporate values of a Danish MNC in a subsidiary in Bangalore (multinational corporation, case study). *Group and Organization Management*, 37(1), 101–132.

Gilbert, X. & Lorange, P. (1994). National approaches to strategic management—A resource-based perspective. *International Business Review*, 3(4), 411–423.

Gonzalez, C.B. (2008). The cultures of international management. *International Business and Economics Research Journal*, 7(7), 95–114.

Gordon, G. & Di Tomaso, N. (1992). Predicting corporate performance from organizational culture. *Journal of Management Studies*, 29(6), 783–798.

Graham, J.L. (1985b), The influence of culture on the process of business negotiations: An exploratory study. *Journal of International Business*, 16(1), 81–96.

Grenness, T. (2011). The impact of national culture on CEO compensation and salary gaps between CEOs and manufacturing workers. *Compensation Benefits Review*, 43(2), 100–108.

Groeschi, S. (2003). Cultural implications for the appraisal process. *Cross-Cultural Management*, 10(1), 67–79.

Groeschl, S. & Doherty, L. (2000). Conceptualizing culture. *Cross-Cultural Management*, 7(4), 12–17.

Guss, C.D. (2002). Decision making in individualist and collectivist cultures. In *Online readings in psychology and culture*, ed. W.J. Lonner, D.L. Dinnel, S.A., Hayes, & D.N. Sattler. http://www.wwu.edu/culture/Guss2.htm (Retrieved 30 January 2013)

Güss, D., Strohschneider, S. & Halcour, D. (2000). Strategies in complex and dynamic decision making: Cross-cultural analyses between India and Germany. Unpublished manuscript. Bamberg, Germany: Institute für Theoretische Psychologies, Otto-Friedrich Universität. http://www.wwu.edu/culture/Guss2.htm (Retrieved 1 February 2013)

Hall, E.T. (1990). *Understanding cultural differences: Germans, French and Americans*. Yarmouth, ME: Intercultural Press.

Hampden-Turner, C. & Trompenaars, F. (1993). *The seven cultures of capitalism*. New York: Double Day.

Herbig, P. & Jacobs, I. (1998). Culture as an explanatory variable for the Japanese innovative processes. *Cross-Cultural Management*, 5(3), 3–28.

Hewett, K., Bruce Money, R. & Sharma, S. (2006). National culture and industrial buyer-seller relationships in the United States and Latin America. *Journal of the Academy of Marketing Science*, 34(3), 386–402.

Hoffman, R.C. & Hegarty, W. (1993). Top management influence on innovations: Effects of executive characteristics and social culture. *Journal of Management*, 19(3), 549–574.

Hofstede, G. (1980). Motivation leadership and organization: Do American theories apply abroad? http://alangutterman.typepad.com/files/motivation-ldrshp-and-orgn-do-american-theories.pdf (Retrieved 30 January 2013)

Hofstede, G. (1983). National culture in four dimensions. *International Studies of Management and Organization*, 13(2), 46–74.

Hofstede, G. (1983). The cultural relativity of organizational practice and theories. *Journal of International Business Studies*, 14(2), 75–89.

Hofstede, G. (1991). *Cultures and Organizations: Software of the Mind*. Maidenhead, UK: McGraw-Hill.

Hofstede, G. (1994). *Culture and Organizations*, London: HarperCollins.

Hope, C.A. & Muhlemann, A.P. (2001). The impact of culture and best practice production operations management. *International Journal of Management Reviews*, 3(3), 199–217.

Inkeles, A. & Levinson, D.J. (1954). National character: The study of modal personality and socio-cultural systems. In G. Lindzey (Ed.), *Handbook of Social Psychology. Vol. 2: Special Fields and Applications* (pp. 977–1020). Reading, MA: Addison-Wesley.

Inkeles, A. & Levinson, D.J. (1969). National character: The study of modal personality and socio-cultural systems. In *The Handbook of Social Psychology*. Reading, MA: Addison-Wesley.

Inkeles, A. & Levinson, D.J. (1964). National character: The study of modal personality and socio-cultural systems. In *Handbook of Social Psychology* (Vol. 2), ed. G. Lindzay & E. Aronson. Reading, MA: Addison-Wesley.

Jaeger, A.M. & Kanungo, R. (Eds.). (1990). *Management in developing countries*. London: Routledge.

Jain, R. & Premkumar, R. (2011). HRD practices in Indian organizations and their impact on 'Productivity' of human resources: An empirical study. *Management and Labour Studies*, 36(1), 5–30.

Kagono, T. (1985). *Strategic vs. evolutionary management: A US-Japan comparison of strategy and organization*. Amsterdam: North Holland.

Kakkar, S. (1974). *Personality and authority in work: The dynamics of subordinate behaviour in Indian organizations*. New Delhi: Somaiya Publishers.

Kakkar, S. (1971). Authority patterns and subordinate behavior in Indian organizations. *Administrative Science Quarterly*, 16(3), 298–307.

Kirkman, B.L. & Shapiro, D.L. (1996). The impact of national culture on employee resistance to teams: Towards a model of globalised self-managing work team effectiveness. *Academy of Management Proceedings*.

Kluckhohn, F. & Strodtbeck, F. (1961). *Variations in value orientations*. Evanstone, IL: Row, Peterson and Company.

Kroeber, A.L. Kluckhohn, C., Untereiner, W. & Meyer, A.G. (1952). *Culture: A critical review of concepts and definitions*. New York: Vintage Books.

Lessem, R. & Neubauer, F. (1994). *European management systems: Towards unity out of cultural diversity*. Maidenhead, Berkshire: McGraw-Hill.

Linton, R. (1945). *The cultural background of personality*. New York: Appleton-Century-Crofts.

Lofland, J. & Lofland, L.H. (2006). *Analyzing social setting: A guide to qualitative observations and analysis*. Belmont, CA: Wadsworth Thomson Learning.

Lok, P. & Crawford, J. (2004). The effect of organizational culture and leadership style on job satisfaction and organizational commitment: A cross-national comparison. *Journal of Management Development*, 23(4), 321–338.

Lumby, J. & Foskett, N. (2011). Power, risk, and utility: Interpreting the landscape of culture in educational leadership. *Educational Administration Quarterly*, 47(3), 446–461.

Mahadevan, J. (2012). Are engineers religious? An interpretative approach to cross-cultural conflict and collective identities. *International Journal of Cross-Cultural Management*, 12(1), 133–149.

Majumdar, R.C. (1980). *Corporate life in ancient India*. Calcutta: Firma Mikhopadhyay.

Malik, M.E., Danish, R.Q. & Ali, U. (2011). Impact of motivation to learn and job attitudes on organizational learning culture in a public service organization of Pakistan. *African Journal of Business Management*, 5(3), 844–854.

Mann, L., Radford, M., Burnett, P., Ford, S., Bond, M., Leung, K., et al. (1998). Cross-cultural differences in self-reported decision making style and confidence. *International Journal of Psychology*, 33(5), 325–335.

Mariamposlski, H. (2006). *Ethnography for marketers: A guide to consumer immersion*. Thousand Oaks, CA: Sage.

Mathur, P., Aycan, Z. & Kanungo, R.N. (1996). Work cultures in Indian organizations: A comparison between public and private sector. *Psychology Developing Societies*, 8(2), 199–222.

Mendonca, M. & Kanungo, R.N. (1996). Impact of culture on performance management in developing countries. *International Journal of Manpower*, 17(4/5), 65–75.

Mendonca, M., Kanungo, R.N. & Aycan, Z. (1999). Culture: The forgotten factor in human resource management. *Journal of Business Perspective*, 3(2), 1–7.

Minkov, M., Hofstede, G.J. & Hofstede, G. (2012). *Cross-cultural analysis*. Thousand Oaks, CA: Sage.

Mohe, M. (2008). Bridging the cultural gap in management consulting research. *International Journal of Cross-Cultural Management*, 8, 41–57.

Morden, T. (1995). International culture and management. *Management Decision*, 33(2), 16–21.

Morden, T. (1995). National culture and the culture of the organization. *International journal of Cross-Cultural Management*, 2(2), 3–12.

Myers, A., Kakabadse, A., McMahon, T. & Spony, G. (1995). Top management styles in Europe: Implications for business and cross-national teams. *European Business Journal*, 7(1), 17–27.

Nazir, N.A. & Lone, M.A. (2008). Validation of Denison's model of organizational culture and effectiveness in the Indian context. *Journal of Business Perspective*, 12(1), 49–58.

Newman, K.L. & Nollen, S.D. (1996). Culture and congruence: The fit between management practices and national culture. *Journal of International Business Studies*, 27(4), 753–779.

Ogbor, J.O. (2000). Organizational leadership and authority relations across cultures: Beyond divergence and convergence. *International Journal of Commerce and Management*, 10(1), 48–73.

Ohbuchi, K.I., Fukushima, O. & Tedeschi, J.T. (1999). Cultural values in conflict management: Goal orientation, goal attainment, and tactical decision. *Journal of Cross-Cultural Psychology*, 30(1), 51–71.

Ouchi, W. (1981). *Theory Z*. Reading, MA: Addison-Wesley.

Ouchi, W.G. & Jaeger, A.M. (1978). Type Z organization: Stability in the midst and mobility. *Academy of Management*, 3(2), 305–314.

Panda, A. & Gupta, R.K. (2005). Measuring organizational culture through peer-induced cognitive pressure: An empirical study. *Indian Journal of Industrial Relations*, 41(1), 1–28.

Pandey, S.K. & Wali, O.P. (2010). Management lessons from Indian epics in context to theory Z. *Journal of Human Values*, 16(1), 57–70.

Parboteeah, K.P., Bronson, J. & Cullen, J.B. (2005). Does national culture affect willingness to justify ethically suspect unethical behaviors? A focus on the Globe National Culture Scheme. *International Journal of Cross-cultural Management*, 5(2), 123–138.

Park, J.S. & Kim, T.H. (2009). Do types of organizational culture matter in nurse job satisfaction and turnover intention? *Leadership in Health Services*, 22(1), 20–38.

Peretz, H. & Rosenblatt, Z. (2011). The role of societal cultural practices in organizational investment in training: A comparative study in 21 countries. *Journal of Cross-Cultural Psychology*, 42(5), 817–831.

Pizam, et al. (1997). Nationality vs industry cultures: Which has a greater effect on managerial behaviour? *International Journal of Hospitality Management*, 16(12), 127–145.

Putti, J.M. (1991). *Management: Asian context*. London: McGraw-Hill.

Redding, S.G. & Pugh, D.S. (1986). The formal and the informal: Japanese and Chinese organization structure. In *The Enterprise and Management in East Asia*, ed. S.R. Clegg, D.C. Dunphy & S.G. Redding. Hong Kong: University of Hong Kong.

Reisinger, Y. & Crotts, J.C. (2010). Applying Hofstede's national culture measures in tourism research: Illuminating issues of divergence and convergence. *Journal of Travel Research*, 49(2), 153–164.

Sadri, G. & Lees, B. (2001). Developing corporate culture as a competitive advantage. *Journal of Management Development*, 20(10), 853–859.

Santha, S.D. (2008). Local culture, technological change and riverine fisheries management in Kerala, South India. *International Journal of Rural Management*, 4(1–2), 25–45.

Schneider, S.C. & DeMeyer, A. (1991). Interpreting and responding to strategic issues: Impact of national culture. *Strategies Management Journal*, 12(4), 307–320.

Schuler, R.S. & Rogovsky, N. (1998). Understanding compensation practice variations across firms: The impact of national culture. *Journal of International Business Studies*, 29(1), 159–177.

Seagrave, S. (1995). *Lords of the rim: The invisible empire of the overseas Chinese*. New York: Putnam.

Shah, S. & Sudhir Bhaskar, A. (2008). Corporate stakeholder management: Western and Indian perspectives: An overview. *Journal of Human Values*, 14(1), 73–93.

Shahzad, F. & Luqman, R.A. (2012). Impact of organizational culture on organizational performance: An overview. *Interdisciplinary Journal of Contemporary Research in Business Institute of Interdisciplinary Business Research*, 3(9), 975–985.

Sharma, S.K. & Sharma, A. (2010). Examining the relationship between organisational culture and leadership styles. *Journal of the Indian Academy of Applied Psychology*, 36(1), 97–105.

Shenkar, O. (2001). Cultural distance revisited: Towards a more rigorous conceptualization and measurement of cultural differences. *Journal of International Business Studies*, 32(3), 519–535.

Shrivastava, R. & Shrivastava, S. (2012). Management practices with Indian work culture: Towards new frontiers in management thinking. *International Journal of Inter science Management Review*, 2(2), 56–62.

Singh, K. (2007). The limited relevance of culture to strategy. *Asia Pacific Journal of Management*, 24(4), 421–429.

Sinha, D.P. (1991). Indian management: Context, concerns and trends. In *Management: Asian Context*, ed. J.M. Putti. New York: McGraw-Hill.Sinha, J.B.P. (1990). *Work culture in the Indian context*. New Delhi: Sage.

Sinha, J.B.P., Sinha, R.B.N. & Bhupatkar, A.P. (2004). Facets of societal and organizational cultures and managers' work-related thoughts and feelings. *Psychology Developing Societies, 16*(1), 1–25.

Smart, J.C. & St. John, E.P. (1996). Organizational culture and effectiveness in higher education: A test of the 'culture type' and 'strong culture' hypotheses. *Educational Evaluation and Policy Analysis, 18*(3), 219–241.

Smart, J.C. (2003). Organizational effectiveness of 2 year colleges: The centrality of cultural and leadership complexity. *Research in Higher Education*, 44(6), 673–703.

Smith, P. (1992). Organizational behaviour and national cultures. *British Journal of Management*, 3(1), 39–51.

Smith, P.B. (1996). National cultures and the values of organizational employees: Time for another look. In *Managing across cultures: Issues and perspectives*, ed. P. Joynt & M. Warner. London: International Thomson Business Press.

Smith, P.B. (2011). Communication styles as dimensions of national culture. *Journal of Cross-Cultural Psychology*, 42(2), 216–233.

Smith, P.B., Peterson, M.F., Thomason, S.J., et al. (2012). National culture as a moderator of the relationship between managers' use of guidance sources and how well work events are handled. *Journal of Cross-Cultural Psychology*, 42(6), 1101–1121.

Som, A. (2008). Innovative human resource management and corporate performance in the context of economic liberalization in India. *International Journal of Human Resource Management*, 19(7), 1278–1297.

Sparrow, P. & Budhwar, P. (1995). Developments in Indian human resource management in the new economic environment. Paper presented in *Conference on Cross-Cultural Perspective: Competitive Management and Organization*, 10–12, NN Henley Management College, Henley-on-Thames, England.

Srivastava, V.N. (2009). Organizational culture as a predictor of managerial motivation in Indian public enterprises. *Management and Labour Studies*, 34(4), 451–470.

Strohschneider, S. & Güss, D. (1999). The fate of the Moros: A cross-cultural exploration of strategies in complex and dynamic decision making. *International Journal of Psychology*, 34(4), 235–252.

Strohschneider, S. & Güss, D. (1998). Planning and problem solving: Differences between Brazilian and German students. *Journal of Cross-Cultural Psychology*, 29(6), 695–716.

Tan, K.C. & Khoo, H.H. (2002). Indian society, total quality and the Rajiv Gandhi National Quality Award. *Journal of Management Development*, 21(6), 417–426.

Tayeb, M. (2001). Conducting research across cultures: Overcoming drawbacks and obstacles. *International Journal of Cross-Cultural Management*, 1(1), 91–108.

Tayeb, M.H. (1988). *Organizations and National Culture.* London: Sage.

Taylor, E.B. (1872). *The primitive culture* (Vol. 1). London: John Murray.

Tran, D.D. & Skitmore, M. (2002). The impact of culture on international management: A survey of project communications in Singapore. *Australian Journal of Construction Economics and Building,* 2(2), 36–47.

Triandis, H.C. (1994). *Culture and social behavior.* New York: McGraw-Hill.

Triandis, H.C. (1999). Dialectics between cultural and cross-cultural psychology. Keynote address to Asian Association of Social Psychology, Taipei, Taiwan. *Asian Journal of Social Psychology,* 3(3), 185–195.

Triandis, H.C. (2001). The study of cross-cultural management and organization: The future. *International Journal of Cross-Cultural Management,* 1(1), 17–20.

Trompenaars, F. (1994). *Riding the waves of culture.* London: Nicholas Brealey.

Turner, H. & Trompenaars, F. (1994). *The seven cultures of capitalism.* London: Piatkus.

Veser, M. (2004). The influence of culture on stakeholder management: Social policy implementation in multinational corporations. *Business Society,* 43(4), 426–436.

Weiss, J. & Delbecq, A. (1987). High-technology cultures and management: Silicon Valley and Route 128. *Group and Organization Management,* 12(1), 39–54.

Wilkins, A.L. & Ouchi, W.G. (1983). Efficient cultures: Exploring the relationship between culture and organizational performance. *Administrative Science Quarterly,* 28(3), 468–481.

Witte, A.E. (2012). Making the case for a post-national cultural analysis of organizations. *Journal of Management Inquiry,* 21(2), 141–159.

Zeynep, A., Kanungo, R.N. & Sinha, J.B.P. (1999). Organizational culture and human resource management practices: The model of culture fit. *Journal of Cross-Cultural Psychology,* 30(4), 501–526.

Index